A Geography of Africa

W. J. Minns

Formerly Geography Master at
Nairobi School, Kenya

MACMILLAN
PUBLISHERS

First published 1978
Reprinted 1980, 1981, 1982 (twice)
New Edition 1984
Reprinted 1984, 1985

Published by *Macmillan Publishers Ltd*
London and Basingstoke
Associated companies and representatives in Accra,
Auckland, Delhi, Dublin, Gaborone, Hamburg, Harare,
Hong Kong, Kuala Lumpur, Lagos, Manzini, Melbourne,
Mexico City, Nairobi, New York, Singapore, Tokyo.

ISBN 0 333 37170 4

Printed in Hong Kong

Photograph credits

The author and publishers wish to acknowledge the
following photographic sources:-
Aerofilms Ltd   pp. 4(L), 19(L), 44(R), 169
Afrique Photo   p. 129
Alcan Ltd   p. 156
Anglo-American Corp (South Africa) Ltd   p. 144
Barnabys Picture Library   pp. 10, 19(R), 84, 120(T),
   122(B)
British Aluminium Corp   p. 154
Cadbury Ltd   p. 50(BL)
Camera Press Ltd   pp. 59, 63(TL), 88, 102, 103, 104,
   105(TL), 142, 164, 173, 175, 184
J. Allan Cash Ltd   pp. 9, 11, 21, 43, 126, 127, 166
Central Office of Information   p. 61(TL)
Commonwealth Development Corporation   pp. 61,
   121, 124(R)
Crown Copyright – Courtesy U.K. Land Forces   p. 175
Douglas Dickens   pp. 44(L), 82
East African Railways & Harbours Board   p. 118
F.A.O.   cover photograph by P. Pittet
Firestone Rubber Co. Ltd   pp. 77, 78
Ghana Information Service   p. 105(R)
Professor Harrison-Church   pp. 92, 148, 188
International Institute for Cotton   p. 67(B)
John Jochimson Ltd   p. 4(R)
Kariba Hydro Electric Authority   p. 105(BL)
Kenya Tea Development Authority   pp. 61, 62
K.W.T. Capetown   pp. 80 and 81

Embassy of the Republic of Liberia   p. 147
Malawi Information Service   p. 185
New African Development   pp. 50 Bottom (R), 152,
   170, 178, 182
Nigerian Information Service   pp. 50(T), 53, 53(TL)
Phototheque C.F.P.   p. 160
Sheila Powell   p. 6, 124(L)
Press Association   p. 15
School of Veterinary Medicine, Edinburgh   p. 115(R)
Senegal Information Service   p. 91
Sennar/Gezira Board   p. 97
Sennar Dam Authority   p. 95
Shell   pp. 67(T), 161, 176
Courtesy of South African Sugar Corporation   pp. 72,
   73
South African Embassy   pp. 112, 122, 123, 137, 178
Satour   pp. 131, 137
Tanzania Information Service   pp. 56, 120(T), 172, 187
Eric Taylor   p. 157
Transafrica Pix   p. 89
United Africa Co. Int.   p. 171
U.S.D.A.   pp. 63(TR), 66
Valco   pp. 140, 155
High Commission for the Republic of Zambia   p. 151

The publishers have made every effort to trace the
copyright holders, but if they have inadvertently over-
looked any, they will be pleased to make the necessary
arrangements at the first opportunity.

Contents

Part B Development studies

**4 Cash crops of Africa: the move
away from subsistance**   47
  Cocoa in West Africa   47
  Palm oil   51
  Coffee   56
  Tea   59
  Cotton   63

5 Plantation agriculture   69
  Sugar   69
    Methods of cultivation   72
  Rubber   75
  Viticulture   79
  Sisal   82

6 Large scale irrigation   85
  The Plain of Death   85
  The Awash Valley Authority   88
  Irrigation on the Senegal River —
  The Richard Toll Scheme   91
  Irrigation on the Niger   92
  Irrigation along the Nile —
    The Gezira Scheme   95
    The Jonglei Canal   99

7 Multi-purpose river development   102
  The Cabora Bassa Dam   104
  The Volta River Project   106
  The Kpong Project   109
  The Kainji Dam   109
  The Aswan Dam   110
    Problems   111
  The Orange River Scheme   113
  The Lesotho Highlands Water
  Project   115

8 Pastoralism   117
  The low grass savanna and semi-
  desert lands — The Fulani   118
  Ranching   121
  The higher cattle lands   123
  Sheep   124
  Goats   125

9 Africa's forests: a case of survival 127
  Tropical hardwoods   129
  The fight against the desert   131

10 The development of industries   134
  Johannesburg and the Rand   134
    Major towns and their manufactured
    goods   139
    Other minerals available to the Rand   142

Part A Africa in general

**1 Africa: the size, shape, position and
physical geography**   1
  The people of Africa   1
  The countries of Africa   2
  Africa: the physical environment —
  the coastal lands, plateau   2
  Africa, the rift valleys, volcanoes
  and their lava, fold mountains,
  Africa's rivers, inland drainage, the
  ice and snow areas, the dry lands   21

2 Africa's climates   24
  The planetary wind system and
  pressure belts   24
  The earth's axis and its movement
  round the sun   25
  The position of the land and sea areas   25
  The Mediterranean climate   26
  The semi-desert and desert climates   32
  The savanna (tropical continental)
  climate   34
  Equatorial climate   36
  Trade winds coast climate (tropical
  and sub-tropical east coast climate)   39
  Mountain climates   39
  The monsoon in Africa   41

3 Africa's natural vegetation   42
  The savanna lands   42
  The equatorial lands   44
  The very dry lands   44
  The Mediterranean lands   45
  The eastern mountains and plateaus   45
  The eastern seaboard lands   46

Further developments 142
Ghana 143
Suez and the Nile Delta Lands 145
Free Zone 146
The Qattara Depression Project 146

11 Minerals and mines 147
Iron ore 147
Copper 152
Zambia's Copper Belt 153
Bauxite 156
Guinea 157
Sierra Leone, Ghana 158
Tin 159
Petroleum: a mixed blessing for
Africa 161

**12 Population and the location of
settlement** 167
Town and city development 170

13 Transport and trade 174
The Gambia 174
The Tanzam (Tazara) Railway 175
The Trans-Cameroon Railway 177
Economic unions 182
The Mano River Union 183
Trade balances 183

14 Fishing 187
Methods of catching fish 188
Index 192

Acknowledgements

The author wishes to acknowledge the help and
encouragement given to him in the preparation of
this book by Mr. Hayden Perrett formerly an
Inspector of Geography in Kenyan schools. He
also wishes to thank the students of Nairobi
School, during the period 1969 – 76, for whom the
basis of this book was written and who were so ap-
preciative.

1 Africa: the size, shape, position and physical geography

Africa is one of the world's largest continents. In fact there is only one larger; and that is the combined landmass of Eurasia: Europe and Asia. In area Africa extends to about 30 300 000 square kilometres. Apart from Eurasia all the other continents are much smaller than this.

Africa's shape is rather unbalanced, in that her northern half is very bulky and wide, while south of the Equator she presents a much thinner, narrower appearance. The Equator almost divides Africa in half, there being approximately 3800 kilometres between Cape Agulhas in the south and the Equator; while between the coast of

Tunisia and the Equator the distance is about 4100 kilometres. A further point about Africa is that she is the only continent where both the Tropics, Cancer and Capricorn, cross the landmass. It is the distance of the landmass along each tropic as shown in Fig. 1 that illustrates the disparity in shape between Africa's northern and southern halves.

The African continent is continued beneath the sea, this submerged portion of Africa is known as the continental shelf. The continent slopes gently out beneath the sea for as much as 300 kilometres in places, before plunging into the depths of the oceans. Many African countries have taken this fact to its logical conclusion and claimed all legal rights of ownership of the seas and sea bed within 200 kilometres of their present coastline.

Group tasks

Study Fig. 1 and your atlas
1 Copy the map Fig. 1. Label, in the correct places, the following Capes — Bon, Agulhas, Vert and Ras Hafun.
2 Find, name and put on your map, six of the biggest islands or groups of islands off the African mainland. Do you think these are part of the mainland? Give reasons for your answer.
3 Label all the lines of latitude and longitude shown on Fig. 1.
4 Find, and label on your map, the following water areas — Mediterranean Sea, Red Sea, Indian Ocean, Mozambique Channel, Atlantic Ocean, Gulf of Guinea, the Straits of Gibraltar.
5 How wide is Africa along each tropic? Use your atlas scale to find out.

The people of Africa

This subject is more suitably discussed in detail in your History lessons. However, a brief reminder of the situation can only be of assistance.

There are many different people and races to be found in Africa; possibly a greater variety than in any other continent. Many archaeologists consider that it was in East Africa that present day man's ancestors began their first faltering steps towards the sort of world we know today.

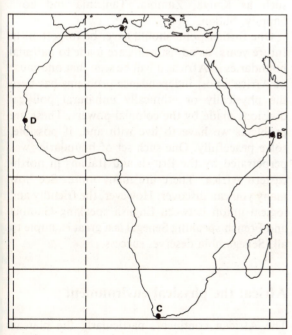

Fig. 1

The small San hunters and gatherers of the Kalahari area seem to have been the first modern men in Africa, although the Pygmies of Zaïre's forests cannot have been far behind. Both these peoples found it difficult to live and compete with the Khoe who arrived later. This is the probable reason for their occupying such inhospitable areas today. The Khoe now largely live in the Namibia region.

In West Africa and the Sudan we find the Sudan negroes, while throughout present-day southern Africa the Bantu negroes are the most numerous people. They have quite dark skins, unlike the peoples of the Sahara and northern Africa who have the palest skins of all Africa's indigenous people. These are the Hamites and the Semites and form the Arab races.

Finally there are many people of mixed Hamite and negro blood who have the features of the Hamites and skin colour of the negroes. The Maasai and Turkana of East Africa are such people. So also are the people of Ethiopia and Somalia.

There are many non-indigenous people in Africa. They have been here for varying lengths of time. The most recent arrivals have been the Europeans and Indians. The Indians only arrived within the last 75 years, while the Europeans have been in Africa since as long ago as the late 13th century. They came to form colonies and to trade. They first came to West Africa and later to South Africa; but in East Africa they were preceded by the Arabs from the Arabian Gulf countries, who traded in goods and slaves long before the Europeans arrived. The Arabs came in their dhows from across the Arabian Sea. They still come and go to this day; only now their journeys are peaceful. The Indians followed the British to Eastern Africa and are now found from Cape Town in the south to Nairobi and Kenya in the north.

The countries of Africa

Because of colonialism most countries in Africa were once ruled by European countries. This largely happened during the last 100 – 150 years. It is only since the end of World War II that colonialism has become a dying force; although the first country to become independent in Africa did so in 1922: Egypt. It was in the mid nineteen fifties that the trickle towards independence became a rushing torrent, sweeping away almost every colonial power in its path.

Some countries had to fight hard for their independence. The struggle in countries like Kenya, Algeria and Mozambique was long and arduous; while in countries such as Ghana, Nigeria and Zambia there was a fairly peaceful transition. They were lucky. Many of Africa's countries had tremendous trouble after gaining independence. Even today, independence has still not brought peace and prosperity to Angola, Uganda, Zimbabwe and what used to be Spanish Sahara.

Ethiopia was never a colony, but was ruled by Italy for a short time. Liberia also was never a colony, but was artificially carved out as a possible home for American negroes who wished to return to their homeland.

Unfortunately some countries are still ruled by minorities, the best known of which is South Africa. Among others are Namibia and Eritrea. Freedom for these countries will take a little time and, tragically, many people may be killed and wounded in the process. But, different races can live together harmoniously and to each other's mutual benefit and happiness. It only requires that greed and the misuse of power should be eliminated. Examples of the success possible in multi-racial cohabitation are seen in countries such as Kenya, Zambia, Tanzania and now, happily, Sudan.

One further point should never be forgotten. In future years, as adjustments are made to national boundaries in Africa, it will be seen that one cause of Africa's post independence problems has been the physically or ethnically unnatural political divisions made by the colonial powers. These are problems we have to live with and, if possible, solve peacefully. One such set of boundaries was perpetrated by the British and Italians in north-eastern Africa. There are many more. See how many you can discover. However, the friendly and logical union between English speaking Gambia and French speaking Senegal is a great example to all. Senegambia deserves success.

Africa: the physical environment

The African continent, particularly the plateau areas and the steep slopes leading up to them, is many millions of years old. The coastal lands, however, are made up of sedimentary rocks which were deposited much more recently; only a few millions of years ago.

Question and answer session

1 What are sedimentary rocks? Sedimentary rocks are formed from the weathered and eroded remains of other rocks. They can also be formed chemically and from the skeletons of dead creatures or dead plant remains.
2 How are they deposited? They are often small and light, tiny particles. The wind can carry them and set them down and rivers and glaciers can easily transport them. Marine creatures die and sink to the bottom of the sea or a lake and their skeletons collect in large masses. Sometimes they are loose but at other times they can be later cemented together.
3 How can we recognise them? Sometimes it is easy. The loose soils in river valleys and all over the surface of the land are sedimentary rocks. Sand is sedimentary. Sometimes it is not so easy because the rocks are hard. The pressure of great weights like sea water can make sands become sandstones. Coral is a sedimentary rock, but it is very hard, so also is limestone. The last two are both formed beneath the sea!! Remember that last point. We will come back to it.

The coastal lands

Almost all of Africa's coastline is very smooth, with very few gaps in it such as we see in North America or Europe. The continental shelf is very shallow and slopes gently, with the result that good harbours are not numerous in Africa. Because of this man has often had to build artificial harbours and one example of this is seen at Takoradi in Ghana.

Not all of Africa's coastline is smooth. On one part of the West African coast there are many gaps and indentations where the sea reaches far inland and the rivers are very deep. These gaps are called *rias*. A *ria* is formed when the sea level rises and invades low parts of the land along river valleys. See Fig. 2. It is also formed if parts of the land sink. In both cases the sea invades the land to find its new level. Freetown and Banjul both lie at

the mouths of rias; while Mombasa lies on an island in the middle of a ria.

On very low, gently sloping coastlines with bays and river mouths, waves and currents helped by the prevailing wind can cause deposits of sand, mud, gravel, etc. to build up across a bay or river mouth. These long finger-like deposits are called *spits* or *bars*. They are caused by a process known as *longshore drift*.

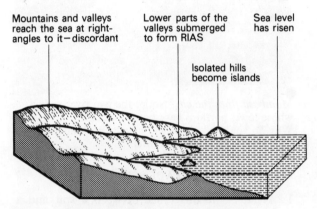

Fig. 2 Simple sketch of a ria formation

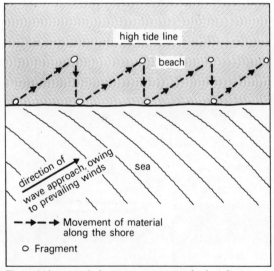

The pebble or rock fragment moves up the beach at right angles to the wave but moves down in the backwash at right angles to the coast. This results in a net movement along the coast

Fig. 3 Longshore drift

Mombasa from the air Notice the two river valleys whose lower portions have been flooded.
Why do you think the island on which Mombasa stands remained above sea level?

Question and answer session

1 What is the difference between a spit and a bar? A spit is joined to the mainland from one side only. Sometimes it is built across a bay or river mouth and joins the mainland on the other side. It is then called a bar.

Monrovia from Mamba Point Notice the bar and the lagoon behind it.
1 What indicates that the bar is many years old?
2 What is the water feature behind the bar called?

2 What is longshore drift? This is the movement of beach materials like sand, gravel, mud and coral pieces along a shoreline. It is caused by winds and ocean currents moving water and the materials along a shoreline. See Fig. 3.
3 How does longshore drift form these narrow deposits? Longshore drift stops when there is a gap in the coastline. Material in the water sinks to the bottom as a result. Gradually the

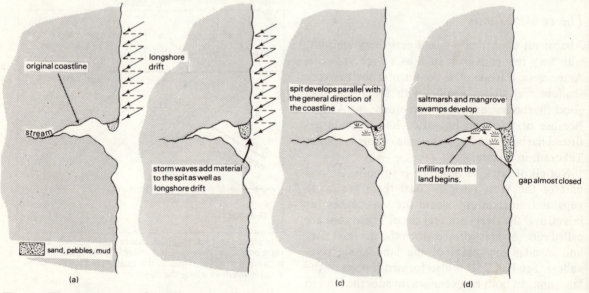

Fig. 4 The formation of a spit

4

deposits build up. Storm waves build them above sea level and the spit is gradually extended as shown in Fig. 4.

Behind the spits and bars long narrow lakes are often formed. They are called *lagoons*. Lagos lies on an island in one such lagoon while Abidjan and Durban are also ports found in lagoons. Another famous area with spits, bars and lagoons is the Nile Delta. Often rivers empty into the lagoon and deposit the materials they are carrying. In this way lagoons tend to fill up with sedimentary deposits which have to be continually dredged and taken away by port authorities. If they were not, the lagoon would soon become too shallow for ships and the port would die. See Fig. 5.

Other parts of Africa's coast have coral deposits, both alive and dead. Coral can only grow in very special areas and under special conditions. It forms a very hard rock which often grows into the shape of a *reef* a few hundred metres off-shore. Coral reefs are very dangerous for shipping. The gaps in them which lead to ports are often very difficult and dangerous to negotiate. Sometimes ships get marooned on coral

reefs as they try to enter a harbour. Such a cargo ship is marooned on the reef off Mombasa. It was blown on to the reef one night many years ago and has been there ever since. Gradually the sea will break up the vessel and it will disappear in years to come.

Question and answer session

1 What is coral? It is a limestone rock composed of the skeletons of minute marine creatures called *polyps*. These polyps live in colonies of thousands and as they die leaving their skeletons behind, fresh coral grows on the old, extending upwards and outwards in many different and beautiful colours and shapes. The dead skeletons are cemented into these shapes by coralline algae (marine organisms) known as *nullipores*.

2 Where can coral grow? Coral polyps can only grow successfully where water temperatures are between 23°C – 25°C for most of the year. This limits present-day coral growth to the western parts of the oceans and seas (eastern shores of continents) between 30°N and 30°S.

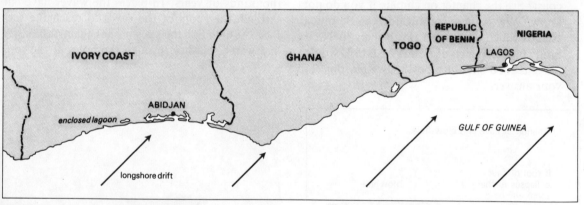

Fig. 5   Spits and lagoons in West Africa

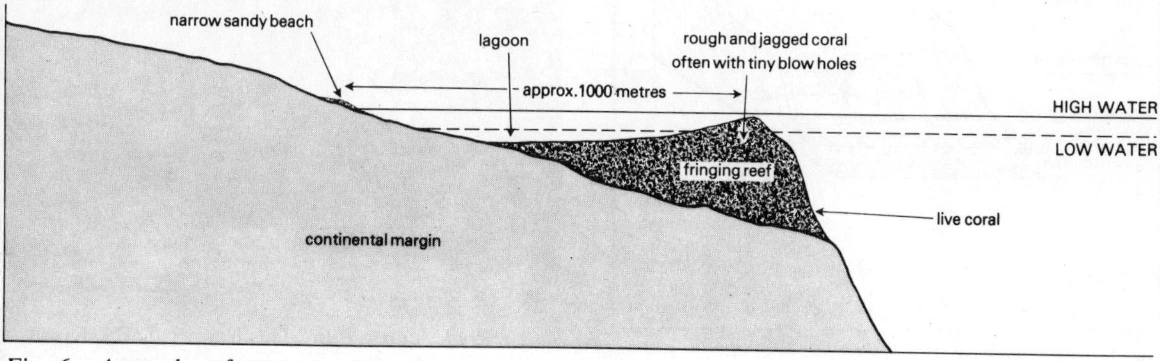

Fig. 6   A coral reef

The water must be *clean, clear* and *salty* and so coral cannot grow opposite the mouths of rivers. There are therefore gaps in coral reefs where rivers enter the sea. Coral cannot withstand exposure to air and so dies if it is exposed at low tide.

3 What is a coral reef? It is composed of a platform of dead coral jutting out from the shore or the continental shelf but which is covered at high tide as shown in Fig. 6. At the seaward edge the actual reef is composed of live coral continually extending out to sea. The water is much deeper on the seaward side. Waves break on the reef and there is always a line of water to be seen where this is happening.

Group tasks

1 Why do rias make good harbours?
2 Explain in your own words how longshore drift is caused and moves rock material along a coastline.
3 Which African countries have a ria coastline?
4 Name 3 countries in Africa which have a coral coast. Why is there no coral on the Namib coast? See the chapter on climate if you do not know. Why is there coral round the Bermuda Islands which are further north than 30°N?
5 Study Fig. 2. Which of Points A, B or C would make a good site for a port? Give reasons for your answer.

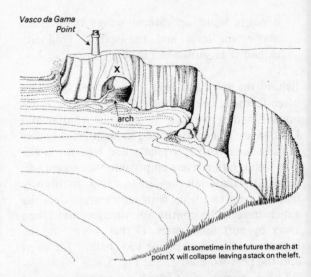

Vasco da Gama Point

X

arch

at sometime in the future the arch at point X will collapse leaving a stack on the left.

Fig. 8   Vasco da Gama Point, Malindi

Some of Africa's coasts have high steep cliffs. Examples of these can be seen along the coasts of East Africa where coral cliffs stand high above the dead coral of the inner reef. They are often undercut, with deep caves cutting into the base of the cliff which fierce waves have carved over the thousands of years. In places the waves have cut through the roofs of the caves to reach the surface. At high tide the sea smashes against the cliffs and water splashes through the holes at the top.

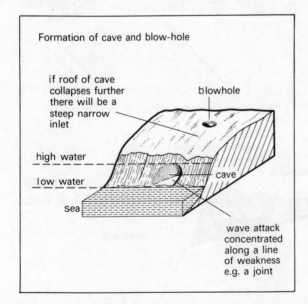

Formation of cave and blow-hole

if roof of cave collapses further there will be a steep narrow inlet

blowhole

high water

low water

cave

sea

wave attack concentrated along a line of weakness e.g. a joint

Fig. 7   A blow-hole

Turtle Rock, Turtle Bay   This is a peculiarly shaped stack formed by wave undercutting.

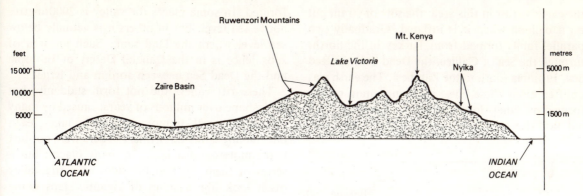

Fig. 9   Sketch section west to east across Africa along the Equator

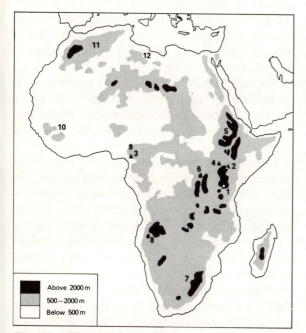

Fig. 10   The relief of Africa

There are known as *blow holes* and are shown in Fig. 7. Good examples of these can be seen on the north coast of Kenya.

It is along this coast also that examples of *stacks* and *arches* can be seen. When the sea attacks a headland caves are cut; and sometimes they are cut right through from one side to another to form an *arch*. After thousands of years wave attack will cause the arch to collapse leaving an isolated pinnacle of rock in the sea separated from the mainland. These are called *stacks*. Study Fig. 8. Watamu, north of Mombasa, has many cliffs, blow holes, arches and stacks where the sea has attacked the dead coral of the mainland as can be seen in the photograph opposite.

Plateau Africa

By far the oldest parts of Africa, with rocks dating back more than 70 million years, are the plateau lands. Most of Africa above 300 metres in altitude is plateau land.

The plateau lands are found at different levels with basement rocks, of differing ages. They often form a series of steps and levels, each one denoting, possibly, a long geological pause in Africa's emergence from the sea. These plateau lands are highest in Eastern Africa and slope downwards to the west, as shown in Figs. 9 and 10.

The rift valleys

Because the rocks of plateau Africa are very old they have reacted differently from younger, sedimentary rocks when pressures and strains from within the earth's crust have been applied to them. Young sedimentary rocks tend to fold if pressure is applied to them, but old rocks are hard and brittle. When pressures and tensions are applied they crack rather than fold.

Such a thing has happened in Eastern Africa from the north-eastern corner of Egypt right to the Zambesi River and beyond. Parts of the earth's crust have been pulled apart, parallel cracks have been formed and there has been displacement along the cracks, or *faults* as geologists call them. The result, over millions of years, has been a rift valley; the longest and biggest in the world as shown in Fig. 11.

Many people think it evolved as follows. First there were great pressures from within the earth's crust and this part of Africa was uplifted from within. This is thought to have put great strain on

7

the earth's crust in this area: the sort of strain put on a balloon when it is inflated. Gradually two parallel faults formed from Turkey in the north, through the Sea of Galilee, the Dead Sea, the Red Sea, Ethiopia south to the Zambesi. The earth was uplifted along these lines, great mountain ranges formed on either side. Between the faults the land did not rise so much and so a rift valley was formed. In some places the valley is 2000 metres above sea level; but in others it is actually below sea level where the land sank. Such an area of subsidence is in the Danakil Desert of Ethiopia and the Dead Sea between Jordan and Israel.

These rift valleys did not form suddenly, but took shape over millions of years; caused by many millions of earth tremors and earthquakes, each one making a tiny adjustment. There were not just two simple parallel faults in many places; but a series of them, so that the sides of a rift valley often look like a series of gigantic steps going down into the valley bottom. In fact they are called *step faults*, and an example is shown in Fig. 12. Even today the movements go on, adjustments are still being made and some of you who live in Eastern Africa may have felt earth tremors in recent years.

The step faulting can most easily be seen not far from Nairobi in Kenya, although it is partly hidden by a lot of surface soil: young sedimentary rock weathered and eroded from the mountain tops.

In Eastern Africa there are two rift valleys: the eastern and western rifts. The western rift contains lakes like Tanganyika and Albert while the eastern rift contains lakes like Turkana, Naivasha, Natron and Manyara. The two rift valleys unite further south to become one and contain Lake Malawi before disappearing as a valley just north of Beira in Mozambique. See Fig. 11.

Some parts of plateau Africa did not develop faults but just sank a little. Lake Victoria was probably formed when the land on either side rose and a depression was formed in between. Lake Chad is another basin or depression like Lake Victoria. Look at the very high and mountainous

Lakes	
1	Turkana
2	Malawi
3	Tanganyika
4	Edward
5	Albert
6	Victoria (*not* in Rift Valley)

X – Volcanoes
Mt. Elgon
Mt. Kenya
Kilimanjaro

0   600 kms

Fig. 11   The Great East African Rift Valley

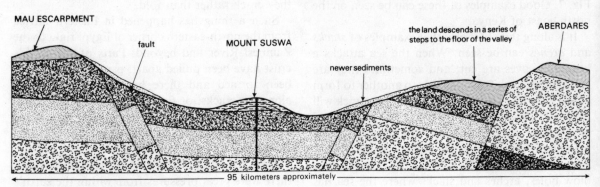

MAU ESCARPMENT

fault

MOUNT SUSWA

newer sediments

the land descends in a series of steps to the floor of the valley

ABERDARES

←—————— 95 kilometers approximately ——————→

Note the displacement of the three main bands of rocks.

Fig. 12   Step faulting near Nairobi

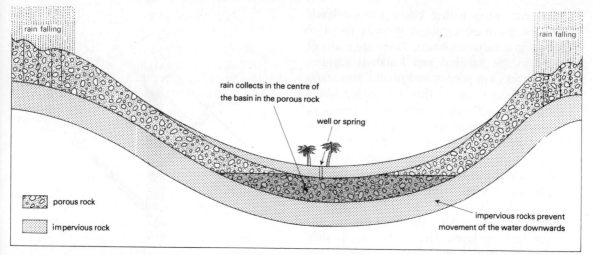

rain falling

rain collects in the centre of
the basin in the porous rock

well or spring

rain falling

impervious rocks prevent
movement of the water downwards

porous rock

impervious rock

Fig. 13   An artesian basin

regions which surround Victoria on almost all sides. As a result many rivers had to change direction and flowed back into the depression to fill it and form lakes like Kyoga and Victoria.

Many mountains often accompany rift valley formation: any sort of faulting in fact. They have a special name and are called *horst* mountains or *block* mountains. The Ruwenzori range is a very good example. In another part of Africa, the Kalahari region, the Great Karas Mountains are good examples.

East African Rift Valley, Kenya   Notice the different levels on the right of the picture.
1   What sort of faulting could this be?
2   What sort of mountain is shown? Give reasons for your answer.
3   Why is the vegetation more luxurious on the valley sides?

Depressions can be caused by other means as well. The Qattara depression in Egypt could have been caused by the earth's crust subsiding a little as some of it is below sea level; but the wind might also have helped. The strong desert winds can carry a lot of desert dust and sand away, particularly if it is loose and dry. It could be that so much loose surface material was blown away that water beneath the ground was nearly reached. Some desert oases are formed like this. There are many thousands of oases in the Sahara regions, both big and small. Huge areas of ground water lie beneath the desert surface.

Question and answer session

1   How do continents move? Many people think that it is because the earth's crust may be made up of different layers like a pile of plates and that the plates are moving. They think that one continental plate often tries to move under or over another. This disrupts the earth's crust; and evidence of this is thought to be provided by the many earthquakes the world is experiencing.

2   Why do continents move? The next time you boil some food watch the movements of the food in the container. The surface material moves to the sides you will find. These are convection currents caused by great heat. Many people now think that the earth's continental plates are moved in a similar way by convection currents set up within the earth's very hot, possibly molten, interior.

3 How can water gather below ground level? One of the most common ways is for it to gather in an artesian basin. There are many of these in the Saharan and Kalahari regions. Some rocks are porous and permit rain water to soak into them. If they are folded like a saucer rain will fall on mountains and soak down to the bottom of the saucer a long way below the surface, as shown in Fig. 13.

4 Why does the water not soak away? Artesian basins also have impervious rocks above and below the porous layer. Thus the water is trapped. It collects in the basin for millions of years and then, maybe, the wind exposes the water bearing layer. Or, as in Libya, men drilling for oil find water instead. Beneath the Libyan Desert there is much water; as much, in fact, as in the whole of the five Great Lakes of North America. This is the reason why the oil fields in the deserts of Libya often have huge farms near them.

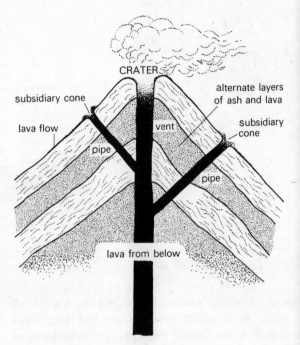

Fig. 14 A composite volcano

Volcanoes and their lava

Plateau Africa has large areas where *vulcanicity* has affected the earth's surface. Many of these areas are now quiet, but there are some where vulcanicity is still active.

Vulcanicity almost always occurs in conjunction with faulting of the earth's crust; and particularly when a rift valley is being formed. When cracks or faults occur in the earth's surface, lava from deep in the earth's crust escapes and can flow for hundreds of miles. The lava often solidifies to form huge plateaus, hundreds of square miles in extent, e.g. the Yatta Plateau in Kenya. The Tibesti and Hoggar Mountains of the Sahara are vast areas of lava. The Ethiopian Highlands form a very large and high volcanic plateau in which rivers have cut many deep gorges. The Aberdare Mountains in Kenya are formed of lava hundreds of feet thick, which accumulated when the first faults began, before the area was mountainous.

Instead of flowing for such long distances lava which is sometimes thick and more solid builds up a volcano when it reaches the surface. The lava cannot flow far before solidifying but, in each eruption, it runs in different directions from a central hole or *crater* in the earth's crust. After

Mount Longonot, Kenya The photograph shows a 'bench' on top of a step fault.
1 What is the physical feature in the far background?
2 What sort of volcano is Longonot?
3 What is the principal human activity on the 'bench'? Explain your answer.

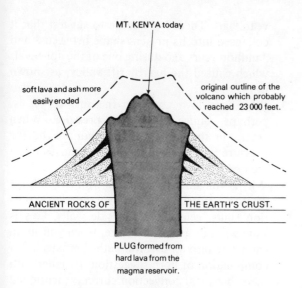

soft lava and ash more easily eroded

MT. KENYA today

original outline of the volcano which probably reached 23 000 feet.

ANCIENT ROCKS OF   THE EARTH'S CRUST.

PLUG formed from hard lava from the magma reservoir.

Fig. 15   Mt. Kenya — a volcanic plug

millions of years and thousands of eruptions the volcano may become very high. Mount Kenya and Mount Kilimanjaro are two good examples. They are called composite volcanoes because they are made up of different layers of lava, dust, cinders and lava pieces as shown in Fig. 14.

At the top of a volcano the crater is found. Its bottom, often flat, is well below the high rim of the volcano. It is from the crater that the eruptions occur; but in dormant or extinct volcanoes trees and vegetation develop on the crater bottom, as on Mount Longonot in Kenya and Mount Ngodoto in Tanzania. Sometimes even a lake is formed on the crater floor as in the crater of Mount Marsabit in Kenya. The lakes are filled by the rain which often falls on high mountains.

The lava in the central pipe of a composite volcano is often very hard indeed; much harder, in fact, than the outside slopes. Sometimes this outside lava is worn away and the hard central core is left standing. The upstanding peaks are called *plugs* and two very good examples of this sort of feature are seen on Mount Kenya's peaks and the peaks of Mount Mawenzi which is part of Mount Kilimanjaro. Further examples occur in the volcanic Hoggar Mountains of the Sahara. Fig. 15 shows how they are formed.

Vulcanicity has provided Africa with one of the finest wild life sanctuaries in the world; an example of the monstrous power which volcanoes can generate, power greater even than that generated by modern nuclear explosions. This is

the Ngorongoro Crater which is not really a crater at all: it is much too big for that. This feature is called a *caldera*. The floor of the Ngorongoro caldera is as much as 16 kilometres wide in places, and is enclosed by cliff-like sides over 600 metres high.

Ngorongoro Crater Tanzania   The home of one of the richest and most varied collections of wild life anywhere in Africa.
1   What is the name given to such a vast physical feature as this?
2   Where does some of the lake's water come from? Use evidence from the picture for your answer.
3   Why is there a rich linear growth of trees in this dry looking area?

Geysers and hot springs

These features are also proof of volcanic activity, and occur when ground water is superheated by volcanically heated subterranean rocks. The water reaches the surface by way of cracks in the earth. Water in these cracks or pipes is superheated at depth to temperatures well above boiling point and pressure builds up. When, eventually, pressure from below forces the water out of the vent at the surface, violent jets of water, spray and steam are propelled into the air. The pressure below is relieved and the process starts to build up again. In East Africa Lake Magadi has many small hot springs and Lake Bogoria (Hannington) has some large boiling pools on its banks of near geyser size. Hot springs and steam jets also occur around Lake Naivasha.

11

Question and answer session

1 Why does some lava flow long distances, while other lava does not? Some lava is not very acidic and is very fluid indeed. It is called basic lava and can flow over great distances. Other lavas are thick and viscous, very acidic and with a high silica content. These cannot flow great distances and usually build high mountains rather than plateaus.

2 How are calderas formed? Many people think they are caused by massive explosions. These are said to occur when acidic lava blocks the pipe. Pressure builds up until it can be contained no longer and a huge explosion takes place which blows off the complete top of the volcano.

Another theory suggests that there is so much space left beneath a volcano after a long and violent eruption that there is nothing beneath it to support its weight and the whole thing just collapses into itself. Certainly, Ngorongoro was about 4600 metres high many millions of years ago. There is evidence to suggest that it collapsed into its present shape between 2 and 3 million years ago during one of the upheavals which caused the nearby rift valley, as shown in Fig. 16.

3 Why does lava come to the surface? It is, perhaps, under very great pressure. When cracks in the earth's crust occur maybe the pressure is released and the lava moves to an area of less pressure.

4 Why is vulcanicity associated with rift valleys? There is a possibility that when the central portion sinks, relative to the side walls, lava is squeezed out as, for instance, when you jump carelessly into an overfull bath. Perhaps it is a combination of both suggestions together with the sub-crustal convection currents mentioned earlier.

Fold mountains

Some mountains are created by a process known as folding, others by faulting, rifting and vul-

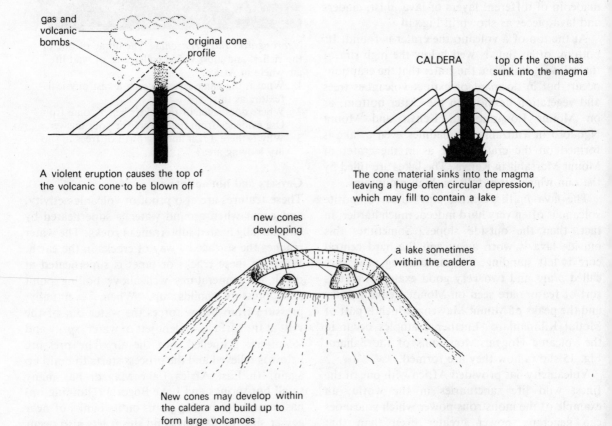

gas and volcanic bombs

original cone profile

A violent eruption causes the top of the volcanic cone to be blown off

CALDERA — top of the cone has sunk into the magma

The cone material sinks into the magma leaving a huge often circular depression, which may fill to contain a lake

new cones developing

a lake sometimes within the caldera

New cones may develop within the caldera and build up to form large volcanoes

Fig. 16   Stages in the development of a caldera

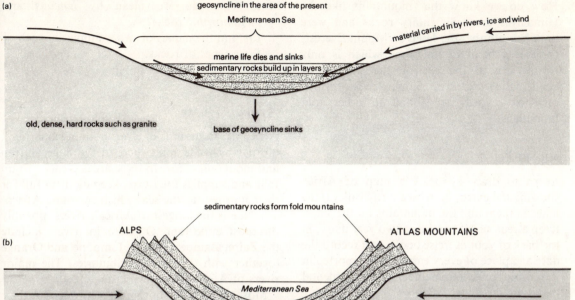

Fig. 17   The formation of the northern fold mountains of Africa

canicity. Africa does not have many fold mountain ranges, which occur when layers of fairly young sedimentary rocks are subjected to tremendous pressures. Fold mountains form the highest mountains and mountain ranges in the world. The Andes of South America, the Alps of Europe and the Himalayas, highest of all, are proof of that.

Africa's fold mountains are found at her northern and southern extremities. In the far south in South Africa there are some very old fold mountains; but the Atlas Mountains of Algeria and Morocco are much younger, and are the product, along with the European Alps, of Africa's northward drift as shown in Fig. 17.

Question and answer session

1   How are fold mountains actually formed? Many geologists consider that a huge, vast, pre-existing and water filled depression in the earth's surface, known as a *geosyncline*, is gradually filled in by wind and water-borne deposits of eroded rock material. Moving ice can play its part in this; and so also can the millions upon millions of sea creatures who die and whose bodies sink to the ocean floor and help the build up, which takes millions of years. Gradually the increased weight of these deposits helps deepen the geosyncline and the bed is depressed still further. This, in turn, is thought to pull the sides of the geosyncline towards the centre. Perhaps the continental plates are encouraged by this to move towards each other. Pressure on the sedimentary rocks is increased and slowly, over millions of years they are crumpled up, folded and uplifted out of the water, high into the atmosphere. So, the Deccan plate of southern India, by its northward movement, has caused the folding of what is now the Himalayas from a geosycline to its north. Africa possibly created the folds of southern Europe in the same way and at the same time, the Atlas Mountains. The suggested series of events are shown in Fig. 17.

2 How do we know that mountains like the Himalayas are sedimentary rocks and were once beneath the sea? High on Mount Everest, there is a band of limestone which is only formed beneath the sea from the skeletons of dead marine creatures! Similar rocks formed only on seabeds are found in other fold mountains.

Group tasks

1 Learn to draw by heart a map of Africa showing the extent of Africa's rift valleys, the lakes in them and the mountains on the sides.
2 Keep a year's or if possible a two year diary, in the back of your exercise book. In it record the date and place of every earthquake reported in the world press. Remember the continental plates are moving...always.
3 Make a record of any lava plateaus or volcanoes in your country.
4 Draw a diagram to illustrate how geysers and hot springs work.
5 Make a list of all the major fold mountain ranges of the world. Discuss it with your teacher.
6 Go to your school library, or ask your teacher. Find out for yourselves two things:

a) What do we mean by *igneous* and *metamorphic* rocks?
b) Find the names of two examples of each of these types of rocks.

Africa's rivers

Africa has thousands of rivers both big and small, all of which rise somewhere in the huge plateau and mountain areas. In these areas plenty of rain falls and supplies the rivers, keeping them full for their journeys to the seas which surround Africa. The Nile is the longest of Africa's rivers, possibly the most important. Other major rivers include the Zaîre, Zambezi, Niger, Limpopo and Orange together with their many tributaries. The major rivers of Africa are shown in Fig. 18.

Most rivers differ in character throughout their course. The same river can present a very different picture near its source to the one it presents as it approaches the sea. At all times we must remember one very important thing; and that is that plateau Africa extends in many places almost to the coast and there is then quite a steep drop to the plain. The Niger is one of the very few African rivers which descend gradually, to the sea and not, like most of Africa's rivers, in a series of steps with waterfalls and rapids at each change in level.

Generally speaking however, most rivers can be divided along their course into three fairly distinct parts the major features of which are shown in Figs. 19 and 20. They are
1 The Upper Course,
2 The Middle Course,
3 The Lower Course.
Some rivers have all three of these stages, while a few, a very few, have two or only one. For instance, some small rivers flowing off the plateau edge in South Africa or West Africa, too small and numerous to name, have only an upper stage and a brief middle stage. Some small rivers flowing in high mountains end their life in a mountain lake and only experience an upper stage. Remember though, that no matter how big or small a river is, no matter which or all the stages it may have, its main task is to erode, to carry and to deposit rock material which has moved down its valley sides and into its water. In this way continents are lowered, washed into the sea and geosynclines are gradually filled up.

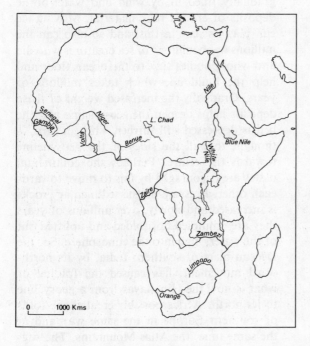

Fig. 18   The major rivers of Africa

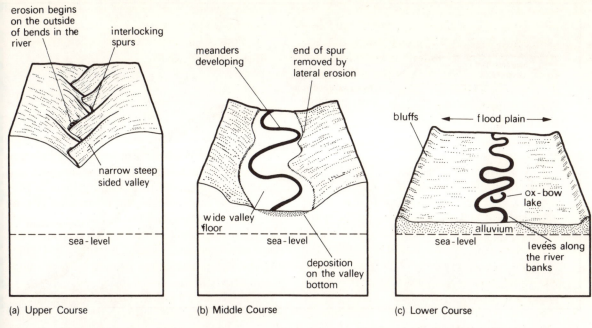

(a) Upper Course (b) Middle Course (c) Lower Course

Fig. 19 Major features of a river valley

The Niger valley from the air
At what stage is this river? Give evidence from the picture.

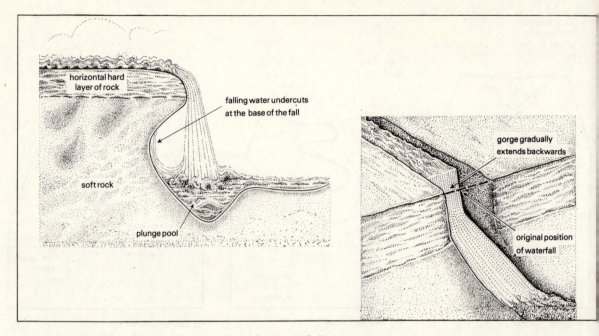

Fig. 20   Diagram to show the recession of a waterfall

Each stage in a river's development has several features which distinguish it from the others. In the upper or mountain stage for instance the river is very fast and very shallow, except in flood. It has a steep gradient and a very narrow, deep valley caused because its speed has allowed it, with the aid of the material it carries, to cut deep into its own bed. There are pot holes to be seen where water-borne rocks have swirled round and carved smooth holes into the bedrock. Interlocking spurs are frequently seen and there are many waterfalls and rapids. The waterfalls often carve out steep sided gorges as they are cut back or retreat. A wonderful example of a gorge is that one created in Uganda by the Murchison (Kabalega) Falls on the Victoria Nile as it enters Lake Albert (Mobutu Sese Seko). Think also of the Victoria Falls and its gorge. There are thousands more, in almost every country in Africa. It is when in flood that these rivers can move huge boulders along their beds by rolling them along: a process known as *traction*.

In the middle course the river is wider and deeper. There is more water because many more tributaries have added to its volume: The valley floor is flat because the river has worn back the interlocking spurs. All of Africa's bigger rivers have a very long length of middle course. The water does not flow so fast but there is more of it. It cannot roll huge rocks along its bed but it can carry, such is its volume, millions of tons of fine sediment suspended in its water. In places there are wide bends or *meanders* where the bank on one side is steep because the river undercuts it as it sweeps round. On the other side, the inside bank is low and shallow with a slight slope. River water always erodes most at the outside bank where the main current is found.

In its lower course the river is very slow indeed because there is almost no gradient as it approaches the sea. You could say it was tired. It is so slow that it cannot carry so much material and sometimes deposits it on its bed. Its flood plain is wide with few, if any, hills in sight. Its meanders are almost complete, though misshapen, circles; and in some places it has broken through the narrow neck of land on the meander to create a newer, straighter path. The old course is left as a curved lake known as an *oxbow*. The Tana in Kenya has many such oxbow lakes. The old river's banks are often very high, as a result of deposition at flood time, and the river flows above its flood plain. The banks are known as *levées* and they are often the sites of settlement: dry areas in a sea of water when the river floods and part of the banks break. This can also be seen on the Tana.

Some rivers have big *deltas*: great triangular areas of very flat, low lying ground, seen where

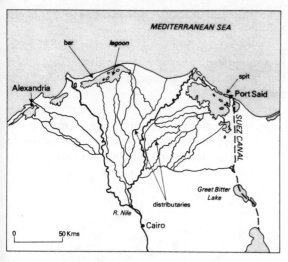

Fig. 21   The Nile delta

the river enters the sea. The deltas of the Nile as shown in Fig. 21, and Niger are very well known indeed but there are many others. The Zambezi has one, so also have the Tana and Rufiji in East Africa, not to mention the Senegal. Deltas form when a river enters the sea (or a lake). The river has its speed checked and so it drops and deposits some of the silt and mud it is carrying. If there are no powerful sea currents this material will gradually build up until the river's path is blocked and it has to divide and flow round the obstacle. Sometimes the river even breaks through it. The river has to do this often, and in this way the many channels or *distributaries* of a delta are formed and the delta gradually extends further and further into the sea.

Question and answer session

1   How do waterfalls cut back on themselves? As the water plunges over the fall it falls heavily into the river at the foot of the fall. There is much splashing and erosion and this undercuts the rock at the base of the fall. A cave is carved out and the top overhangs it as shown in Fig. 20. After many years there is no support for the top and it falls in. The process then starts again.

2   How are oxbow lakes formed? They are formed when the neck of a meander becomes very narrow. There comes a stage when the river floods heavily and also flows faster. It sweeps across the narrow neck to form a new course.

When the floods subside the lake is left separate from the river.

3   How are levées formed? Whenever the lower course of a river overflows its banks in flood periods small amounts of deposition occur on the banks. During low water periods the river deposits material on its bed. Over the years both banks and beds are built up above the surrounding plain.

Group tasks

Study the big African rivers in an atlas.
1   In which highland region does each rise?
2   Which river flows through most countries?
3   Which rivers flow through deserts or semi-deserts?
4   Rivers often form borders between countries. Can you find and name some examples?

Inland drainage

Many of Africa's smaller rivers are unable to reach a river's normal destination: the sea. Instead they flow into lakes. There are many examples of this in Africa and you can easily find some by looking, in your atlas, at Lake Chad or the Okavango Swamplands in Botswana. There are also several examples of inland drainage in the great rift valley regions. All water contains mineral salts and, if the climate in an inland drainage area is very hot there is great evaporation. When this happens the mineral salts are left behind and the lakes sometimes become very saline (salty) indeed. Lake Magadi in Kenya for instance, is full of solid salts and there is very little water. Namibia and Botswana have many salty basins for the same reason. Study your map and try to find an example.

Lakes Victoria and Malawi are among many lakes which are not salty. Discuss why this is so and search for other examples.

The ice and snow areas

Africa is often considered to be quite a hot country, and so it is almost everywhere. However there are certain small parts of Africa where, because of great altitude, much snow and ice is found. All examples are found in East Africa where the altitude is 4750 metres or more. Above this height there is permanent snow which has formed glaciers in many places. All these places are quite near the Equator, in fact the Equator crosses one of them: Mount Kenya.

The glaciers on these mountains used to be much bigger when the earth was much colder than it is now. They reached much further down the mountains. Glacier ice moves downhill, flowing like water, though very much more slowly; and as it moves it scrapes and grinds away at the rock beneath it and at its sides. It also has rock tools to help it.

The result of thousands of years of ice erosion in a mountain valley is a steep sided valley with a flat floor. These valleys are known as *U shaped valleys*.

U shaped valleys are not the only features created by moving ice and snow. Small basin shaped depressions are sometimes enlarged when snow and ice gather in them later to form a small

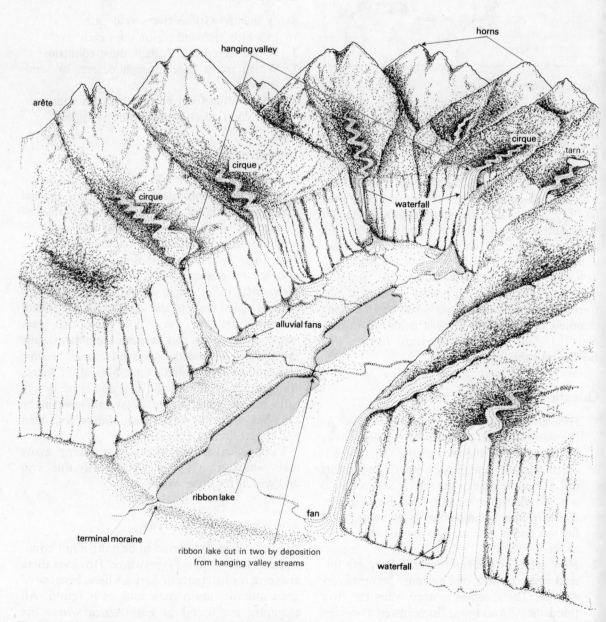

Fig. 22 Features at the head of a glaciated valley

A different view of Mount Kenya
Discuss it with your teacher and pinpoint: a pyramidal peak, an arête, a cirque, scree slopes, a trough end and a 'U' shaped valley. Make a diagrammatic sketch and label these features.

moving glacier. They are called *cirques*. They are widened and deepened by the freezing and thawing of water in cracks in the rock walls. The sides of a cirque are quite steep and when there is more than one cirque on a peak these steep sides sometimes become very sharp knife-like ridges between the cirques. When several cirques are situated all round a mountain there is usually a very sharp, high and pointed peak rising above them. It is called a *pyramidal peak* or *horn*. If the ice later melts in a cirque a small lake is often formed. This is known as a *tarn*, and very often a small steam flows from it and plunges headlong into the valley below by means of a waterfall or very steep gradient. These are known as *hanging valleys* because they are high above the main valley. All these features are shown in Fig. 22.

Question and answer session

1   What are a glacier's tools? These are pieces of rock, both big and small, which fall from rock faces onto the glacier. They sink to the bottom of the glacier and are carried with it as the glacier moves. They assist in the grinding and scraping action of the ice.

2   What causes rocks to fall into glaciers? Rocks are always breaking off from mountain sides. A weathering process known as frost shattering causes the break up.

3   What causes frost shattering? At night water frequently freezes in little cracks on mountain sides. Water expands in volume when it freezes, widening the cracks. There is more room for water when the ice melts. When it freezes again the crack becomes even bigger. This goes on until a piece of rock is broken off and falls. In the highest mountains of Africa it is a 24 hour process with night time freezing and day time melting. In this way cirque side walls retreat to meet each other and the back walls retreat to produce a pyramidal peak. The peaks of Ruwenzori and Mount Kenya have been sharpened in this manner. There are hundreds of small cirques and tarns all over these mountains.

Glaciers carry their tools of erosion with them as they move. And, like the wind, the sea and rivers they have to put them down sometimes: deposit them in fact. Every piece of rock a glacier carries is deposited at its snout: the place where the ice melts. This material builds up into a large pile of

Kilimanjaro with Kibo and Mawenzi
1   In which approximate direction are we looking?
2   Notice the jagged peaks of Mawenzi. What weathering process produces these?
3   Name the mountain in the distance. What sort of mountain is it?
4   Which is older: Kibo or Mawenzi — why do you say so?

material called a *terminal moraine*. Many rock pieces are deposited where a glacier touches the side of a valley and this is called a *lateral* or *side moraine*. These features are shown in Fig. 23.

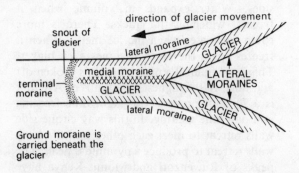

Fig. 23 Moraines

Group tasks

1 Are there any examples of inland drainage in your country? If so make sure you know their names and where they are.

2 Make a list of all the permanent snow areas in Africa.

3 Which African countries might experience snow falls for part of the year? How high are their highest parts?

4 Go to your library. Find out what *scree* is. It has something to do with frost shattering.

The dry lands

In a country like Africa the dry lands are deserts or semi-deserts. The little rain that falls is soon lost by evaporation, and so running water is not such an important agent of erosion as in wetter areas. The most important agent of erosion in the deserts is the wind. The wind uses tools, just like ice and water. It picks up small rock pieces, sands and dust and hurls them against hills and mountains. The wind is always very powerful in the desert and, with its tools, it carves many wonderful shapes in upstanding rock. With its rock tools it has been known to cut down wooden telegraph poles. Valley sides are always steep in deserts because the wind blown sands and stones

Fig. 24 A desert basin or wadi

cut away at the base until the top falls down: just like a waterfall.

Water does help erode in the desert as well. It rarely rains in these regions, but when it does the storms are very heavy although they do not last long. Flash floods quickly build up and, for an hour or so, rocky valleys in plain and mountain become raging torrents of water carrying thousands of tons of *scree* by traction, suspension and saltation. They soon die out and sink into the ground, leaving their rocky, sandy load where they sink as shown in Fig. 24.

The wind also deposits material. It builds up sand dunes into shapes which look like a half-moon, called *barchans* or *crescent dunes*. There are thousands upon thousands of square miles of them in the Sahara, and together they are called *sand seas*. Barchans are created by a prevailing wind. Sand collects around an obstacle or clump of vegetation and piles up on the windward side falling over to the other slope to form the *slip off face*. The sides of a barchan creep forward faster than the middle because there is less wind resistance encouraging deposition.

Inselbergs are very important features of the dry lands. They are lonely, isolated hills or mountains standing up above the general level of the plain. Some represent the remains of older, higher levels of land while others have been exposed because the land surface has been eroded from around them. They are also an important feature of the savanna lands of Kenya. Some of the inselbergs have very flat tops and concave sides as shown in Fig. 26 and

A Libyan sand sea
1 What are the deposition features shown?
2 Is there any possible evidence of human activity in this picture?
3 What evidence is there to suggest this photo was taken long before midday? Look at shadows, the deposition features and think of prevailing winds.

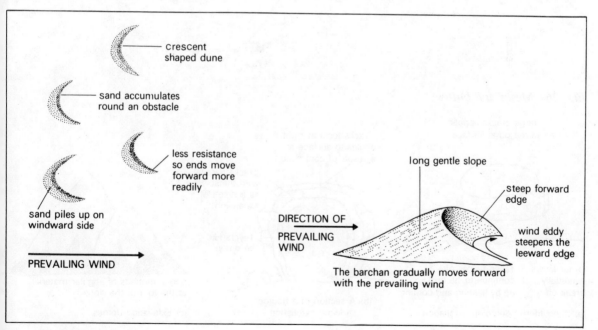

- crescent shaped dune
- sand accumulates round an obstacle
- less resistance so ends move forward more readily
- sand piles up on windward side

PREVAILING WIND

DIRECTION OF PREVAILING WIND

long gentle slope

steep forward edge

wind eddy steepens the leeward edge

The barchan gradually moves forward with the prevailing wind

Fig. 25 *Barchan dunes*

21

are called *mesas*. The tops are of hard resistant rock which lies on top of softer rock. The flat tops protect the soft rock beneath from erosion by wind and water. These mesas are all that is left after thousands of years of erosion have carved away the rest of the higher surface level.

Some inselbergs are smooth and round; quite unlike the flat topped mesas. They are the product of *exfoliation*: another weathering process which depends on great changes in temperature each day. There are many to be seen in Kenya's northlands, in Zimbabwe in the Matopos Hills and in Tanzania.

Question and answer session

1 What is saltation? This occurs when tiny pieces of rock are partly rolled and partly suspended by a moving force: either water or wind. The small rock pieces are light enough to be lifted but too heavy to stay lifted.

2 What is weathering? This is the means whereby water, temperature, chemicals, bacteria and animals combine or act singly to bring about the break up of rocks and, in the end, the formation of soil.

There are different types of weathering. Mechanical or physical weathering largely concerns temperature changes, e.g. freeze and thaw or the action of burrowing animals. Chemical weathering concerns the solvent effect that water has on soluble minerals in rocks. Biotic weathering is a form of chemical weathering when bacteria from animal droppings and acids from decaying vegetation and animal droppings act on the mineral constituents of rocks.

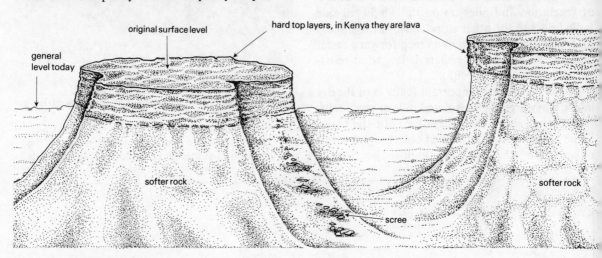

Fig. 26 *Mesas and buttes*

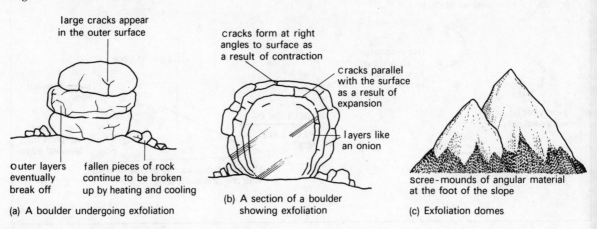

(a) A boulder undergoing exfoliation

(b) A section of a boulder showing exfoliation

(c) Exfoliation domes

Fig. 27 *Exfoliation features*

3 What is exfoliation? This is a form of mechanical weathering by temperature change, assisted slightly by water. Daytime heating of the surface layers causes rocks to expand. Cracks parallel to the surface are formed. At night a drop in temperature occurs. The rock contracts and cracks form at right angles to the surface. Over the years layers of rock peel off from the main rock, giving a smooth rounded surface. The chemical action of any water in the cracks greatly assists this process.

Group tasks

1 Have a class discussion on how animals and plants can assist weathering.
2 Go to your library. Ask your teacher. Find out all you can about *tors*.
3 Which types of weathering might be most important in
   a) the Zaïre rain forests and
   b) the Tibesti Mountains.
   Give reasons for your answer.

2 Africa's climates

Before we deal with the climates of Africa we must first look at the earth as a whole. By doing that it will be easier to understand the climates of Africa.

The planetary wind system and pressure belts

What has to be understood first is that the equatorial region of the earth is an area of low atmospheric pressure. The pressure of the atmosphere on the earth's surface there is very light. In this region the greatest, most consistent, heat from the sun is received. The hot surface heats the air near to it and so the air expands and rises. This rising air splits up in the upper atmosphere and moves either north or south. As this air moves away from the equatorial regions in the upper atmosphere it seems as if it is deflected slightly to the east by the earth's rotation. However, just north of the tropic of Cancer and south of Capricorn, this upper atmosphere air becomes dense and heavy. This is because

a) of the continued arrival of air from the equatorial regions and

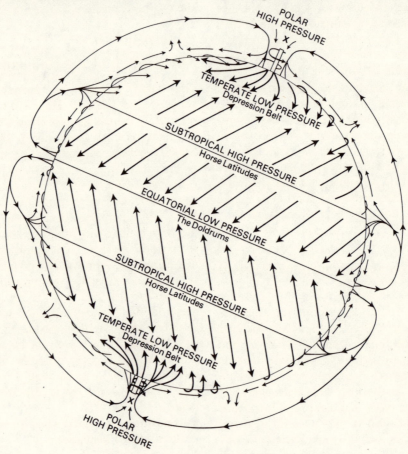

X   The axis is inserted to show the direction of rotation

Fig. 28   The planetary wind system

b) an ever increasing centrifugal force which, because the air is rotating round the earth's axis faster than the earth itself, tends to restrict a further movement to the poles.

For these two reasons much of the air above the tropical and sub-tropical areas of the earth descends to the earth's surface. Thus areas of the surface just outside the tropics become High Pressure zones as shown in Fig. 28. On reaching the surface this air splits up. One body of air heads polewards, being deflected to the east all the time. These are the south-west winds of the Northern Hemisphere and the north-west winds of the Southern Hemisphere. The other air body heads towards the Equator, being deflected westwards all the time. These are the North-East (Northern Hemisphere) and the South-East (Southern Hemisphere) Trade Winds.

The remaining air in the upper atmosphere over the tropics keeps moving polewards, becoming colder all the time. This air meets and concentrates at the poles. It becomes extremely dense and heavy and even colder; and there descends and creates a high pressure area at each Pole. On the surface air swirls outwards towards the Equator and is deflected westward all the time. This air becomes the North-East winds in the northern hemisphere and the South-East winds in the southern hemisphere. At the point on the earth's surface where they meet the westerly winds an area of low pressure is formed: the Temperate Low Pressure Belt. These pressure belts and resulting winds are shown in Fig. 28. Unfortunately it is not as simple as that. Two factors alter the basic pattern.

Factor 1

The earth's axis and its movement round the sun

The earth moves round the sun one complete circuit every $365\frac{1}{4}$ days. Because its axis is inclined from the vertical *either* the northern *or* the southern hemisphere is often facing more towards the sun than the other. This means one hemisphere becomes hotter than the other. One hemisphere has winter while the other has summer. *Insolation* (heating from the sun) is thus unequal in either hemisphere for much of the year. Because of this the heat equator (the area receiving maximum insolation) is often north or south of the mathematical equator. It thus follows that the

Doldrums, that area of rising air and thus low atmospheric pressure, is *also* either north or south of the mathematical equator for much of the year. This, in turn, means that the meeting place of the North-East and South-East Trades is, for much of the year, either north or south of the mathematical equator. In fact, this all results in the whole planetary system of wind belts moving slightly north or south during the year according to which hemisphere is receiving greatest insolation.

The Trade Winds can and do (in places) cross the Equator. The Westerlies also move north or south during the year. The Polar winds advance and retreat to and from the equator. Look back at Fig. 28. It shows the earth tilted on its axis and the wind and pressure belts equi-distant from the Equator. This sort of thing occurs when the sun is overhead on the Equator in March and September. At other times of the year the winds and pressure belts move north or south according to the overhead position of the sun.

Factor 2

The position of the land and sea areas

The earth presents an unequal relationship between land and sea. Huge land areas are surrounded by even bigger sea areas. Land changes its temperature much more quickly than the sea, as solids generally change their temperature much quicker than water.

So, when the sun is overhead in the northern hemisphere the land becomes hotter than the northern hemisphere seas. Because the surface affects the air in contact with it air over the land is heated. It expands, becomes less dense and lighter and therefore rises. Atmospheric pressure on the land is thus *LOW*. Over the seas pressure is *HIGHER* because the sea, and thus the air, is cooler than over the land and tends not to rise. In the southern hemisphere at this time it is winter. The land, cooling quicker than the sea (losing heat by radiation loss) is colder than the sea. Pressure is therefore *HIGH* over the land. Pressure over the seas is lower as the sea is now warmer than the land.

This position is reversed when the sun is overhead in the southern hemisphere.

You could rewrite the whole of the above paragraph to show this. BUT DON'T. There is a slight problem involved...

The northern land masses are bigger than the southern land masses: look at an atlas map of the world for proof. The result of this is that the northern lands' winters are colder than those of the southern hemisphere. Pressure is therefore much higher. Similarly, in northern lands summers become much hotter than those in the southern lands. Pressure, accordingly, becomes much lower. What does all this mean?

It means that the seasonal movements of the planetary wind system and its pressure belts are also unequal in extent. The thermal (heat) equator moves some considerable way north (in the northern hemisphere summer) where huge land masses lie to the north. It does not move an equal distance south because the land masses to the south are smaller. If there is no land mass to the immediate south and a big one to the north the heat equator tends to remain, in fact, just north of the mathematical equator, even in a southen hemisphere summer as will be shown in West Africa.

Thus north-south movement of the wind and pressure belts is not simple. In some areas it is a plain north-south movement, but in other areas, Asia for instance, pressure changes are so great that winds experience a complete reversal of direction during the year. In East Africa we are greatly affected by this as air flows from eastern Africa *into* Asia during the northern hemisphere summer. In the northern hemisphere winter air flows *from* Asia towards eastern Africa. All this is because air flows from high pressure areas to low pressure areas. In Asia and eastern Africa this movement is called the *Monsoon*.

Let us now look further at Africa's climates. Africa has hundreds of different climates because of her huge spread of latitude, the great differences in her altitude, the large mass of her land area and the different ocean currents which wash her shores. On a general level however we can satisfactorily reduce these to less than 10 major types. To a large extent Africa lies within the Trade Wind belt of winds. It is only at her northern and southern extremities that there is any real change. It is with these extremities that we will deal first. In these regions, for a few months of the year, Africa experiences cool and wet conditions because of the seasonal movements of the wind and pressure belts. For most months, however, they experience warm and dry conditions. A climate such as this is known as Mediterranean.

The Mediterranean climate

Another name given to this sort of climate is Warm Temperate Western Margin. In these areas

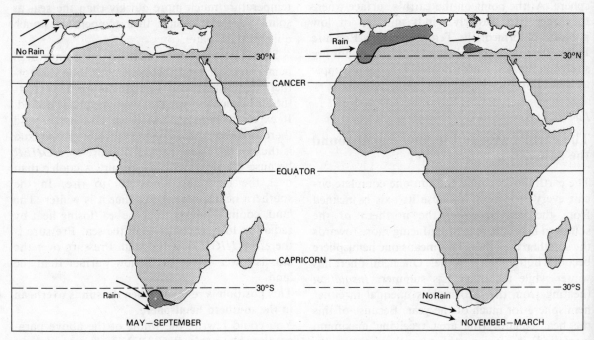

Fig. 29   Mediterranean regions of Africa

they have warm to hot, dry summers and cool to mild, wet winters.

To a large extent this is because in the winters there are onshore winds while in summers winds are offshore. As we have seen, the wind and pressure belts move slightly north and south with the sun during the course of a year. From May to September they move north. This means that the northern belt of westerlies moves northwards away from North Africa. At the same time the southern belt of westerlies moves northwards as well: towards South Africa and they just manage to blow onshore at the south-west trip around the Cape Town region, as shown in Fig. 29. Between November and March the wind and pressure belts move slightly south. The northern belt of westerlies moves south to blow onshore along the north west African coastal margins. The southern belt of westerlies also moves south into the southern ocean and does not affect Africa's south-west tip. At this time, there are offshore winds from a surface high pressure area over the sea to the south, plus cool descending air which is becoming warmer, which comes from a high pressure cell stationed permanently in the atmosphere over South Africa: even in summer. A simplified diagram of this is shown in Fig. 30. Remember that offshore winds do not bring rain because as they blow from the land to the sea they are dry and have very little moisture. Onshore winds often bring rain because they come from the sea to the land and contain much moisture. Rain in winter is also brought to these lands by depressions.

Summers in the Cape Town area are cooler than normal because temperatures are lowered by the cold Benguela ocean current which flows northwards along South Africa's west coast shown on your atlas map of ocean currents. Below is a set of statistics for both Mediterranean areas in Africa.

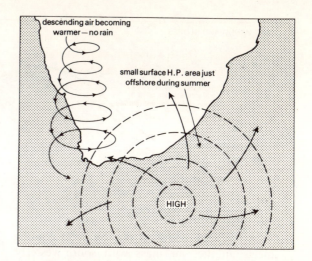

Fig. 30 High level atmospheric pressure in South Africa

Question and answer session

1   What is relief rain? This occurs when damp air is forced up a mountain side by strong winds. The air cools as it rises and its water vapour condenses to form clouds. As it moves higher the droplets of water vapour coalesce until eventually they are too heavy and fall from the cloud as rain as shown in Fig. 31.

In Africa the Atlas mountains of the north west and mountains like the Langerberg in the south-west cause this type of rainfall.

2   What is a depression? This is very difficult to explain. You must read this slowly and carefully to make sure you understand. Depressions are usually formed in temperate latitudes. They occur when two air masses meet. The line along which these air masses meet is known as a *front*. In the northern hemisphere one air mass with cold north

ALGIERS — North-west Africa

Temp. °C	12	13	15	16	19	22	25	26	24	20	17	15
Rain mm	150	87	87	60	30	12	—	—	25	75	110	140

CAPETOWN — South-west tip of Africa

Temp. °C	21	20	20	17	15	13	12	13	15	16	18	20
Rain mm	12	12	15	50	90	110	87	87	50	35	20	15

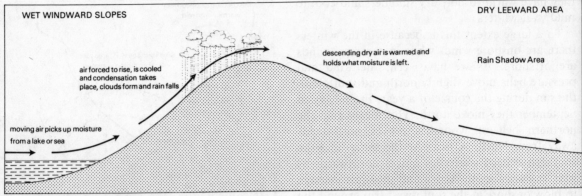

WET WINDWARD SLOPES

DRY LEEWARD AREA

air forced to rise, is cooled
and condensation takes
place, clouds form and rain falls

descending dry air is warmed and
holds what moisture is left.

Rain Shadow Area

moving air picks up moisture
from a lake or sea

Fig. 31   Relief rainfall

-easterly winds coming from the polar regions meets another air mass with south-westerly winds from warm sub-tropical regions. When these two air masses meet along with the winds, considerable turbulence is set up by their interaction. The formation of depressions is shown in Fig. 32.

The earth's rotation on its axis, together with these two wind streams attacking each other helps to set up a rotational effect. The general result is that pockets of warm sub-

tropical air are almost surrounded by cold polar air attacking mostly from the rear. These pockets of warm sub-tropical air are pushed eastwards along the front by the prevailing westerly winds.

The pockets of warm air are areas of low pressure and they are surrounded almost completely by cold air and high pressure. Each pocket of low pressure is known as a depression. You cannot actually see them of course but if you could they might look something

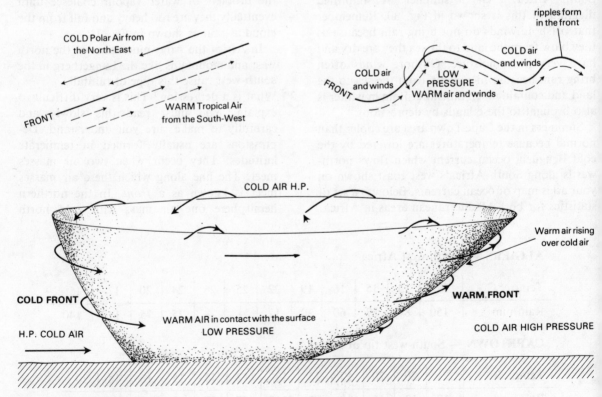

COLD Polar Air from
the North-East

FRONT

WARM Tropical Air
from the South-West

ripples form
in the front

COLD air
and winds

FRONT

COLD air
and winds

LOW
PRESSURE
WARM air and winds

COLD AIR H.P.

Warm air rising
over cold air

COLD FRONT

WARM.FRONT

H.P. COLD AIR

WARM AIR in contact with the surface
LOW PRESSURE

COLD AIR HIGH PRESSURE

Fig. 32   Frontal formation

like a basin or saucer shape.

3 Can depressions be shown on a map? Yes. They are shown by drawing *isobars* on a map. Isobars are lines on a map which join all places on the surface which are experiencing the same atmospheric pressure. In a depression isobars often form a concentric pattern on the earth's surface as shown in Fig. 33. The figures on the isobars are millibars. These are measurements of atmospheric pressure. 1000 millibars is about average. Above that, pressure is high and below it, pressure is low.

4 How do depressions cause rain? The cold air which attacks the rear of a depression is known as the *cold front*. Where the warm air at the front of the depression rides up over the cold air it is known as the *warm front*. The whole of the depression moves from west to east; but

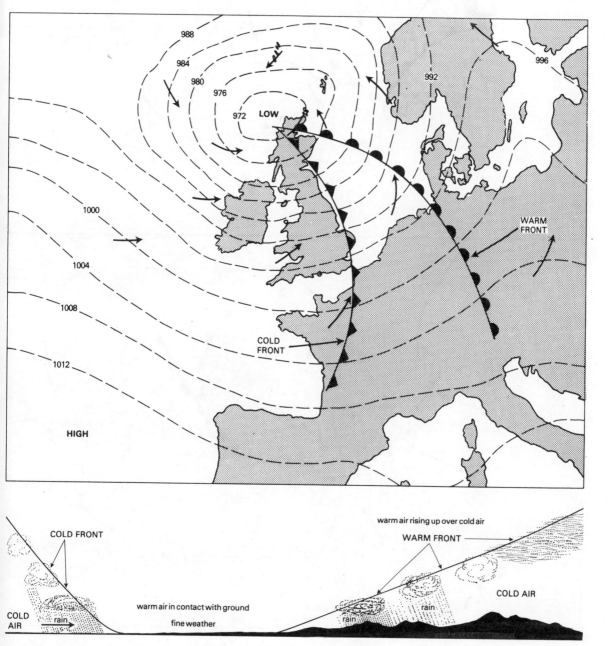

Fig. 33 Section through a front and the associated weather map

29

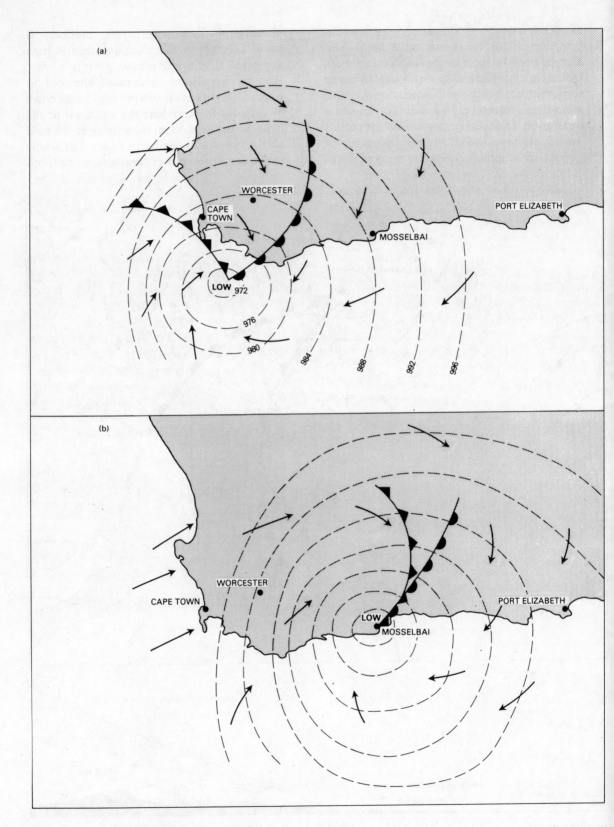

Fig. 34 A day's weather in South Africa

the cold front moves fastest for some reason. It wedges under the warm moist air of the depression and makes it rise. The air cools, so does its water vapour. Clouds form and rain falls. The warm front air has to rise over the cold air in front of it. Again, for the same reasons rain falls. However the heaviest rain is caused when a depression is *occluded*. This occurs when the cold front catches up with the warm front and lifts it completely off the ground. Heavy, dark cloud forms and rain falls heavily. The weather associated with, and the formation of fronts is shown in Fig. 33.

As a depression approaches and passes over a certain place, different weather conditions are experienced. Let us look at a depression's path across the south-west of South Africa. Remember this mostly occurs in the winter months. Study Fig. 34a first and look at a relief map of the area.

i) At Cape Town it is probably quite cold as winds are from the south. It is also probably wet as the cold front is near at hand and also onshore winds are rising over the hills and mountains.

ii) Between Worcester and Cape Town it is warmer as winds are from the north, nearer the Equator. It is also drier as air is not being forced to rise in the low pressure area.

iii) East of Worcester it is warm with winds from the Equator's direction. It is also raining a little as the warm front rises over the cold air ahead.

iv) At Mosselbai it is warm because of the same north winds. It is also dry because winds are offshore.

Now look at Fig. 34b. It is the same depression but a few hours later and has moved a few miles further east.

i) At Cape Town it is still cold but skies are quite clear. Perhaps there is a little relief rain on hills and mountains.

ii) Worcester is cool and dry. Skies could be clear.

iii) The south coast between Mosselbai and Cape Town is cold with onshore winds bringing relief rain on the hills. Just north-east of Mosselbai the depression has partly occluded. It could be raining heavily there. Along both the fronts there is probably a little rain.

iv) East of Mosselbai it is warm and dry.

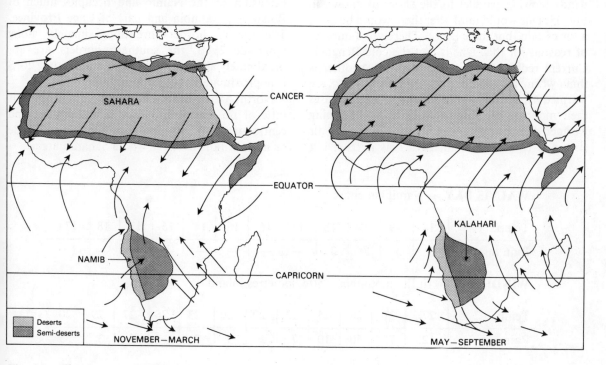

Fig. 35   The deserts of Africa

The semi-desert and desert climates

Once again, read the text very slowly and refer continuously to the maps shown in Fig. 35. Most of the world's deserts are to be found on the western sides of continents and Africa's deserts follow this pattern fairly closely. The Sahara extends across the whole of the continent; but remember North Africa lies to the south-west of the largest continent of all: Eurasia.

The hot deserts of Africa fall into two categories: Marine and Continental. They generally lie within the Trade Wind belt where winds blow from east to west.

Marine Type – Namib Desert

The Namib Desert is found in south-west Africa (Namibia) along the coast. It is rarely wider than about 160 kilometres. Like all marine deserts, the Namib coast is washed by a cold ocean current. This flows towards the Equator and is known as the Benguela Current.

Although the South-East Trades are supposed to blow across the continent and to be very dry by the time they reach the Namib region, in fact they do not generally blow this far south. There are, strangely, combinations of onshore winds or winds blowing parallel to the shore as shown in Fig. 35. One would think that there would be quite a lot of rain, but there is not. There are a number of reasons for this. One is that the cold Benguela Current reduces evaporation slightly. Another is that when the winds blow onshore they are warmed by the hot land in summer. This increases their moisture carrying capacity as air becoming warmer does not part with its moisture. Hot air rises and cools you might say. This is true; but

here in South Africa it is not allowed to do so to a very great extent. Above southern Africa there is a high pressure cell, mentioned earlier and shown in Fig. 30, about 9200 metres up in the atmosphere. From it cool air descends, even in summer, and becomes warmer. Air which is becoming warmer does not produce rain. This descending air stops air rising from ground level. There is thus little rain in summer. In winter this descending air repels any air coming in from the sea and there is again almost no rain at all. The effects of this cell are clearly shown in Fig. 36.

Continental desert and semi-desert climate

In Africa these types of climate are found in and around the Sahara region in the north and the Kalahari area in the south. The Sahara extends right across North Africa from the Red Sea westwards to the Atlantic Ocean. The northern borders are the Mediterranean climate region of the north African coast lands. Its southern borders are found approximately along latitude 15°N. Along the west coast conditions are similar to those of the Namib. The cold Canary Current has the same sort of effect here as does the Benguela in the south.

The Kalahari semi-desert is an eastward extension of the Namib and occupies much of Botswana, Namibia and part of Cape Province. The eastern borders are approximately along longitude 25°E, the southern borders are approximately along latitude 30°S, and latitude 20°S is approximately the northern limit.

North Africa is very large indeed and there is little or no marine influence in the eastern and central areas. Winds rapidly become dry and little or no rain falls over the whole Saharan area.

WALVIS BAY — Namibian coast

Temp. °C	18	19	19	18	17	16	16	14	15	17	18	17
Rain mm	3	3	7	3	—	—	—	—	—	—	—	3

WINDHOEK — In the mountains 250 kilometres inland

Temp. °C	27	27	26	25	22	20	20	23	26	27	29	30
Rain mm	125	75	50	10	7	5	3	3	—	7	3	35

Above is a set of statistics for two places in Namibia.

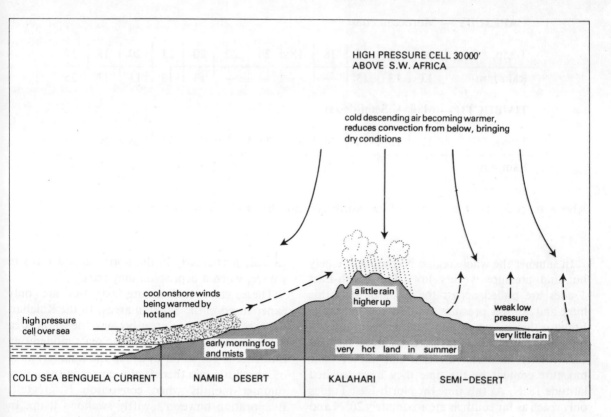

Fig. 36 Summer atmospheric conditions over south-west Africa

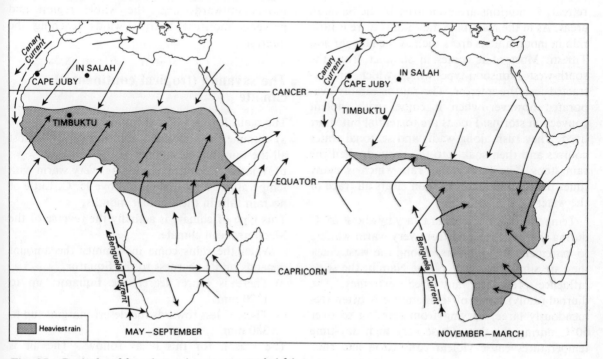

Fig. 37 Periods of heaviest rain over central Africa

33

CAPEJUBY — Moroccan coast

Temp. °C	16	16	17	18	18	20	20	20	21	20	18	16
Rain mm	13	13	13	—	—	—	—	13	13	13	13	25

TIMBUCTU — Mali — Semi-desert

Temp. °C	12	15	20	25	30	35	37	36	33	26	20	16
Rain mm	—	—	3	10	10	35	85	50	13	12	—	—

Above are two sets of statistics for the North African dry lands, which are located in Fig. 37.

In summer the whole region becomes extremely hot and pressure is very low. The South-East Trades are pulled across the Equator into this huge and hot low pressure area. As they cross the Equator they become south-west winds of a monsoon type and reach as far north as about latitude 18°N. They have lost most, if not all, of their moisture content by the time they have reached latitude 18°N. At this time the North-East Trades only reach as far south as approximately 20°N and are dry as well.

In winter the North-East Trades advance as far south as latitude 8°N and the south-west winds retreat. Conditions are even drier in the Saharan areas. As in the Namibian mountains there is little rain in mountainous areas such as the Hoggar and Tibesti. Most of it comes in summer from the south-west monsoon-type winds which are attracted into the interior. The rain is rapidly evaporated however when it comes with violent convection storms. Floods are torrential but short lived. They rush along wadis and seasonal water courses and then soak into the ground when the rain stops. The evaporation rate which is many times the rainfall amount, soon clears all trace of the water.

Temperatures in the Sahara vary by about 25°C during the year; ranging from very warm winters to extremely hot summers. Along the west coast they are similar to those of the Namib: the sea's influence preventing any great extremes. The diurnal (daily) range of temperature is often tremendously large; varying from freezing to over 50°C during the day. These very high day-time temperatures cause violent convection and thus very strong winds. Sometimes sandstorms are caused, particularly in the north Sahara areas in winter, when a depression may pass.

These great temperature extremes are only experienced in the Saharan areas. In the Kalahari they are not quite so great because the whole area is smaller and narrower and the sea's moderating influence is not so far away. In the Kalahari most of what little rain there is also comes in the hotter summer months when convection is greatest. Evaporation however, swiftly swallows it up. In winter the high pressure cell above southern Africa becomes very intense indeed. Cool descending air becoming warmer reaches the surface and moves outwards over the whole region and prevents moisture bearing winds reaching the interior.

The savanna (tropical continental) climate

The main features of a savanna climate are:—
a) Summers are very hot: well over 25°C. Almost all the rain falls in summer.
b) Winters are warm, sometimes very warm with temperatures almost always above 15°C. Little or no rain falls in these cooler months.
This type of climate is actually the reverse of the Mediterranean climate.

When the rains come in summer the amount depends on its nearness to the Equator.
 i) There is more nearer the Equator: up to 1270 mm.
ii) There is less towards the desert margins: up to 380 mm.
The reason for this is as follows. The air is moisture laden as it comes in from the sea. By the

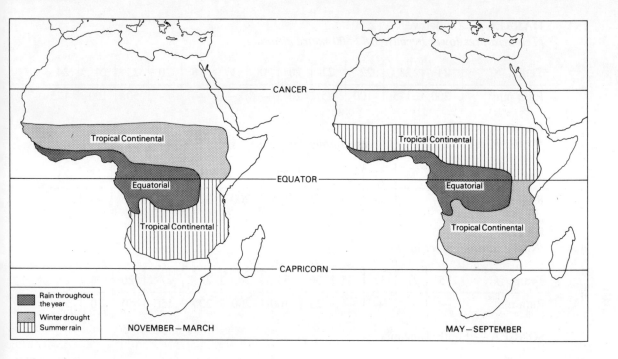

CANCER

EQUATOR

CAPRICORN

Tropical Continental

Equatorial

Tropical Continental

Tropical Continental

Equatorial

Tropical Continental

Rain throughout the year

Winter drought

Summer rain

NOVEMBER—MARCH

MAY—SEPTEMBER

Fig. 38   Equatorial and savanna (tropical continental) regions of Africa

time it has moved a long way inland there is very little left. There is almost none left when this air reaches the desert lands.

What causes a savanna climate? Look frequently at Figs. 38 and 39 as you read this account.

As the sun apparently moves north to settle over the Tropic of Cancer the land in the northern tropical areas becomes very hot and heats the air in contact with it. This heated air rises and a vast low pressure area results. The pressure is so low that air from the south of the Equator is attracted to this low pressure area. Remember the Sahara desert passage? This air has often travelled over the sea and has a high moisture content. When it reaches the hot land it is forced to rise and rain falls for two reasons.

i) Convectional rain because of heated air rising and then cooling.
ii) Relief rain when mountain barriers force it to rise.

In the **northern** tropical regions this happens between May and September. See both Figs. 37 and 38. During the same period there are cooler conditions south of the Equator.

Pressure is high over southern Africa. Air is

blowing outwards from land to sea and prevents rain bearing winds from entering. Thus there is winter drought in the southern savanna lands and summer rain in the northern savanna lands as shown in Fig. 38.

When the sun makes its apparent journey south to settle over Capricorn, the area of lowest pressure moves south as well. There is considerable convection (though not so much as in the North African summer: see desert passage on Kalahari) and wet winds from the Indian and Atlantic oceans are pulled into the interior to bring summer rainfall. This happens between November and March. See Figs. 37 and 38. At the same time the North-East Trades extend much further south over the Sahara: as far as Latitude 8°N, remember? These winds are dry and thus the cool season (winter) in North African savanna areas is also one of drought, as shown in Fig. 37.

In West Africa the South-East Trades still cross the Equator but only just reach the coast to bring a little cool season rainfall. Because of this the West African coast receives rainfall all year round and has an equatorial climate. On page 36 are four sets of statistics for the savanna lands: two north and two south of the equator.

HARARE — Zimbabwe
(Temperatures lower because of 1 500 metre altitude)

Temp. °C	24	23	22	21	20	18	17	18	20	23	24	24
Rain mm	200	175	100	25	20	—	—	—	—	50	100	175

KANO — Nigeria
(Notice heavy rain slightly lowers summer temperatures)

Temp. °C	22	24	27	32	31	27	26	25	26	26	25	23
Rain mm	—	—	—	25	75	125	200	325	150	25	—	—

KAYES — Mali
(Notice rainfall effect again)

Temp. °C	25	27	32	35	36	33	28	27	27	26	26	25
Rain mm	—	—	—	—	25	100	200	200	150	50	10	5

SONGEA — South Tanzania

Temp. °C	22	23	22	21	19	18	17	18	21	22	23	23
Rain mm	275	212	225	100	10	—	—	—	—	3	25	185

Notice that in all these examples there is rainfall in the hot season (summer) and very little indeed in the cool season (winter).

Equatorial climate

This type of climate occurs largely in those lower regions found between latitudes 6° – 7° north or south of the Equator. Look again at Fig. 38. Within these latitudes can be found the belt of a warm, moist rising air known as the Doldrums. Also it is within this belt that the Trade Winds meet and rise for much of the year. Study Fig. 38 and also Fig. 37.

You will see that the equatorial region shown in Fig. 38 is shown by Fig. 37 to receive rainfall throughout the year. Because of this the equatorial region gets more rain than the savanna lands to the north or south.

Rain does not fall evenly in the equatorial regions. It is usually heaviest just after the sun has been overhead.

Temperatures are remarkably even throughout the year. There is rarely more than a 3 – 4 degree difference between the hottest and the coldest month. It is often only 1–2 degrees. This is because equatorial regions are rarely without a very high noonday sun. After all, the apparent movement of the overhead sun is only between the Tropics. It must, therefore, spend a long time *over* or *not far from* the equatorial latitudes mentioned earlier.

Diurnal temperatures often reach 35°C or more, but monthly average temperatures work out at around 29°C at sea level. Temperatures are rather lower at higher altitudes but are still *just as even*.

Rainfall is largely convectional and falls in the late afternoons on many days. Total amounts vary between 1750 mm – 2250 mm, but if there is also a strong prevailing onshore wind then amounts are often higher by the addition of relief rainfall, e.g. Freetown 3875 millimetres or Douala 10 000 millimetres.

On page 37 are three examples of equatorial climate statistics. Note that the first and second have two heavy rainfall periods, and even temperatures. Note the lower temperatures of Entebbe, 1170 metres above sea level.

LIBREVILLE — Gabon coast

Temp. °C	30	31	31	31	30	29	28	28	29	29	29	30
Rain mm	250	250	325	300	213	25	25	25	100	275	380	200

ENTEBBE — Uganda, Lake Victoria

Temp. °C	27	27	27	26	25	25	25	26	27	27	26	26
Rain mm	65	85	150	250	225	125	75	75	75	112	125	125

FREETOWN — Sierra Leone coast
(Note the effect of strong winds)

Temp. °C	30	31	31	30	29	28	27	27	28	29	30	30
Rain mm	25	25	50	100	275	500	900	925	700	300	125	25

Question and answer session

1   Is the high pressure cell over southern Africa something to do with the sub-tropical pressures shown in Fig. 28? Yes.

2   Is there something similar above North Africa? Yes.

3   What is convection? It occurs when the sun heats the land. The land becomes hot and heats the air in contact with it. Hot air expands and becomes less dense. It becomes lighter and rises up into the atmosphere. The greater the heating the greater will be the upward convection currents of air.

4   How does convection cause rain? In just the same way as relief rainfall is caused. In just the same way as depression rainfall is caused. Air is forced to rise. It cools. Water vapour in the air condenses to form little droplets of water. They join together and clouds form. The droplets get bigger and fall out of the clouds.

5   Is rain only brought by winds from the sea? No. It can be caused by moist air being drawn from a nearby lake. A lake the size of Lake Victoria produces a lot of rainfall over the adjacent land. Copy Fig. 39 and study the following statements.
a) Convection currents of damp air rise over hot land.
b) Rising air is cooled. Clouds form. Rain falls.
c) Moist air from lake is drawn to hot land.
d) Cool air falling, becomes warmer.
e) Air evaporates water.
Now put letters a) to e) in the proper places on the diagram.

6   Learn to draw all the diagrams which show how rainfall is caused. Make up and learn a

Fig. 39

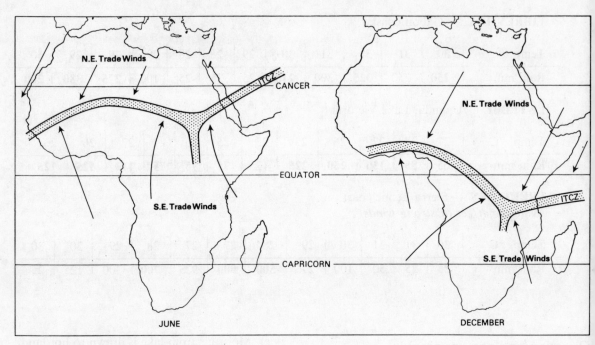

Fig. 40   The position of the I.T.C.Z.

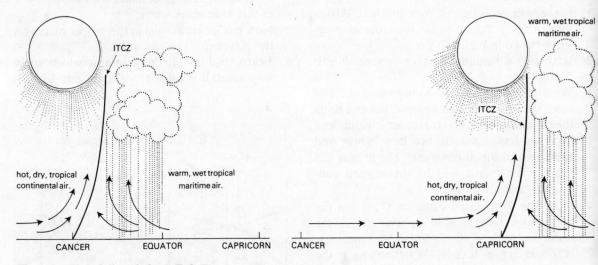

Fig. 41   Rainfall and the I.T.C.Z.

paragraph in your own words, which describes each of the three main ways by which rain is caused.

7   Why do many equatorial areas have two extra heavy rainy periods as at Libreville? This is closely connected with the position of the I.T.C.Z. These letters stand for the words *Inter Tropical Convergence Zone*. This zone is the place where the North-East Trade Winds and the South-East Trade Winds converge on each other: this is the area where they meet

each other. The I.T.C.Z. moves throughout the year. When the sun apparently moves to the southern tropic the I.T.C.Z. moves southwards as well. When the sun moves to the northern tropic the I.T.C.Z. moves northwards as well, as shown in Fig. 40. In fact in any one month this meeting place or convergence zone is roughly where the sun is overhead: and that is where it is hottest. It is therefore true to say that this is where convection is greatest and rainfall is heaviest. See Fig. 41.

8   Do the Trade Winds have a different moisture content? Yes, they do. The North-East Trade Winds are largely dry over Africa because they come from another continent: Eurasia. The South-East Trades are largely damp because they have blown over large sea areas. It is the damp air which brings the rain as it advances or retreats, northwards or southwards. The I.T.C.Z. crosses equatorial regions twice; once on the sun's apparent northward journey and once on its apparent southward journey. That is why there are often two extra heavy rainy periods in equatorial areas.

9   Why does the heaviest rain fall just after the sun has been overhead? For much the same reason as a pot of water takes a little while to boil. It takes time to heat up! Convection over the land also takes time to build up to a maximum.

Trade winds coast climate (tropical and sub-tropical east coast climate)

This type of climate can be found along the east coast of Africa roughly between Dar es Salaam and Durban. Onshore winds, mostly Trade Winds, blow all the year round and so rain falls all the year round, as shown in Fig. 42. However, these areas lie largely within the tropics and are affected by the same controls as a tropical continental climate. Thus rainfall is heavier in the hot season (summer) when rain bearing winds are attracted inland to the inland low pressure areas. Read the passages on savanna areas again and check what happens. (Page 35)

Temperatures in these areas are very warm all the year. Summers are hot and wet while winters are warm and drier. Temperature ranges are far greater than in the equatorial areas but not so great as in the savanna (tropical continental) lands owing to the modifying effect of the sea.

Below are three examples of this type of climate. Their positions are shown in Fig. 42.

Mountain climates

There are many high mountains and plateau regions in Africa. One has only to think of the Ethiopian Highlands or the Drakensbergs. We have also mentioned mountains like Kenya and Kilimanjaro.

Almost everywhere the mountains tend to take on the characteristics of the climate region in which they are situated: *with two important exceptions*. Their altitude changes and affects their temperatures and their size and altitude affects the distribution of rainfall over large areas.

Temperatures *decrease* with *increasing* altitude. Thus we find permanent snow and ice on Africa's highest peaks. Temperatures *increase* with *decreasing* altitude. Thus we find some of the highest temperatures in Africa in the Danakil desert in

LINDI — South coast, Tanzania

Temp. °C	26	27	25	24	24	23	23	23	24	25	25	26
Rain mm	160	112	175	180	35	12	10	5	10	10	55	160

MOZAMBIQUE

Temp. °C	28	27	27	26	24	23	23	23	25	26	26	27
Rain mm	300	325	275	150	50	25	25	35	100	150	225	250

DURBAN — Natal coast

Temp. °C	25	26	24	22	20	17	17	18	19	21	23	24
Rain mm	112	125	135	85	50	25	25	37	75	125	125	125

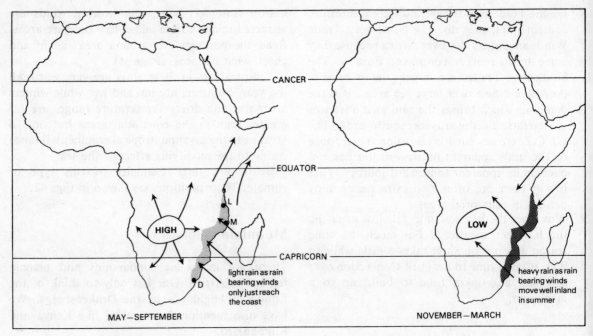

Fig. 42 Areas of Trade Wind coast climate

Within the figure (left map, MAY—SEPTEMBER):
CANCER
EQUATOR
HIGH
L
M
CAPRICORN
D
light rain as rain bearing winds only just reach the coast
MAY—SEPTEMBER

Within the figure (right map, NOVEMBER—MARCH):
LOW
heavy rain as rain bearing winds move well inland in summer
NOVEMBER—MARCH

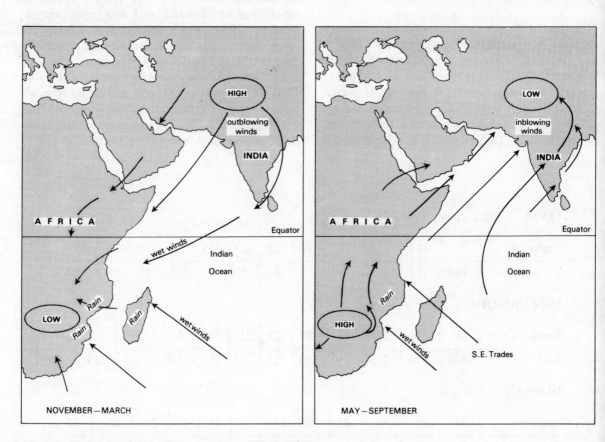

Fig. 43 The monsoon affected areas of East Africa

Within the figure (left map, NOVEMBER—MARCH):
HIGH
outblowing winds
INDIA
AFRICA
Equator
wet winds
Indian Ocean
Rain
Rain
Rain
LOW
wet winds
NOVEMBER—MARCH

Within the figure (right map, MAY—SEPTEMBER):
LOW
inblowing winds
INDIA
AFRICA
Equator
Indian Ocean
Rain
HIGH
wet winds
S.E. Trades
MAY—SEPTEMBER

Ethiopia where large areas are below sea level.
Memorise the following fact:
TEMPERATURE CHANGES BY ABOUT 2°C
FOR EVERY 300 METRES ALTITUDE.

It is no surprise to learn that on the higher levels
of Ruwenzori, Kilimanjaro and Kenya we might
see a 5000 metre temperature chart which reads
roughly as follows:

Temp. °C	1	1	1	0	−1	−1	−1	0	1	1	0	0

The above figures were worked out on the basis
of Entebbe being roughly 1200 metres above sea
level. The difference between that and 5000 metres
is 3800m.
Thus 3800 ÷ 300 = roughly 13
    13 × 2 = 26
We then took 26 away from each Entebbe temperature figure. Check it out for yourself. It is a
rough and ready method of comparison which
gives an idea of the temperature difference caused
by altitude.

Mountains, mountain ranges and high plateaus
cause much of the relief rainfall. The slopes which
face rain bearing winds are very well watered
indeed, but on the far side, away from these
winds, there is often much less rainfall, as shown
in Fig. 31. By the time rain bearing winds have
reached the peaks of high mountains like those
mentioned above there is little moisture left in the
air. *Thus the very tops of these mountains do not
receive as much rain/snow as the lower slopes.*
Another point is that as the air falls down the
other side of the mountains it becomes warmer
(remember how altitude affects temperatures) and
air which is becoming warmer does not lose its
moisture: particularly if its moisture content is
already low. Thus we see that *windward* slopes are
often wet but *leeward* areas are often very dry.
These dry areas are known as *rain shadows*.

The monsoon in Africa

As previously stated, the monsoon type of climate
involves the complete reversal of wind direction,
from one direction to another, during the course
of the year. This is caused because great pressure
systems change from high to low and back again:
pressure systems so powerful that they can even
interfere with the planetary wind system.

With the sun in the northern hemisphere, the
Indus–Ganges valley of India and Pakistan
together with central Asia becomes a vast low
pressure area. Air pours into Asia from the Pacific
Ocean, Australasia, the Indian Ocean and South
and Eastern Africa. This occurs between May and
September. As in West Africa the South-East
Trades are pulled across the Equator to become
South-West Winds heading towards India. They
come in off the Indian Ocean and bring rain to
East Africa before moving on towards India, as
shown in Fig. 43. When the sun is in the southern
hemisphere, Central Asia with its extremely cold
winters, becomes a great area of high pressure.
There is then a great flow, a great outward
movement, of air from Asia into the Pacific
Ocean, to Australasia, to the Indian Ocean and to
South and Eastern Africa. This occurs during
November to March; and, as the I.T.C.Z. moves
south as well, so eastern Africa receives another
extra heavy period of rain.

Those then, are the basic climates of Africa. But
there are hundreds of smaller climatic types within
each region. As you study your particular part of
Africa more closely you will learn, with your
teacher's help, how latitude, altitude, distance
from large bodies of water, winds, mountain
barriers and ocean currents can create climatic
changes and differences over very small areas as
well as large ones.

Group tasks

1 Study Fig. 31. Draw a diagram similar to it.
   On it show:
     i) Conakry
    ii) The Futa Djallon Highlands
   iii) Bamako
    iv) The Atlantic Ocean
     v) The S.W. winds
    vi) Leeward and windward sides
   vii) Heaviest rainfall and rain shadow.
2 Discuss with your closest friends how man can
   affect, purposely or accidentally, a region's
   climate. Check with other people in your class
   and *pool your ideas.*
3 Work out a rough temperature graph for the
   Drakensberg Mountains in Lesotho at about
   3000 metres altitude. Use the Durban figures.

3 Africa's natural vegetation

There are many types of vegetation, most of which are either trees, bushes or grass. Anything which grows from the soil is vegetation, even the crops which men plant; but **natural** vegetation is the sort which has grown and developed naturally. Natural vegetation is not planted by man. He has little or nothing to do with it; except of course, to destroy it in one way or another. Natural vegetation is a natural product and grows of its own accord. All natural vegetation develops, and has developed over the years past, in accordance with the climate and the soils in which it grows. Man can destroy natural vegetation but he cannot make it.

Different climates create different types of natural vegetation. If the climate of a region changes, as has proved to have happened during the millions of years gone by, then natural vegetation will also change. So also will soils. At one stage in its pre-history the Sahara region was a grassy plain with forested mountains. The grasslands of the present day Transvaal were once covered with the thick, dense, hot, steamy forest typical of an equatorial climate. That was many millions of years ago; because now the remains of those forests form the basis of the great Transvaal – Natal coalfields and are found thousands of feet below the surface.

We, however, are largely concerned with the present. We know that Africa has many different climates; a few basic ones, but hundreds of subdivisions with which we cannot be concerned at this stage. For this reason Africa has developed hundreds of different types of natural vegetation; for our purposes, we can reduce it to just a few basic types which are very closely connected with the basic climates with which we have just dealt.

The savanna lands

Probably the most widespread type of natural vegetation in Africa grows in the tropical continental areas; the savanna lands. We have, in fact, called it savanna vegetation. If you look at Fig. 38 you will see that the savanna lands occupy a huge slice of Africa and form a broad arc which all but encloses the equatorial lands.

The savanna lands are Africa's great grasslands; but, scattered amongst the grass are trees, as

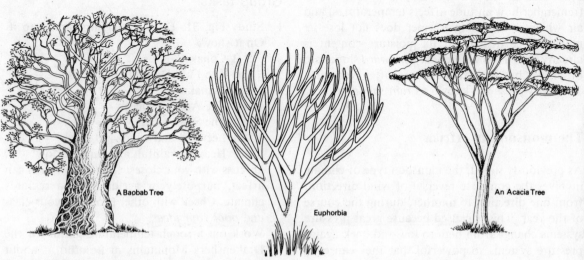

A Baobab Tree

Euphorbia

An Acacia Tree

Fig. 44   Plants of the savanna lands

An acacia tree, typical of savanna vegetation

shown in Fig. 44 and the photograph opposite. Sometimes the trees are tall and thickly scattered and this is because the rainfall is plentiful; even though, as you know, it only comes for one period in the year. Towards the desert margins the trees, the most common of which is the acacia, grow smaller and are much more widely scattered. This is because rainfall is less generous.

The height of the grass also depends upon the amount of rainfall. Towards the equatorial margins it is rich and tall; so tall that it is often called elephant grass. But towards the desert lands it is short and thin and has little food value.

The grasses spring to life when the summer rains arrive. Bare earth with a desert appearance quickly becomes a sea of green and plains animals, cattle and sheep feed well for several months. When the rains stop the grass develops seeds, just like corn, wheat, millet and barley, which are dropped onto the ground. The thorn trees lose their leaves; so also does the huge thick-waisted

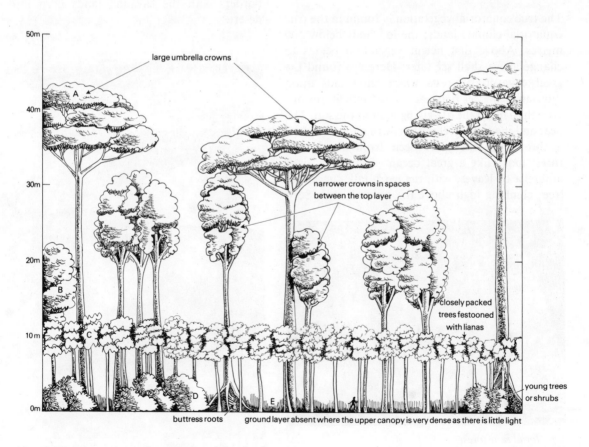

Fig. 45   A sketch section of an equatorial rain forest

baobab tree, shown in Fig. 44, which stores water in its soft fibrous trunk. But, the following year when the rains again arrive, everything springs to life again. The many pronged euphorbia cactus tree, also shown in Fig. 44, pays little attention to all this. It stands grey-green and tall year in year out.

This sort of natural vegetation grows where there is a warm dry cool season followed by a very hot and wet season: the tropical continental climate. On some of the plateaus of East Africa it has also developed over wide areas. Instead of one wet and one dry season there are two wet and two dry seasons. The monsoon and altitude have interfered with, and interrupted, what would normally have been an equatorial climate. The result has been large areas of savanna vegetation with two wet and two dry seasons instead of one of each.

The equatorial lands

The true equatorial vegetation is found in the true equatorial climate lands: the lowlands below 500 metres. Above that height vegetation begins to change as we shall see later. Here are found the great equatorial forests where thousands upon thousands of trees fight each other in their upward growth to reach the life giving light of the sun. The heat and the rain accelerate growth and encourage it throughout the year. Seen from above, the forest looks like a great ocean of green; a giant umbrella of leaves, with the extra tall, successful trees climbing high above the general level. Seen

from below it is a dark, damp underworld of roots, lianas and dripping water coming from the leaves above; with here and there a shaft of sunlight stabbing through to the ground. Rivers criss-cross the forests; and, seen from a boat, bright red flashes of bougainvillaea and other colourful plants interrupt the green. Fig. 45 and the photo on the left below give an impression of these forests.

The equatorial forest is green throughout the year; not because all the trees are evergreen themselves, but because many of the trees which shed their leaves, do so at different times of the year. Why do you think this is so? Thus there are always some leaves on the deciduous trees, plus those which are, in fact, evergreen.

The very dry lands

The vegetation of the semi-desert lands and the desert lands extends, in many places, from the borders with the savanna lands deep into the desert.

Equatorial rain forest
Notice how dense the vegetation is.

Desert oases in Algeria

44

After the short, painfully inadequate rains, on the savanna margins, grasses spring up, and for a few weeks the desert can be green; until the burning sun brings the grasses to seed. They drop and all is yellow-brown again until the following year. Here and there a cactus might struggle for survival, or even a tiny thorn bush. But in deepest Sahara or in the Namib there is nothing; just mile upon mile upon mile of bare rock, stones or sand sea.

All over these desert wastes there are thousands of oases, big and small, where the bubbling water can support some plant life. But it is almost all plant life put there by man; for all natural vegetation will have been removed and replaced with more valuable plants like the date palm or the lemon tree. The date palm is the natural vegetation of the Saharan desert oases, but it ceases to be natural when man cultivates the trees in great oases plantations.

It is always very difficult to decide where the savanna lands, or any grassland for that matter, end and semi-desert and desert begins. Perhaps as good a rule as any is one which says that the desert begins where a continuous vegetation cover becomes discontinuous: where in fact, bare patches of soil begin to appear and grow larger in area. You can see then that between climatic regions and also natural vegetation regions, there is no clear cut line which divides them. Instead there is almost always a blurred, unclear, shadowy zone where one merges imperceptibly into the other. This is also illustrated when we move polewards from the desert.

The Mediterranean lands

The Mediterranean lands have a very special vegetation. It is found along the Algerian and Tunisian coasts and is also seen in Morocco and around Benghazi in Libya. In the south this sort of vegetation is found in a very small area around Cape Town; within no more, and sometimes less, than 200 kilometres of that city port.

The climate of these lands does not make it easy for growth. The rain arrives in the winter months; but these months are frequently too cold for much growth to take place. In the summer months temperatures are high and ideal for growth: but there is little or no rain.

And so, as elsewhere, we find a natural vegetation which stores water for summer use in many cases, or can reach deep into the ground for it. There are trees with shiny waxy leaves which, by reducing transpiration, conserve the limited water supply. The cork oak, from which bottle corks are made, has thick cork bark which does the same thing. Almost all of them have long tap roots which reach far beneath the ground in search of water. Some plants have large fleshy bulbous roots which also store water. All these things are developments designed to guard against prolonged drought.

The eastern mountains and plateaus

Natural vegetation in the eastern mountains and high plateau regions of eastern Africa is rather different. Once again altitude plays its part, permitting a type of vegetation which is more often seen in the temperate zones. The high veld grasslands of South Africa provide one such example.

The Drakensberg Mountains of South Africa and Lesotho have many large forests of both coniferous and other evergreen trees. Similar forests are found in the mountains of East Africa and Ethiopia, particularly on windward slopes. On mountains like Kilimanjaro, Kenya, Elgon, Ruwenzori and those in south-west Uganda great rain forests occur, only slightly different from those of lowland equatorial land; the trees still have the long air roots known as lianas and beneath them it is just as dark and damp.

Above the forests of the equatorial highlands, at about 3750 – 4000 metres, it is much colder and rather drier. Only tough grasses and small mountain plants grow; the sort of vegetation which is called moorland in western Europe. It is also on these equatorial mountains above the tree line that we see the giant groundsel plants; plants which in Europe are tiny weeds a few centimetres high, but which grow to heights of 3 metres in these mountains.

On the mountain tops there is desert again, but this time a cold desert. There is no vegetation at all, just stones and rocks and a lot of scree on steep slopes. In the highest parts of course there is permanent snow and ice. Nothing can grow because it is far too cold and far too windy.

There are other high plateau lands than those of

South Africa's High Veldt (1800 metres). The Trans-Nzoia and Uasin Gishu of Kenya (2300 metres) are two examples, while there are hundreds of square miles of even higher plateau land in Ethiopia. On these plateaus strong rich grasses grow which are similar to those of the prairies of North America: where they have not been ploughed up.

The eastern seaboard lands

A tremendous variety of natural vegetation is to be found along Africa's east coasts. In Egypt, Sudan, Eritrea and much of Somalia the vegetation is that of the semi-desert or desert lands. The winds which blow over these lands are either hot or dry or both. They bring little rain. But further south the winds come from the sea, either from the North-East or South-East Trade Winds. They bring considerable though not great rainfall and it is always warm, sometimes hot.

The coast at Malindi, Kenya
1 Name the two types of tree shown.
2 What evidence is there to suggest that the sea is often higher than it appears here?
3 What evidence suggests that it is windy?
4 Is it late morning or early afternoon?

There are many trees although they are not as thick and dense as the equatorial forests.

This type of vegetation can be seen all the way from the Kenya coast south to beyond Durban. Coconut palms abound for the whole length of the coast, thriving in the warm damp climate. The tall, thin, graceful casuarina trees, grey-green of leaf, tower above patches of rich green thorn forest; while in creeks and inlets all along these coasts, as on West Africa's coasts as well, vast areas of mangrove swamps occur on the tidal mudflats.

Group tasks

1 Discuss with your friends the ways in which man can destroy natural vegetation in a planned or accidental way. Check with other people in your class and pool your results.
2 Ask your biology teacher to advise you on the possibilities of transpiration from vast forests, causing rainfall.
3 Trace two outline maps of Africa. Use these notes and an atlas to help you divide Africa into
   a) basic climatic regions and
   b) basic natural vegetation regions.
   Neatly label each zone.
4 You can have fun testing each other as well. Many of you live in boarding schools where there is always some spare time. Practise your outline maps of Africa and have a competition with your friends. Ask each other questions like, 'What climate is *there*?' 'Which way does the wind blow in July here?' 'What sort of savanna grasses grow on this spot?' 'What is the name of this ocean current?' 'Would you see mangrove vegetation at this point?' 'Is it a cold desert there?' or 'What sort of pressure is *there* (point it out) in December?' There are hundreds of questions like this that you can ask each other, and your teacher can settle the arguments.

4 Cash crops of Africa:
the move away from subsistence

We have had a brief look at Africa in general and you now know a little about the environments in which people live in Africa. Climate and the shape of the land form a major part of what we call environment; and, later on, we will be looking more closely at how it affects where people live and how different environments affect people in different ways.

As you know, it is climate which has a large say in how natural vegetation develops. Most of man's plant foods were, at one time, natural vegetation; and for thousands of years before man settled down to become a cultivator of crops he was a collector. He looked for his food. He hunted for it. Of course, he had to kill for his meat; but his vegetable foods, in greater or lesser quantities, were there around him, he just had to collect them. The plant foods which he ate and to which he became accustomed, were determined largely by the climate of his homeland and the soils in which they grew. In fact even the soils were, to a very great extent, the result of the climate in which they were developed.

When man finally developed a cultivator economy he had realised, at last, that he could have a greater degree of control over when and what he could eat. It had become obvious that it was better to have one's food near at hand and all in one place. As a result, everything then became that much more reliable. For many years man was happy to grow what he wanted; and, perhaps, exchange surplus produce for other things which he could not produce himself: utensils, weapons, different foods. This went on all over the world; specialised food crops being produced because

they could naturally grow in a particular area or country. Then man invented sturdy ships which could travel fairly safely on the world's great oceans. The Mediterranean peoples were some of the first in this respect and their limited travels brought them new experiences in food and many other aspects of human existence. They grew to like the new foods. The other European nations developed even bigger ships and gradually the world became smaller. They explored, they traded and, in many respects, they exploited a lot of what they found for their own benefit. In this way nonetheless, different foods from different climatic regions crossed the oceans and were enjoyed by other people.

This was so in Africa's case; and, as elsewhere, it gradually became obvious that the old ways of subsistence agriculture were a little unsatisfactory. It became plain that greater efforts could be made to grow more of certain crops, as they would bring in money resulting in a higher standard of living to the grower.

The development of cash crop agriculture has proceeded along several different lines which vary from small individual ownership, the co-operative idea, para statal organisations, down to the massive, privately or company owned estates devoted entirely to the making of profit; whether fair or exorbitant. Let us look at some of them.

Cocoa in West Africa

Cocoa production in West Africa is essentially a small farm activity; and nowhere is more typical of this than Ghana. Most of Africa's cocoa comes from Ghana and Ivory Coast, although almost all other West African countries produce at least some. Ghana and Ivory Coast are the world's leading producers, followed by Nigeria and Cameroon. Between them they produce roughly 75% of the world's output.

Cocoa is a native of Brazil and was first grown in Africa on Sao Tomé island. In 1874 it was first produced in Nigeria, but did not arrive in Ghana unitl 1879; brought by a blacksmith called Tetteh Quarshie.

Ghana's main cocoa lands are found in the south west where rainfall is heavier and the land a little higher than elsewhere: part of Africa's plateau lands in fact. There is another cocoa area

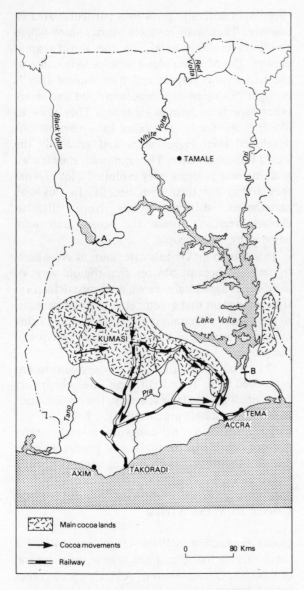

Fig. 46   The cocoa growing lands of Ghana

Main cocoa lands

Cocoa movements

Railway

0   80 Kms

long wait for the farmer. It takes at least five years from the time the seeds are planted in the nursery beds to the time that their pods may be harvested, from trees which have been transplanted into permanent positions.

Many cocoa villagers do not own their farms. They do all the work and receive, perhaps, a third of the crop for themselves. Of course, they sell it. They have to work very hard indeed to make a living, and equally hard to grow food for themselves on the village food plot. But whether they own their own farms or not, their lives are governed throughout the year by the tasks necessary to achieve a successful crop. Leisure pursuits, cultivating food plots, a little fishing perhaps, all have to be fitted in with the demands of the cocoa crop. As a result there has been a slow drift away from the farms into better paid jobs in industries like construction and oil.

Throughout West Africa further problems have arisen. Feeder roads often become flooded in the rainy season. Recently, some farmers have had to take a reduction in payments for their crop, have not been able to afford so much fertilizer and insecticide and quality has suffered as a result. There has been less rain in recent years and so bush fires have also caused problems.

West Africa's Cocoa Crop (000 Tonnes)

	1980	1981	1982
Ghana	280	170	258
Ivory Coast	380	400	445
Nigeria	157	143	181
Cameroon	115	113	120
Totals	932	826	1004

to the east of Lake Volta on the border with Togo, as shown in Fig. 46.

Cocoa farms are not very large, averaging in Ghana, between $2\frac{1}{2}$ and 4 hectares in area. They are often found in groups which are based near or around a small village. The whole complex is located in clearings in the rain forest, as shown in Fig. 47. The tall forest trees, towering above the clearing, give shelter to the cocoa trees from the blazing equatorial sun and the strong winds of the hot rainy season. Most farms are now well established but, if he wants some new trees, it is a

The cocoa pods grow from the trunk and the main branches of the tree, as shown on Page 50. The pods become yellow-orange when ripe and about 40 per tree reach this stage during each year. There is no set time for ripening and both flowers and pods can be seen on the tree. However there are two main harvesting periods: the main crop is collected between October and February while another harvest is carried out between May and August. These are very hard working periods for the village and even children join in. First the pods are cut from the tree and taken to the pod splitting area. There they are split open with a panga and the cocoa beans scooped out by hand. There are about 40 white beans in each pod and they are covered with a slimy juicy pulp which has to be removed. All the family helps in this task which involves placing the beans on a mat of banana leaves, later covering them with leaves as well. During the next five or six days the juicy pulp ferments and drains away. After this the beans are placed on tables and covered with rush mats. They are turned frequently and, as they dry out in the hot sun, they slowly turn brown.

After drying, the beans are put in sacks and taken, sometimes on a man's head, to the nearest government buying agent. This can involve walking through forests and crossing streams on the way. At the agency they are weighed and graded into three grades: 1, 2 and sub-standard, depending on how dry and free of defects they are. The farmer is then paid according to the grade of his cocoa and the price ruling at the time. The price is not always a good one as world prices for cocoa often fluctuate a great deal. When the price is low, times are very hard for the cocoa people

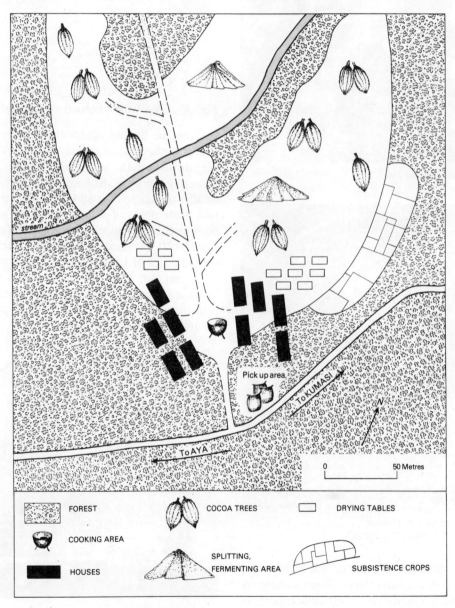

Fig. 47   A village in the cocoa region of Ghana

A heavily laden cocoa tree

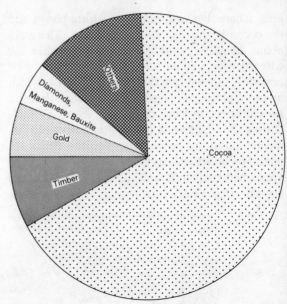

Fig. 48   The major exports of Ghana

From the buying agents the beans are sent in lorries to the nearest railway station. This can be very difficult in the heavy rainy seasons. The main collecting centre is Kumasi, but there are many smaller ones; and they all finally lead to one of the two great ports of Ghana, both of which have been artificially built: Takoradi and Tema. From these ports the beans are sent to Europe which uses millions of tons of cocoa every year.

So you see, because Europe wants cocoa and because Ghana can grow it, Ghana can make a profit out of what used to be just part of the natural vegetation of Brazil.

Cocoa beans drying in Ghana
Why is the girl moving the beans?

because they have nothing else to sell. If the world cocoa price is low it also affects Ghana's economy because cocoa is Ghana's most valuable export, as shown clearly in Fig. 48.

Loading cocoa at Tema

50

Temp. °C	25	27	27	27	27	26	24	24	24	26	26	26
Rain mm	20	58	145	180	190	200	110	80	170	180	94	20

Question and answer session

1 What is the cocoa bean used for? It is principally used for two manufactures. One is a beverage (drink) which is actually called cocoa, and the other, of course, is chocolate. There are other uses but these are the most important.

2 How are cocoa and chocolate made? It is very complicated really; but put simply, the beans are roasted and then crushed into a paste which is called 'mass'. For cocoa some of the oil, known as butter fat, is squeezed from the mass. What is left is dried and ground to a find powder which makes a very nutritious drink when mixed with water, milk and sugar. For chocolate extra cocoa butter fat is added to the mass together with milk and sugar. It dries into hard, tasty and very nutritious slabs which are good to eat.

3 Why cannot Europe grow its own cocoa? Cocoa needs the following conditions for successful growth. Conditions number (i) and (v) are impossible in Europe because of her latitude.

   i) Consistent great heat and humidity are needed. Average temperatures must not fall below 20°C and there must be *at least* 1125 millimetres of fairly *evenly distributed* rain throughout the year: preferably lots more.

   ii) The seedlings must be sheltered from strong sunlight.

   iii) The trees must be sheltered from strong winds.

   iv) Soils must be well drained and porous.

   v) Night temperatures must not fall below 12°C.

   vi) At least five years must elapse before harvesting starts.

4 Are there any diseases which attack cocoa? Yes. The worst is 'swollen shoot disease'. To counteract it the Ghana Government sells cheap sprays and spraying machines to the farmers. If the worst comes to the worst, infected trees are dug up and burned. Capsid is an insect pest which attacks the leaves, particularly if there is a dry spell.

Group tasks

1 How could all-weather feeder roads help Ghana's cocoa farmers and Ghana's economy?

2 Make a combined bar and line graph for the climate figures for Kumasi, altitude 287 metres, shown above.
Your teacher will show you how.

3 Make a list of those African countries which have a climate suitable for cocoa. Where are most to be found?

4 Discuss among your friends the dangers and problems of monoculture. Ask your teacher to collect and list your combined efforts on the blackboard.

5 See Fig. 48. Work out as accurately as you can the percentages for each item shown.

6 Which of dams A and B shown in Fig. 46 is the Bui Gorge Dam?

7 Discuss future problems if Malaysia, by using plantation farming, becomes the world's leading cocoa producer within 20 years.

Palm oil

Another good example of natural vegetation which provided early man with food in equatorial Africa is the oil palm. It is grown throughout the lowlands of equatorial Africa to the west of the great rift valley, even up to heights of 1000 metres. However, the really important areas are the coastal plain regions of Gulf of Guinea countries and south to Zaïre.

The oil palm is often very tall, sometimes well over 8 metres, but it takes some years to achieve heights beyond that. The fruit grows in large bunches, each one of which can have on it up to a thousand fruit and weigh more than 50 kilogrammes. The fruit is oily to the touch and each one is egg shaped. When the fruit is ripe it turns a bright orange-red and, after processing, produces a greater percentage of oil than any other vegetable oil crop.

The oil palm is an important subsistence food. Most rural or village households have at least one oil palm growing in the garden. The trees are rarely destroyed.

In most Nigerian coast and delta villages there is also a communal grove of oil palms. This often provides the only cash crop of the village, the proceeds of which are shared. Many villages have their own oil press and the oil is sold to traders who arrange for its export. In the villages individual families usually prepare the fruit in the traditional way. The women pound the fruits to pulp, which is then boiled in water until the orange coloured palm oil floats to the surface. It is then skimmed off and put into containers for future use, the principal one of which is cooking. The palm oil has quite a high protein content and is used in much the same way as other countries use butter and other animal fats. Inside the fruit itself there is a hard nut which contains a kernel. The women crack the nuts which, after drying are then sold in bags to the nearby trader. When crushed these kernels yield another valuable oil: palm kernel oil.

Most West African villages in the equatorial belt have their origins in a subsistence economy, and those in Nigeria are no exception. Each house-

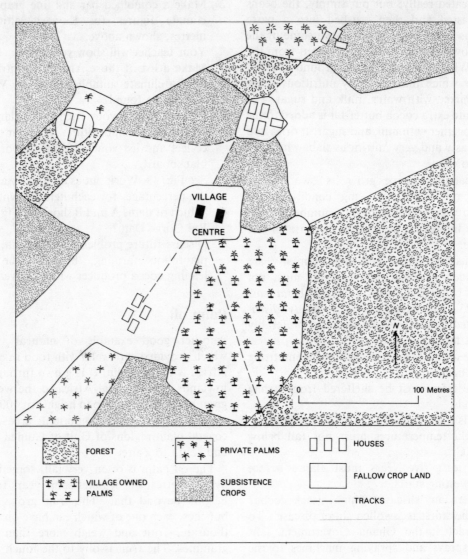

Fig. 49 *A typical village in an oil palm area*

FOREST

PRIVATE PALMS

HOUSES

VILLAGE OWNED PALMS

SUBSISTENCE CROPS

FALLOW CROP LAND

TRACKS

VILLAGE CENTRE

0   100 Metres

The oil palm and its fruit
1 What is the man doing?
2 Is this photograph of a plantation or small farm?
  Give your reasons.

holder or farmer spends a lot of his time producing subsistence crops like yams, rice, bananas, cassava, maize and vegetables, as shown in Fig. 49. The cassava is particularly important because if all else fails, by reason of weather or disease, the cassava can be relied on for food. Nigerian farmers, in common with other farmers in the West African equatorial zone, cannot keep cattle and so the people's protein must come from elsewhere. If they live near the coast or a stream then fish can help in this; otherwise chickens and the lower protein content of the oil palm and the other food crops have to suffice. It is, however, only the oil palm which has helped, and is helping, certain Nigerian farmers to introduce a cash element into an otherwise subsistence economy.

Efficient production is essential for the oil palm to be an export crop. Thus plantation cultivation has become increasingly important.

Plantation development has thus increased in recent years. In Zaïre the Unilever corporation has huge plantations near the coast. In Ivory Coast there are over 80 000 hectares, making her Africa's largest producer and second only to Malaysia in the world. There are also plantations in Ghana and Nigeria.

In Ghana however, there have been problems. Only 2000 acres of the State Farm Corporations 27 500 acres of oil palm were harvested in 1982 because of extreme labour shortages. The rest was overgrown by bush. But now there is hope. Eastern Region's Okumaning plantation has been reclaimed. At Twifo Praso a new mill now produces 30 tonnes an hour, while E.E.C. finance is helping the renewal of the Pretsea plantation. New seedlings will come from the Oil Palm Research Centre at Kusi in Eastern Region.

On the plantations the one year old seedlings are planted approximately 9 metres apart in neat rows which are also 9 metres apart. They grow quickly and may be harvested after three years have elapsed. The best variety of oil palm for Nigerian purposes has been produced by the Nigerian Institute for Oil Palm Research near Benin City. It has crossed two types, the Dura and Pistifera, to achieve the best qualities of both. It is called

An oil palm seedling
1 What material is the bag made of?
2 Is this photograph taken on a small farm? Give reasons for your answer.

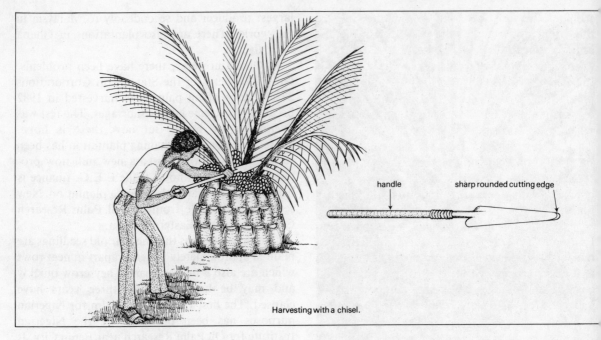

handle   sharp rounded cutting edge

Harvesting with a chisel.

Fig. 50   Harvesting from a low oil palm tree

Tenera, the fruit from which yields 25% oil and up to 1250 kilograms of oil per hectare in the plantations. N.I.F.O.R. produces and sells thousands of these plants every year.

Six months after flowering the fruit is generally ripe and is then harvested. This is quite difficult as a man has to climb each tree and cut off the ripe bunches. To do this he uses a long belt which supports him as he jerks himself up the tree, carrying his panga with him. On the plantations more modern methods are used.

N.I.F.O.R., as it is called, has introduced two methods which involve least damage to the tree (yields decline if branches are cut off). One is for the younger trees before they become too tall, as shown in Fig. 50, the other is for trees which

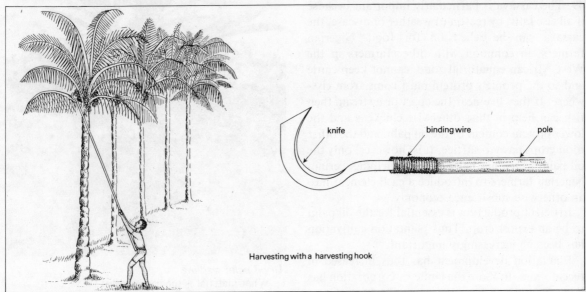

knife   binding wire   pole

Harvesting with a harvesting hook

Fig. 51   Harvesting from a tall oil plam tree

would otherwise necessitate climbing by the dangerous and time wasting traditional method and is shown in Fig. 51.

An important feature of plantation farming is the amount of crop processing done on the plantation, involving expensive machinery. The oil plantations have modern factories (mills) which process up to 60 tonnes of fruit an hour. They achieve a more efficient yield than village methods, producing up to 2 tonnes of oil from 10 tonnes of fruit. The dried fibre from the fruit and cracked shells from the nuts fuel the factory boilers.

Both palm oil and kernel oil are exported to Europe and North America. Palm oil is used to make margarine, soap and candles. The kernel oil is used in expensive toilet soaps, margarine and cosmetics. In Africa the tree has yet another use. Villagers tap the trunk, rather like tapping a rubber tree. The sap which drains out is collected and fermented into a strong alcoholic drink.

Discussion points

1 What possible connection is there between the development of Nigeria's petroleum industry and labour shortages in Ghana? How might recent events in Nigeria affect this shortage?

2 What possible connection is there between the development of Nigeria's petroleum and the following facts. In 1982 Nigeria imported about 25 000 tonnes of palm oil. This, plus imports of soya beans and groundnuts cost over 20 million Naira. In 1979 over 450 million Naira was spent on imports of rice, meat, fish, cereal flour, milk and dairy products. See also Chapter 7.

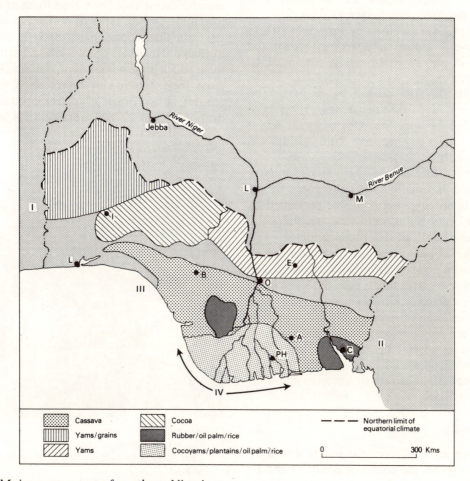

Cassava		Cocoa	
Yams/grains		Rubber/oil palm/rice	
Yams		Cocoyams/plantains/oil palm/rice	

Northern limit of equatorial climate

0   300 Kms

Fig. 52 Major crop areas of southern Nigeria

Question and answer session

1 Why can cattle not be kept in the West Africa equatorial lands? The problem is the tsetse fly, whose bite is extremely harmful, and sometimes fatal, to cattle. See the chapter on Pastoralism.
2 Are the conditions for successful growth similar to cocoa? Yes, except that not so much protection from sun and wind is necessary; and it can grow on the equatorial—savanna margins where it is drier. However, yields are then not so good.
3 Where are the most important oil palm lands in Nigeria? See Fig. 52 for your answer. It also shows you other major crop areas of Nigeria. Remember, the map shows you the most important areas. All the crops are grown in all the areas to a lesser extent; they are however, the *major* crop in the areas shown.
4 Do any diseases attack the oil palm? Yes! There are three very dangerous ones.

Anthracnose is caused by fungi and attacks the leaves, turning them yellow, brown and black. It can be lethal but is prevented by spraying.

Freckle is also caused by a fungi and discolours and shrivels leaves. It is also controlled by spraying. Obviously, if leaves cannot function properly fruit yields will suffer badly.

Blast is a root disease which attacks nursery beds and is usually fatal. The roots decay. There is no cure, but it can be prevented by careful cultivation, growing seedlings in polythene bags and watering efficiently.
5 Does the oil palm need any special care? Yes, but only on plantations. It needs a great deal in its early years. Weeding is essential when it has just been planted out. Regular spraying must be carried out to prevent disease, and fertilizers are essential to maintain good yields. A leguminous cover crop also helps, as it contributes nitrogen and humus to the soil and helps prevent the growth of a deep rooted weed known as siam.

Group tasks

1 Use your atlas to name the towns shown by dots in Fig. 52, the countries labelled I and II, water area III and coastal feature IV.

2 In which areas of Ghana and Ivory Coast do you think the oil palm is most important?
3 Study your atlas. Which other countries might have considerable palm oil production?

Coffee

Coffee is another crop, supposedly originating in Ethiopia, where it was once part of the natural vegetation, which is successfully helping to lead Africa away from the subsistence agriculture of old, into the higher standard of living of a cash crop economy. Like the oil palm and other crops we shall mention later, it forms the cash element on many small farms, particularly in East Africa.

Coffee is grown in most of the equatorial lands of Africa where it thrives in the hot damp conditions. However, it is not like cocoa as it can also grow successfully where, sometimes, temperatures are often somewhat lower than those of equatorial lowlands. Certain types of coffee can manage on less rain than cocoa, particularly if irrigation is available. However, there is one climatic requirement which is most important, and that is freedom from frost, which kills coffee. It is one of the reasons why Brazil's coffee production has dropped from 1 200 000 tonnes in 1978 to 1 067 000

Coffee picking in Tanzania
1 Which large towns are not far away?
2 What is the approximate height of these coffee bushes?
3 What evidence suggests that rainfall is abundant?

tonnes in 1980. This of course, has been a golden opportunity for Africa to attempt to take Brazil's place as the world's largest producer, and many countries are working very hard at doing so. No one African country can hope to do this, but collectively the position is slightly less of an impossibility. One thing is certain; the coffee farmers of Africa, whether big or small, have been receiving higher prices for their coffee than ever before. Coffee is an immensely popular beverage; and as it is in short supply there are plenty of people in the world prepared to pay high prices for it.

The most important coffee countries in Africa are Ivory Coast, Ethiopia, Uganda, Cameroon, Kenya, Zaïre and Angola in that order.

Until 1977 cocoa took second place to coffee products, as Ivory Coast's most important export. It grows in the hot damp lands of Ivory Coast's south. The two most common types of coffee are Robusta and Arabica. Robusta is the most widely grown in Africa and is always found at altitudes of less than 1500 m. This means that all of Ivory Coast's production is Robusta; so also is the production of most of lowland Cameroon and Zaïre. Angola only produces Robusta. It is the predominant type of coffee in Uganda. Arabica is different, and in Africa it is an equatorial crop in the highlands in between 1400 and 2000 metres. It does not need the heavy rainfall of the Robusta and also thrives in the slightly cooler temperatures of those altitudes.

Coffee Production 1977/8 — 1981/2 (000 bags)

	1977/8	1978/9	1979/80	1980/1	1981/2
Colombian Milds					
Colombia	11 152	12 750	12 181	13 068	14 000
Kenya	1 356	1 232	1 651	1 715	1 703
Tanzania	840	839	788	1 059	1 057
Other Milds					
Latin America	16 096	17 726	16 459	17 484	17 455
Burundi	342	456	347	621	558
Rwanda	322	453	502	467	478
Other countries	3 263	3 068	3 768	3 033	3 982
Unwashed Arabicas					
Brazil	18 451	21 074	19 342	25 764	26 069
Ethiopia	3 169	3 150	3 120	3 304	3 367
Robustas					
Angola	951	572	289	721	344
Indonesia	4 575	4 801	4 954	5 576	5 648
Cameroon	1 369	1 637	1 658	1 968	2 300
Central African Rep.	186	131	218	221	250
Ivory Coast	3 270	4 894	4 125	6 184	5 500
Madagascar	796	1 238	1 162	1 270	1 398
Sierra Leone	102	221	169	155	221
Uganda	1 829	1 839	1 942	1 918	3 300
Zaïre	1 034	1 279	1 328	1 519	1 500
Totals	72 383	80 662	77 687	89 726	93 422

Compiled from International Coffee Organisation and U.S. official sources.

Above 2000 metres there is a danger of frost on the Equator and so little, if any, coffee is grown above that height. Most of Africa's Arabica is grown on mountain slopes the best areas of which have rich volcanic soils. Mount Kilimanjaro, Mount Kenya, Mount Elgon and the Aberdares of Kenya provide excellent examples and are all to be found in East Africa. In Zaïre Arabica is grown in the mountains alongside Lakes Edward, Kwu, and Tanganyika where the soils are also volcanic.

All Africa's coffee lands have rain in every month and the amount varies, usually between 1000 mm and 1750 mm for the whole year. None of Africa's coffee lands ever gets really cold. They are usually quite warm, while in the Robusta lands it is always hot: over 22°C, as shown in Fig. 53. After flowering average temperatures must always be above 19°C for both Arabica and Robusta. Coffee is easy to grow and anyone can quickly learn how. Moderate delays between picking and processing do not harm the crop. All this makes it an ideal crop for a small subsistence farmer who wishes to introduce a cash element on to his farm. Small farmers are receiving every encouragement in Ivory Coast, and in the East African highlands it is as much a small farm crop as a plantation crop. Often the little farmer sells his crop to the plantation. Sometimes co-operatives are formed so that each co-operative has a processing plant which is fed by the small farmers who belong to it.

When the seedlings are eighteen months old they are planted out into the deep soils of well drained slopes and hillsides. This allows easy spreading of the root system. After this there is then a wait of about three years before the trees are established enough to be harvested. During the life of the tree, over 20 years, it must be kept free from weeds, as these use the soil foods which the coffee tree needs. In fact, the trees also have to be fertilized regularly otherwise crop yields will decline. The bushes are set about 3 metres apart, and pruned to about 2 metres high, which makes life easier for the pickers. The bushes flower at different times according to altitude and it is also no strange thing to see flowers, green berries and red berries all at the same time. Actually it takes about eight to nine months after flowering for the 'cherries' as they are called, to ripen. In East Africa the picking season can last from the middle of November until early March.

Altitude largely decides harvesting time as ripening is delayed higher up the hillside. The picking season is very busy indeed and hundreds upon hundreds of women and children are employed on the plantations during this period. Extra labour is brought from nearby villages by buses and lorries hired by the plantation. The workers are a very colourful sight in the coffee fields with their baskets hanging from their shoulders. As they empty their baskets each time so a supervisor gives them a metal token. These are exchanged for money at the end of the day, when they all gather at the plantation headquarters.

After picking, the cherries are passed through sets of rollers which crush the flesh without damaging the beans. They are then left to ferment and the flesh just drains away; rather like the fleshy material round a cocoa bean. After this the beans are dried by warm air blasts being forced through them. In the village co-operative drying is done in the sun on tables or on the ground. After drying, the beans go to the 'hulleries' where the green skin or 'parchment' is removed.

Finally the bean is roasted to turn it into a brown colour ready for grinding. It is then ready for grading and sale by auction at big centres like Nairobi and Abidjan, where the world's buyers assemble.

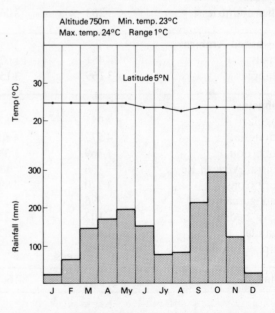

Fig. 53 Climate graph for Yaoundé (Cameroon)

Coffee pickers: the end of the day
These beans will be weighed and the pickers paid for their collection. What evidence suggests that it is the end of the afternoon?

Question and answer session

1 Have any coffee-based industries developed in Africa? Not enough. It seems silly for Ivory Coast to send coffee to France and then import it back again before she can drink what she produces. Instant coffee is one of the allied growth industries and already Brooke Bond in Kenya and Nestlé in Tanzania are producing it very successfully.

2 What do the plantation coffee workers do when picking is finished? Most of them remain employed on the plantation, pruning, weeding and fertilizing. Maintaining machinery and roads is also important. They also cultivate their food crops.

3 What diseases attack coffee? The most important one is coffee berry disease, and regular spraying during the heavier rains is essential to keep it away. Leaf rust is another disease which sometimes attacks low lying Arabica. In fact this is one of the reasons for

Arabica being cultivated above 1400 metres.

4 How is instant coffee made? Put at its simplest the bean is ground to an extremely find powder and then immersed in water. The soluble elements dissolve while the insoluble elements float to the surface and are skimmed off. The water is then evaporated off and the soluble coffee is left.

5 How are Robusta and Arabica different? Robusta can withstand higher temperatures than Arabica, but also needs greater rainfall as its root system is shallower than that of Arabica and cannot reach so far down into the earth for moisture. Arabica's milder flavour is preferred by many people. Kenya is Africa's largest producer of the Arabica known as 'Colombia Mild'. Tanzania is Africa's second largest producer, but the 1983 coffee berry disease epidemic may affect this.

Group tasks

1 Discuss with your friends the possible effects on coffee farmers of the following fact. World coffee production in 1982 was nearly 15 million bags more than world consumption.

Try to discover what the International Coffee Organisation (I.C.O.) did about this imbalance.

2 Trace a map of Africa to include political boundaries. Put in the coffee figures for 1980 – 1 in each producing country. Lightly shade in those countries to emphasise them. Label a port which would handle the exports.

3 Extract from the passage as much information as you can about the conditions under which coffee can be successfully grown. Make a list of them and learn it.

4 Drawn twin bar graphs to compare the total crop of Africa's top six coffee producers with that of Brazil for 1980 – 81 and 1981 – 2 using the statistics on Page 57.

Tea

Tea is yet another crop, a tasty and popular beverage throughout the world, which is grown with great success in many parts of Africa. It is another crop which is helping in the development of a cash economy for Africa's small farmers.

Tea is not only an equatorial crop. It is well known that some of the greatest tea growing lands in the world are to be found in northern India, as far north as Latitude 27°N. Tea was first grown in Africa in Malawi; and it is therefore not surprising that that country should be one of Africa's biggest producers. Other African producers include Mozambique, Zimbabwe, Zaïre, and the island Mauritius. However, most of Africa's production is found close to, or not far from, the Equator in East Africa. Kenya is the biggest producer of all and, as shown in the table below and along with Tanzania, Uganda, Rwanda and Burundi, produces more than 58% of Africa's total production.

African Tea Producers (000 Tonnes)

	1979	1980	1981
Kenya	99	90	91
Uganda	1.8	1.5	1.6
Tanzania	18	17	16
Malawi	33	30	32
Mozambique	20	19.5	22
Zimbabwe	10.2	9.9	10.3
Zaïre	6	5	5
Mauritius	5	4.4	4.7
Rwanda	5.8	7	7
South Africa	6.2	6.3	6.8
Cameroon	1.9	1.8	2
Burundi	1.6	1.4	2.2

The great tea lands of northern India lie in the foothills of the Himalayas and receive the full blast of the summer monsoon. It is in these lands that some of the highest rainfall totals in the world are experienced. At Cherrapunji in the Assam Hills, another great tea area, up to 12 500 mm often falls during the rainy season.

You can see that tea needs a lot of rain. In fact, the minimum it can survive on successfully is about 1250 mm, but it prefers between 1600 mm and 2000 mm. In equatorial Africa the tea areas need rainfall in every month; even if only a little. This is because in the equatorial lands growth is

possible throughout the year; unlike the tea lands of northern India which experience a winter cold enough to bring growth to a halt.

As you can now imagine tea does not need such high average temperatures as oil palm or cocoa. In fact temperatures must be slightly lower for really successful growth. That is why tea is so successful in Malawi, Africa's second largest producer, and it can grow at 2150 metres in the equatorial regions of East Africa. Kericho, whose climate statistics are shown in the table below, is the most famous tea growing district in East Africa and has been known to experience slight frosts on occasions. Although slight frosts are not harmful it can equally be said that they do no good and so it is best that tea is grown in areas where they are not frequent. Tea is grown both on lower, gentler slopes of mountains and on rolling hilly country where the soils are deep and well drained.

Although tea needs a lot of rain it dislikes water-logged soils and so good drainage is essential. It also prefers slightly acidic soils and certain of the rich volcanic soils of East Africa are perfect in this respect. In Uganda the tea lands between Kampala and Jinja are only gently sloping, while in Kenya and Tanzania the tea is found in steep ridge and valley lands, in the Aberdare Mountains and on Mount Kenya as well.

In Malawi the tea is grown on large plantations in the Mount Mulanje area and south of Blantyre; whereas the most important plantation lands of Kenya are found in the countryside around Limuru and the Nandi Hills as well as Kericho. The small farmers are not forgotten however, and tremendous governmental encouragement is being given to them, particularly in Kenya. They abound around the big plantations for instance, and sell their tea to the plantation factories as soon as they have plucked it.

In the Aberdares and Mount Kenya regions small farmers are in the majority, with perhaps, only a quarter of a hectare of the farm given over to tea. The Kenya Tea Development Authority, a para statal body, has built factories in central locations and the tea is delivered to them by the

KERICHO — Kenya

Temp. °C	24	24	25	24	23	22	21	21	22	24	24	24
Rain mm	75	115	155	240	205	160	160	185	150	135	110	65

A tea bush nursery on the slopes of Mount Mulanje in Malawi

Tea smallholdings on the slopes of Mount Kenya

1 What volcanic feature is represented by Mount Kenya's peak?
2 Give photographic evidence to suggest that this area is well watered.

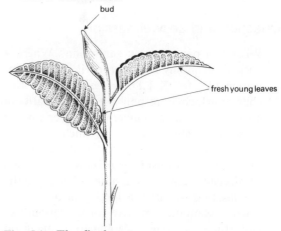

Fig. 54   The flush

small farmers for processing. In Kenya alone there are now over 90 000 small farmers who produce tea and who provide at least half of Kenya's total production. Every year hundreds of hectares of new land are being planted with tea.

Most tea bushes are now developed from cuttings which are called 'clones', and which are taken from the very best of the mature bushes. They are kept in individual polythene bags beneath large polythene covered frames for up to two years. They are then planted out in the fields at about 12 000 to the hectare. They must not be picked for another three years, but after that they will go on producing tea for at least a further forty years.

It used to be thought that big trees should be dotted throughout the tea gardens in order to provide shade; but now it is not considered necessary and, in fact, many existing trees on the older plantations are being destroyed by 'ring-barking'.

The bushes are carefully pruned while they are developing, to ensure a thick growth of branches. They are usually kept to a height of about 90 cms which is the height at which the pluckers can work most efficiently. Weeding must be thoroughly done and nitrogenous fertilizer applied at regular intervals. The biggest danger is hail. At certain times of the year, when convection is at its most rapid and violent hailstones form in the clouds instead of rain. This can tear a tea bush to shreds and so the Brooke-Bond company in Kenya tried to stop hail by 'seeding' storm clouds with nitrous oxide crystals to prevent the hail stones forming. After five years they stopped as the success rate was so poor and it was not worth the expense.

Plucking goes on all the year round in the equatorial regions of Africa, for the simple reason that growth goes on throughout the year. Each bush is picked roughly every 5 – 7 days and, as for coffee, tremendous numbers of people are required for this purpose. On the small farms of course, just as for coffee, the farmer and his family carry out this task. Only the top two leaves and bud are picked. This portion, known as the flush, is shown in Fig. 54.

Tea pickers in Kenya
1 What is the approximate height of the bushes?
2 Is this a small farm or a plantation? Give reasons for your answer.

Question and answer session

1 What is a para statal organisation? Where a nation's economy is concerned it is an organisation like the K.T.D.A. mentioned in this chapter which is responsible to the national government, has a number of civil servants in its senior administration but which is, nevertheless, expected to organise and administer itself on a profit-making basis: all excess profits either going to the state or back into the organisation for further development.

2 What is plantation life like for the labourers? Unfortunately, if tea is going to compete on world markets like cocoa and coffee it must be as cheap to buy. As a result the hundreds of workers on a plantation are not very well paid; but at least they are very well looked after. There are often plantation schools, hospitals, and other medical services and sports facilities. Their houses are often of a better standard than those in the other districts. All these facilities are often provided free of charge. Life is very hard however, and children who are good at school usually leave for university, or a better paid job in the city. Plantations are often as much as 300 hectares in area and for one of this size at least 300 pluckers would be needed. In the factory perhaps another 100 are also required.

3 Is picking a skilled job? It requires great care as no hard twig must be included which might impair the quality of the tea. The pluckers (pickers) carry a long thin pole which they lay across the bushes they are picking. This helps them to keep the bush tops fairly level. It is often a very wet job and for protection they wear large brightly coloured plastic aprons.

4 Who buys Africa's tea? Study the table.

Origins of British tea imports 1981

	Tonnes
India	39 514
Bangladesh	2 258
Sri Lanka	18 012
Indonesia	4 029
Kenya	41 346
China	6 003
Tanzania	7 297
Malawi	15 192
Mozambique	5 308
Mauritius	1 634
African others	4 807
Others	15 608
Total	160 408

Sources: International Tea Committee; Thompson Lloyd & Ewart.

It shows that Britain is a very large purchaser. She buys more than any other country and gets almost half of her tea from Africa. Kenya is the world's third largest producer.

5 How is tea processed? From the time it arrives at the factory, and deliveries take place throughout the day, it takes less than three hours for it to be ready to be used for a drink.

First the leaves are spread over long wire trays and dried by blasts of warm air from beneath. They are then passed through a set of rollers which have cutting edges and which chop up the leaves. After cutting they are placed in containers and allowed to ferment for twenty minutes, during which time they turn a greeny brown colour. The last stage is to pass them on conveyor belts through a very hot tunnel where air heated to over 100°C turns the chopped leaves the colour we see them when we buy a packet in the shop.

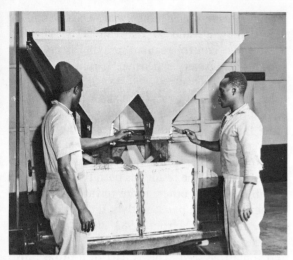

A tea leaf grader The tea falls through sieves which have holes of different sizes. The next stage is to send the tea chests to Mombasa for export.

Mechanical cotton harvesting in U.S.A.
Why is this generally not possible in Africa?

After this the tea is graded by sifting it through trays with different sized holes and putting each grade in different sacks. Finally the tea is packed in thin aluminium foil lined boxes and delivered to the port for export.

Group tasks

1 Show Africa's 1981 tea production
   a) as percentages on a pie graph and
   b) as totals on a bar graph.
   Which method do you prefer?
2 Study the section on tea, including the climate statistics. Make a list of the factors necessary for successful growth and processing of tea in Africa.
3 Discuss with your friends the problems which could occur later, because of Africa's rapidly increasing number of hectares devoted to tea production. Ask your teacher to list your findings for the benefit of the class.

Cotton

Cotton, like cocoa, coffee, tea and several other crops we shall mention, is ideally suited to production under plantation conditions, but with a minimum of manual labour. It is a plantation crop in the U.S.A., where almost every function from ploughing through to planting, weeding, fertilising, harvesting and processing is carried out by machinery.

Hoeing the cotton crop
1 Why is this necessary?
2 What food crop can be seen in the background?
3 What sort of climate is experienced here?

However, here in Africa it is a small farm crop; and, apart from processing, almost all the work is done by hand, as African farmers cannot afford large items of expensive machinery. Of course, huge schemes like Gezira and Rahad in the Sudan are rather different and will be dealt with separately in a later chapter. In many countries, African farmers do not produce enough cotton; in many areas production could be very much higher than it is; and in some countries the local textile mills are so short of raw cotton that they have to import it from other countries.

There are several reasons for this, not the least of which is the fact that cotton growing is very hard work indeed, from start to finish. The ground is usually hard and has to be ploughed and broken up before seeds can be sown. At the end of a dry savanna winter this can be very tiring. The ground must be kept free from weeds at all times; and as cotton grows in the hot wet season, weeds spring up very quickly if given the chance. The soil easily becomes exhausted and therefore expensive

fertilizers are applied every year. Disease can be very damaging, and so also can pests. To keep them under control regular spraying is necessary and this also is very expensive. If rain falls on the open cotton it is ruined.

So you can see that cotton growing has many difficulties and disappointments, and yet many more farmers would grow it, were it not for one last very discouraging factor: the rather low price the farmers receive for their cotton when they come to sell it. The result has been that if it proves possible to grow other, more rewarding crops, a farmer will do so; particularly if the work is not so hard. In Kenya, from 1983 onwards, cotton farmers will receive more money for their produce and some free seed. This is part of a project also designed to improve transportation, storage and

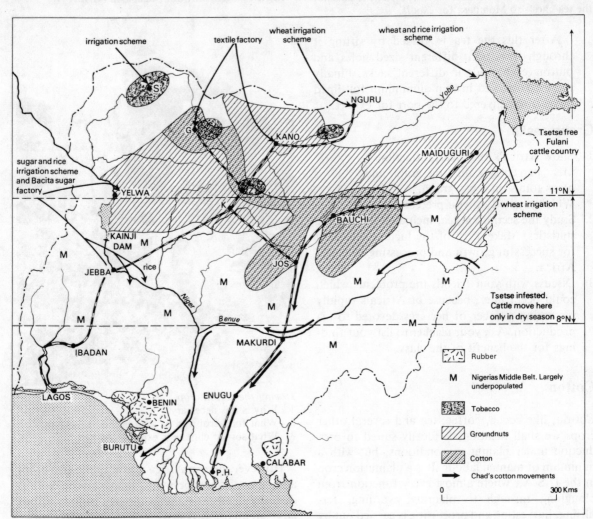

Fig. 55   Nigerian crops and related industries

ginning facilities. Hopefully Kenya's mills will remain in full production, using Kenyan cotton, thus saving valuable foreign exchange spent on cotton imports.

Despite all these problems there are many countries in Africa where cotton *is* one of the leading agricultural products, and where the small farmers are happy to grow it. On many of these farms cotton is one of the only two, or perhaps three, cash crops it is possible to grow without irrigation. These farms are in some of the more remote savanna lands like north-west Uganda or parts of northern Nigeria. Southern Chad is another such area where, apart from tobacco,

cotton is the only cash crop possible. There are over 200 000 hectares of cotton in the lower lying plains of southern Chad, and the farmers are very happy to receive their payment for it, low though it is: about $50 per year to the average farmer, whose yields are rather low.

Low yields are a serious problem for the small farmer, who can ill afford expensive fertilizer. Some, like the farmers of Sukumaland in northern Tanzania, partially overcome this problem by grazing their cattle on the harvested cotton lands; but this is impossible if the tsetse fly is prevalent. However, in north-west Uganda the land that each farmer can spare after growing subsistence crops

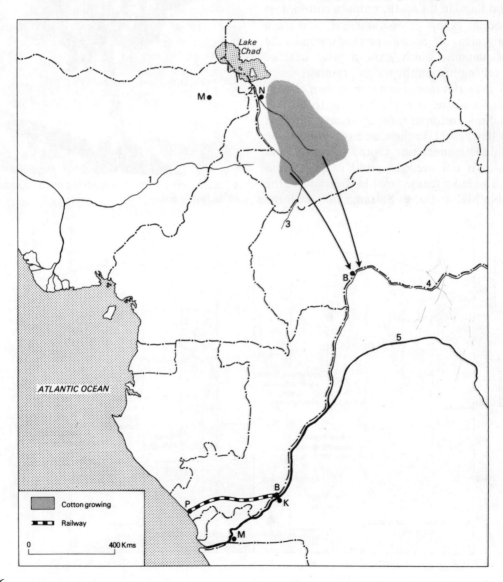

Fig. 56

is so small that his entire cotton crop can be taken to the ginnery on the back of his bicycle. Uganda's overall production is slowly recovering from the troubles of recent years. From a production of only 20 000 bales a year it has risen to 200 000 bales in 1982. Greater production is expected as British Overseas Aid funds the application of Ripcord, a pyrethrum based insecticide. Transport, storage and ginning must be improved as well if the crop is to be successfully marketed.

Almost all the savanna countries produce some cotton, as it is quite well suited to that type of climate as you will see. In Zaïre for instance, much of the available cash crop land, betwen the rivers Zaïre and Kasai in the south, produce cotton. It is an important export of Mozambique, and there are many areas of Sudan, particulary near the Nuba mountains, which grow a great deal of cotton, relying just on the natural rainfall.

Many countries manufacture their own cotton. They are fortunate. It is much better to do that than send raw cotton to another country and then have to buy it back in the shape of clothes. The mills at Jinja manufacture Uganda's cotton, and that which is not needed is sold to Japan and Russia. The most famous mill in Tanzania is the Friendship Mill at Dar es Salaam, built with the

A cotton boll   Later it will spring open to expose the white fluffy lint.

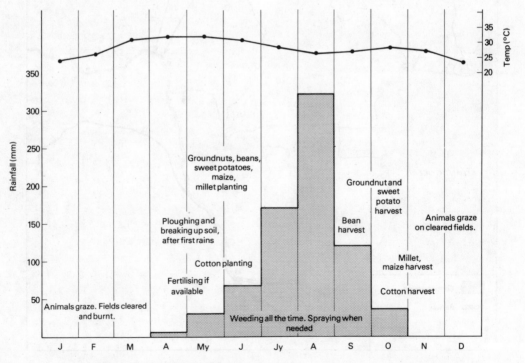

Fig. 57   A year on a West African cotton farm

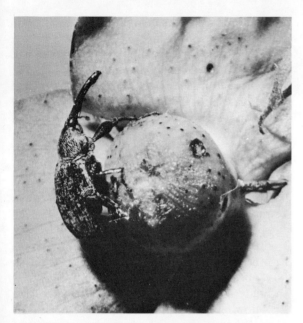

The boll weevil It eats into the boll and destroys the lint.

A textile mill in Kaduna: Nigeria
1 Are these spinning or weaving machines?
2 Why is it necessary to concentrate them all in one factory?

assistance of China and which now produces many millions of metres of printed cloth each year. There are others at Mwanza and Arusha which help manufacture some of Tanzania's crop. In 1980 cotton production was 51 000 tonnes: all produced by small farmers who received in payment an average of Sh 1.50 per kilogram.

It is clear therefore that cotton is an important crop in Africa; and after reading Chapter 6, you will see just how important it really is. But for the moment we are dealing with Africa's small farmers, for whom cotton brings in much of what little cash they earn. Two countries who have many such farmers are northern Nigeria and, to a much greater extent, Chad, as shown in Figs. 55 and 56.

Yields in the two countries are not good, largely because fertilizers are so expensive; but perhaps the new fertilizer factories being built in Nigeria will help improve matters, for Nigerian cotton anyway.

After early season ploughing and breaking up the soil baked hard by the winter's drought, the seeds are sown, as cotton is an annual crop. Five to six months later the *boll*, a hard brown case which develops after the plant flowers and which contains the cotton wool, breaks open to expose the white and fluffy cotton which is known as the *lint*. As the bolls open the lint is picked. After picking the lint is taken to the village ginnery. Here it is ginned — the lint is separated by machine from the many little cotton seeds to which it is attached. The seeds are not wasted as they contain a valuable vegetable oil. To obtain this oil the seeds are crushed and the waste is then fed to the farm animals.

After ginning the cotton is packed into bales weighing approximately 190 kilograms, and sent either to Lagos for export or to the great cotton mill towns of Kaduna, Kano and Gusau where it is manufactured into cloth for Nigeria's own use. In 1975–6 Nigeria's cotton farmers produced 300 000 bales of which about 150 000 bales were used by Nigeria's own textile industry, while the rest were exported. But in 1982 – 83 the 200 000 tonnes produced was insufficient to keep all her mills working and some were closed. See page 64 again.

In Chad there are no textile mills and all the farmer's production is exported. It is the need to export which causes Chad's farmers to receive less money than those of other countries. Transport costs are very high, particularly so, because all Chad's imports and exports have to go by way of other countries as Chad is landlocked. Some of her cotton goes by rail to Maiduguri in Nigeria and then on to Port Harcourt. Some of the cotton goes by river, down the Benue and Niger to Burutu, as shown in Fig. 55. There is a further route to be mentioned later. Whichever way it goes it costs a lot of money and there is not much profit left for the farmers.

Question and answer session

1 What pests harm the cotton plant? There are two insects which are particularly dangerous. One is the 'boll weevil' which thrives in areas which receive a lot of rain. This insect, shown in the photograph, eats into the boll and destroys the lint inside. The other pest is the 'stainer' which also attacks the lint and discolours it, making it useless for manufacture.

2 Why is the tropical continental climate so suitable for cotton? It is only suitable in areas which receive adequate rain of course, otherwise irrigation is necessary, as will be seen in a later chapter. The cotton plant requires about 750 millimetres of rainfall in these high temperatures during the growing season which lasts 5–6 months. The cotton areas of northern Nigeria and Chad receive rather more than this. Frost kills the cotton plant but fortunately there are no frosts in the rainy season of tropical continental countries. During the final month of the cotton plants' growth average temperatures must be at least 20°C; they are considerably more than that in these regions. There should be a reliable dry period for harvesting as rain ruins the cotton wool (lint) after the boll has burst. At the end of the growing season in these climates the rain has almost finished.

The tasks performed by a cotton farmer and the associated climate can be seen in Fig. 57.

3 Does cotton grow only in tropical continental Africa? No. It flourishes in very dry conditions, even in deserts: *if* it can be efficiently irrigated.

Group tasks

1 Study Fig. 56. Label rivers 1 – 5. Label towns shown by dots and capital letters. Label all countries.

2 Study Fig. 56. Describe in your own words the other way in which Chad's cotton reaches an export port: Pointe Noire.

3 Study the table below and answer the following questions:
a) What is the total production tonnage of Tanzania's 1978 crops?
b) What percentage of that is cotton?
c) Which type of crops, cash or food, made the greatest improvement in 1980?
d) Which four crops made the highest production in 1977 and 1979?
e) Can you think of any reason for the decline in cotton for 1978?

TANZANIA — production of major foods and cash crops (000 Tonnes)

	1977	1978	1979	1980
Maize	968	1 041	900	800
Paddy (rice)	194	260	250	180
Wheat	62	52	55	48
Cassava (manioc)	4 250	4 450	4 550	4 600
Groundnuts	74	70	72	75
Sesame	6	15	18	15
Castor	2	6	8	8
Sunflower	6	59	31	40
Cotton Lint	65	56	60	51
Cashew Nuts	97	68	57	46
Tobacco (leaves)	18	17	17	18
Coffee	49	52	50	52
Tea	17	18	18	17
Sisal	115	92	81	115

5 Plantation agriculture

Many of the crops that we have discussed in the previous chapter were entirely suited to plantation agriculture; but their chief importance, as far as Africa is concerned, is the opportunity they afford to the millions of small farmers on the African continent, to make a little money from their labours and thus achieve a better standard of living, than if they were subsistence farmers, pure and simple.

We saw in the last chapter how many small farmers, living near to the plantation, grew the same crop as their huge neighbour and got money by selling it to the plantation. The same thing happens with some of the crops we are going to consider now; but to a much smaller extent. The crops are those from which the greatest benefits accrue if they are grown on a massive scale; and which undergo a considerable degree of processing on the plantation by means of extremely expensive machinery. In fact if these crops were not grown and produced on a huge scale the world might not be able to consume such large quantities. First let us consider sugar.

Sugar

Most of us think of sugar as something we put in our tea, coffee or cocoa to make it taste sweet and thus increase our enjoyment in drinking these beverages. But sugar is important for much more than that, as you will see when you look at Fig. 58. If you only memorise a quarter of what you see it will give you a greater understanding of what sugar means to the modern world. Look at Fig.

58, long and hard. You will then understand why countries and big multi-national companies go to such great expense to make thousands upon thousands of hectares of normally unproductive desert and semi-desert land produce this crop. Sugar cane needs a lot of water. To bring this water to the desert takes a lot of hard work, time skill and money as you will see Chapter 6.

Many countries all over Africa grow sugar to a greater or lesser extent. It grows more easily along Africa's trade wind coasts and with fewer artificial aids than anywhere else. Sugar is a type of grass, a very tall one, and grows well in these areas. Temperatures are warm enough, over 15°C in the coolest months, and there is rainfall in every month: a very important factor.

At Bacita, near Jebba, on the River Niger, there is a very big plantation, as shown in Fig. 55 in Chapter 4. Rainfall is not sufficient in this part of Nigeria and so the plantation takes advantage of the huge and permanent water supply provided by the man-made lake created by the Kainji Dam. Bacita now supplies at least a quarter of Nigeria's sugar requirements. Incidentally, why is rainfall a problem there? Check in the climate chapter on tropical continental climates if you are confused.

Most of Zaïre's sugar is grown on plantations in the well watered regions along the railway line between Kinshasa and Zaïre's only large port, Matadi. Much of Angola's sugar is also grown near the coast between Luanda and Zaïre. Both of these areas receive rain bearing winds for much of the year, but in Angola a certain amount of irrigation is needed in some months. Can you work out which months these could be?

A great deal of sugar is normally grown around Jinja in Uganda; and on the Kano Plains not far from Kisumu in Kenya there are thousands of hectares of both plantation and small farmer's sugar cane. The Kilombero valley in Tanzania now produces most of Tanzania's sugar along with projects at Mtibwa, Arusha-Chini and, since 1983, at Kagera.

Almost all Zambia's sugar is grown near Mazabuka, which is on the flat, polder-like land on either side of the River Kafue close to where it joins the Zambezi. Irrigation is vitally necessary there as rainfall is insufficient and irregular. It is supplied by water from the lake behind the great Kafue Dam. Sugar cane needs at least 1000 milli-metres of rain each year and prefers much more.

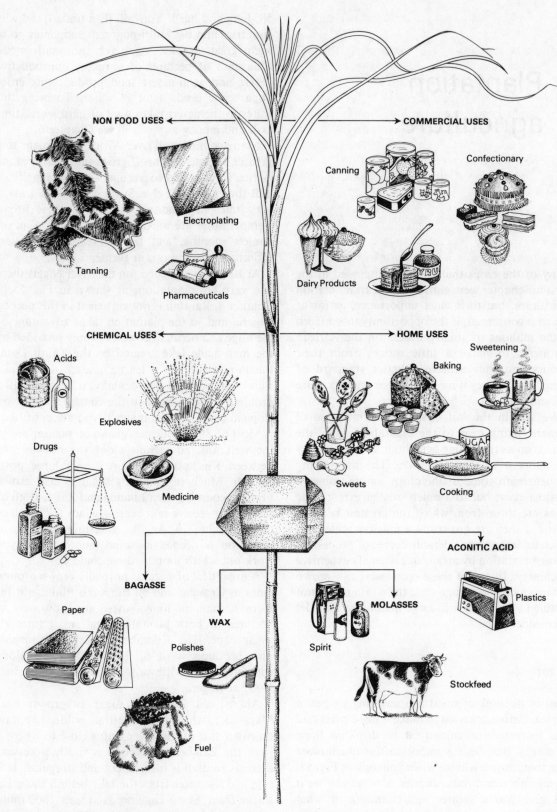

NON FOOD USES

COMMERCIAL USES

Tanning

Electroplating

Pharmaceuticals

Canning

Confectionary

Dairy Products

CHEMICAL USES

HOME USES

Acids

Explosives

Drugs

Medicine

Sweets

Sweetening

Baking

Cooking

ACONITIC ACID

BAGASSE

Paper

Fuel

WAX

Polishes

MOLASSES

Spirit

Plastics

Stockfeed

Fig. 58   The many uses of sugar

70

A climate like that in southern Zambia cannot provide it. Why?

In Africa sugar cane was first grown in the West Coast countries and on islands of the west coast, the Canary and Cape Verde Islands. This first occurred under the Spanish and Portuguese who later took sugar cane across the Atlantic to what are now known as the West Indies. These islands now form one of the largest cane sugar producers in the world; an achievement largely due to the warm and moist tropical marine climate experienced there.

It is a coastal area just outside the Tropic of Capricorn which, at the moment, is the most important cane sugar producing area in Africa. This is Natal, a province of South Africa, where sugar cane was first grown in 1851.

Natal is further away from the Equator than is normal for successful sugar cane growth. But the two factors responsible for the success are the warm southward flowing Mozambique Current and the onshore winds which blow over them, bringing warm moist conditions to the Natal Coast.

Most of Natal's sugar is grown on the coastal plain between Margate and Lake St. Lucia: a distance of some 400 kilometres. The sugar belt also extends inland as far as 25 kilometres and up to 750 metres altitude around places like Pietermaritzburg, as shown in Fig. 59. Soils vary from the flat fertile alluvial soils of coastal delta lands through porous sandy soils to the thin, less fertile soils of the hill and valley sides further inland.

Rainfall in the sugar lands varies a great deal from place to place, ranging from 500 – 1500 millimetres. It is also unreliable at times. On the coastal plain temperatures are always warm and often quite hot, Fig. 60 confirms this. Irrigation, therefore, is frequently necessary. Further inland towards the 750 metre level slightly lower temperatures mean a rather slower growth rate; but irrigation can still be just as necessary, as 'run-off' is greater and evaporation still quite high.

There are well over 362 000 hectares of Natal's farmland devoted to sugar cane, about half of which is harvested each year. Yields averaged between 85 and 95 tonnes of cane per hectare in 1979 while the sugar yield works out at approximately 1 tonne of sugar for 9.1 tonnes of cane.

The sugar cane industry in Natal is administered by the South African Sugar Association, which

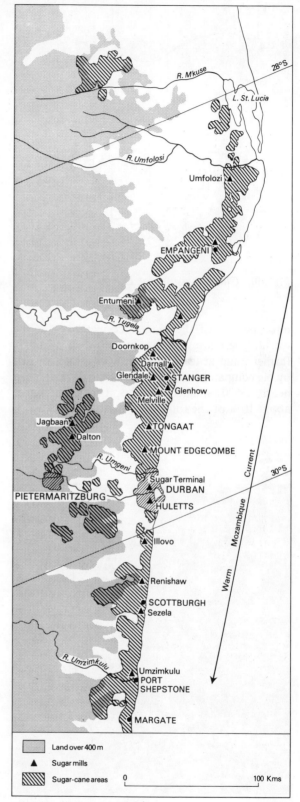

Fig. 59 Sugar in Natal

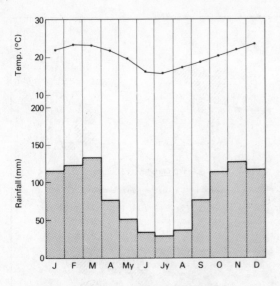

Fig. 60 Climate graph for Durban

must be one of the biggest cooperatives in the world. There are very big farms owned by single farmers, and at least 25 vast sugar estates owned by big companies. On a smaller scale there are also nearly 6500 smaller farmers producing cane: about 10% of the total.

Collecting sugar cane from the fields

Dotted throughout the sugar belt are 20 sugar mills, to one or other of which all Natal's sugar i sent for primary processing. The biggest of all o these is the mill at Tongaat. It produced 209 000 tonnes of raw sugar in 1979 which, with most o the sugar from the other mills (three have thei own refineries) is sent to the huge Huletts refinery in Durban, which has an annual capacity in excess of 500 000 tonnes. South Africa cannot possibly consume all the sugar she produces. It is stored i the new Bulk Sugar Terminal in Durban' dockland area and most of it is exported to Japan

Methods of cultivation

When land is to be re-planted with new cane all the old cane roots have to be ploughed out first and burned. The soil has to be deep ploughed to about 60 cms to allow it to 'breathe' and absorb water.

Contour ploughing is the rule and contour strip cropping the general practice. In this process wide strips of cane are grown at *different* stages. Thus when one strip is ready for harvesting, other strips on either side are at different stages; in this way sloping ground is never left bare and exposed to erosion forces. Where slopes are steep, artificia banks are built along contours. Grass contour strips are also used to act as fire breaks because cane can be very prone to fire outbreak. For instance, in 1976 a great fire destroyed over 4000 tonnes of Zaïre's sugar crop. Also, whatever the shape of the land there are always drainage channels.

Preparing seed cane for planting is a complicated business and no mechanisation is possible. The cane is selected from perfect specimens in the fields. With repeatedly disinfected knives the cane is chopped into 40cm lengths and then immersed for two hours in hot water (50°C) to prevent the later development of disease. It is then dipped in a fungicide/insecticide solution and planted. After roughly one year it is ready for use in the fields. Once again it is chopped with disinfected pangas and dipped in fungicide/insecticide before planting.

Contoured furrows are dug; each row being about 135 cm apart. Fertilizer is added and the 40 cm 'setts' as they are called, are planted end to end along the furrow and covered with soil. On the really big farms and estates this is often done mechanically; but on other farms it is done by hand. Weeding is essential from the start because weeds use exactly the same nutrients as the cane. Constant hoeing also allows water to percolate into the soil and keeps it aerated.

The sucrose content of cane in Natal is greatest during the period September – November and so it is best if the cane can be harvested then. However, this is never completely possible; and, in fact, harvesting usually takes place between May and December.

Several crops are possible from the same plant. The first crop is called *plant cane*; and then, after cutting, the root will sprout again. These crops are called the *rattoon* crops and anything up to three or four rattoons are harvested before the field is ploughed up and rested for several months.

The cane is cut by hand, the leaves removed and the cane stacked neatly on the ground in bundles. The cut leaves, called *trash*, are left to cover the land. Trash prevents loss of moisture, keeps weeds down, helps prevent erosion by deflation or rain-wash and provides humus for the soil when it rots.

Tractors and trailers, even small trains, collect up the sugar cane from the fields for delivery to the mills. At a mill like Tongaat, north of Durban, the cane is chopped and then passed through a series of contra-rotating rollers which squeezes out the juice. The fibrous waste is called *bagasse* and is used to fire the mill's boilers. As a result the mills need little or no other fuel.

Lime is mixed with the juice to help purify it. The impurities sink to the bottom. This material is called 'mud' and is returned to the fields as fertilizer.

The remaining juice is boiled until sugar crystals are produced. These are removed and the mix is boiled yet again until more crystals are produced. At the finish the only thing left is *molasses* which can be used as a stock food, fertilizer or in the manufacture of alcohol.

The raw sugar is then transported to Huletts refinery in Durban for the last refining process before export by way of the sugar terminal which can load sugar on to ships at the rate of 500 tonnes an hour.

Recently, however, sugar producers have had their problems. In 1974 – 75 world sugar prices reached £650 per tonne. With Cuba, South Africa, Russia and the E.E.C. reaching high production

The refinery's reception centre The cane will now go to the crushers.

The Tongaat sugar factory near Durban

levels other African countries were encouraged to increase production. Then, within three short years the price fell to £80 per tonne; rising to £90 in 1982. This is below the overall cost of production and, as a result, some African producers are suffering.

For special reasons countries such as Ghana and Nigeria are not self sufficient (see Discussion Points P. 55) but other producers have problems. Recently some countries seem to have found a partial answer. Malawi, Kenya and Zimbabwe produce alcohol (ethanol) with their surplus sugar. In Zimbabwe it is processed at Triangle: 60 000 tonnes of cane producing 120 000 litres of alcohol each day. In Harare it is mixed with petrol, sometimes to a 20% mix, saving money on petrol imports. The fermented waste (stillage) is

73

mixed with irrigation water, increasing cane yields by 6%. Solid waste is used as cattle food and in the factory boilers. This whole scheme is a fine example of adaptation to the current African economic nightmare of expensive fuel oil and excess sugar production. It even offers export potential.

Question and answer session

1 How are the cane fields irrigated? There are three basic methods. One is by means of perforated pipes laid in between rows of cane.

Irrigating sugar at Bacita, Nigeria

Water sprays from the holes upwards and outwards. Another is by means of a rotating rain gun fixed to a permanent supply of water. As the nozzle rotates, water is hurled over a circular area of at least 30 metres in radius. Both these methods reduce transpiration and give an even cover of water. A different method is that of furrow irrigation in which controlled flooding of certain furrows between rows of cane takes place. Water is supplied by small main concrete lined channels with sluice gates controlling entrances to the cane fields. These methods are shown in Fig. 61.

2 Why is good drainage so necessary? It is necessary no matter what crop is irrigated. Good drainage methods shown in Fig. 62 remove excess water and allow bacteria to work on the breakdown of organic matter. Excess mineral salts will be removed. Ordinary river water, if applied at the rate of 1250 millimetres per year per hectare will, if drainage is not efficient, in tropical and sub-tropical lands, deposit in the soil an average of 1 tonne of mineral salts per hectare. Thus efficient drainage is a must on irrigated land, particularly where the evaporation rate is greatly in excess of normal rainfall. If it is not efficient gradually increasing salinity will cause both crop and soil deterioration.

Overhead irrigation from pipes laid in between rows.
The pipes have holes and the water sprays upwards and outwards.

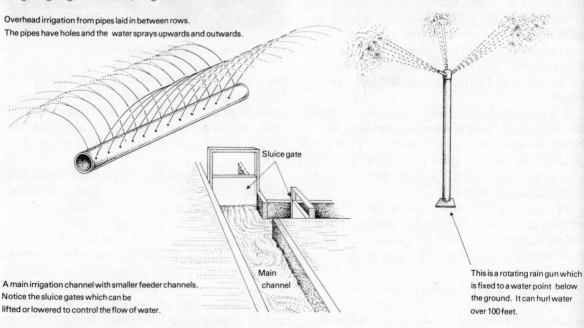

Sluice gate

A main irrigation channel with smaller feeder channels.
Notice the sluice gates which can be
lifted or lowered to control the flow of water.

Main channel

This is a rotating rain gun which is fixed to a water point below the ground. It can hurl water over 100 feet.

Fig. 61 Methods of irrigating sugar cane

What drainage methods are used in Natal? See Fig. 62.

What pests and diseases affect sugar cane? The most infamous disease is *rattoon stunting* which inhibits the normal growth of the cane. This is caused by various pests, one of which is the *Mealybug* which sucks juice from the cane. Other sucking insects are the *Leafhopper* and *Green Leafsucker*. Two leaf-eating insects are the larvae of the *Trashworm* and the *Army Worm*. Great care when planting the setts will avoid many of these problems, spraying with insecticides like D.D.T. can also control them.

How does the South African Sugar Association help growers? It organises marketing and negotiates prices. It gives advice to farmers on all matters connected with cane cultivation. Its research institute at Mount Edgecombe develops new varieties of cane, experiments with pest and disease control and also soil improvement and fertilizer techniques. All their findings are continuously passed on to members of the association.

Group tasks

Which country, south of the Sahara, is *least* likely to grow sugar cane? Give reasons for your answer.

2 Why are sugar cane, and many other crops, planted round hillsides and not up and down them?

3 Do you have any crop marketing boards or growing associations in your country? If so find out how they work and what benefits they bring.

4 In which months is irrigation likely to be necessary in Natal?

5 Get together with your friends and work out how a large shallow tank of water with milli-metre measurements marked on the inside might, by studying daily evaporation rates, help to decide *if, when* and *how much* irrigation is needed.

Rubber

Rubber is another agricultural product, a tree crop, which is best suited to plantation methods; although in one country we shall study, Liberia, well over half the area devoted to rubber cultivation is owned by small farmers with individual plots. The fact that they are not so successful as the big estates is a great pity and we shall be looking at the reasons for this.

Rubber is a very useful material and can be used for many purposes. For those of us connected

POLE DRAIN

Large poles are laid along a pre-dug trench and surrounded by brushwood and stones. Soil covers it to the surface. Because the wood rots after some years they have to be periodically reconstructed

TILE DRAIN

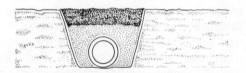

These are clay pipes laid end to end along a pre-dug trench. They are laid on a bed of, and surrounded by, sand.

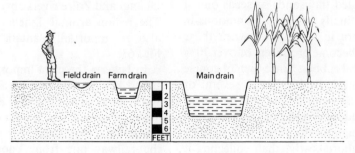

Fig. 62   Methods of drainage in sugar cane areas

with schools and education its most well known use is for rubbing out mistakes in our exercise books. It is used for the soles of shoes and for making all sorts of vehicle tyres, both big and small, without which the world's transport system would not run so efficiently. Rubber is thus another example of how man has exploited and domesticated natural vegetation for his own benefit by cultivating it in large, controlled and concentrated areas.

Unfortunately, like so many other inter-tropical crops, rubber depends a great deal for its marketability upon the low wages paid to the men who actually work on the farms and plantations. It is a sad fact that rubber, in common with many other crops grown in such countries, needs a large supply of cheap labour. If labour suddenly became expensive it is possible that the world might well turn to other substitutes. Rubber, in fact, is a good case in point. Until the world price of oil began its catastrophic rise in 1973 rubber growing countries had had to compete with synthetic rubber made from oil by the great industrial countries. Now natural rubber is in greater demand again and makes up 68% of all rubber made; but it is unlikely that the farm worker will receive much financial benefit.

The Manihot tree, Ceara tree and several others, all grow wild in the wetter parts of Africa. However, the best and most productive rubber tree is not a native of Africa. It is the Hevea tree, now known as Hevea Braziliensis because it was, and still is, part of the natural vegetation of the Brazilian rain forest areas. Its arrival in Africa was achieved by very complicated and, some would say, rather illegal methods. Brazil guarded her wild rubber trees jealously and forbade their export because she wished to maintain a stranglehold on world rubber sales and production. However in 1876, Sir Henry Wickham, an Englishman, smuggled thousands of seeds out of Brazil. They were finally sown on plantations in Malaya and Sumatra in 1890; since when those two countries have become producers of over 70% of the world's natural rubber. Since then of course it has been brought, quite legally, to several of Africa's countries. By contrast Brazil is no longer an important producer: collecting rubber from trees scattered throughout the forest is far less efficient, and much more costly, than collecting it from concentrated groups of trees on plantations.

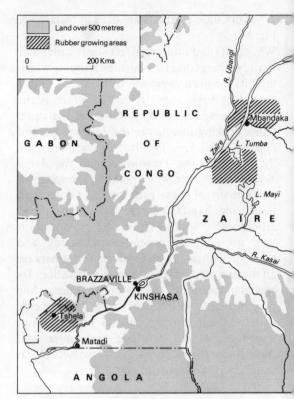

Fig. 63   *Zaïre's rubber growing lands*

As you know, rubber is an equatorial crop; bu it is still very demanding in its requirements. I must have deep, fertile, well-drained lowland soils: preferably the slopes of gentle hills. It mus have well over 1750 millimetres of evenly distributed rainfall, preferably with at least 5(millimetres in every month. It must have average temperatures which never fall below 21°C. From these demands you can see that only Africa's hottest and wettest lands are suitable for it cultivation.

Zaïre produces a great deal of rubber, particularly along the Zaïre river itself in the swampy low lying regions around Mbandaka; where the Ubangi and Zaïre rivers coverge upon each other The region around Tshela, north of Matadi, is also an important plantation area, as shown in Fig. 63.

In Nigeria the most important rubber areas are found between Benin City and Sapele and in the south east near Calabar, as shown in Fig. 55. There is also a big plantation near Yaoundé in Cameroun, the factory for which is at Edea, or the railway line from Yaoundé to Douala, as shown in Fig. 64.

A Firestone rubber plantation in Liberia
What advantages does the site have?

Ivory Coast started plantation rubber less than 25 years ago diversifying away from a near total dependence on cocoa and coffee. In that time the para statal company SOCTACI, aided by French money has planted thirty-five thousand hectares. A 13 500 hectare plantation at Bereby in the south-west had its first tapping in 1979. There are plantations at Sassandra, San Pedro and Abidjan, while another 4800 hectares were planted near Grah Rapids in 1979 and a factory erected. 25 000 tonnes of rubber were produced in 1982 and the aim is for 41 000 in 1985 and 77 000 tonnes by 1990.

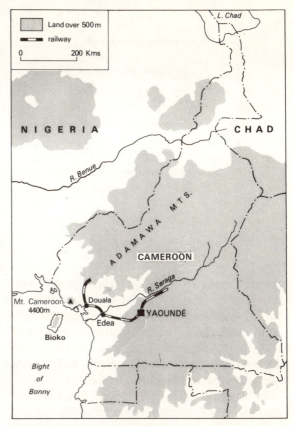

Fig. 64   Cameroon's rubber growing lands

All these rubber producing farms and plantations look small beside the rubber production of Liberia. There, nearly 120 000 hectares of land are devoted to rubber production; of which 60 000

Liberian Rubber Production 1975

Source	Planted area (acres)	Area in tapping (acres)	Concession production (lb.)	Total purchased from farmers (lb.)	Exports (lb.)	Yield (lb./acre)	1978 expected production
The Liberia Co.	5 831	4 643	5 618 929	—	5 049 450	1 210	7 000 000
Firestone	90 024	52 602	73 483 895	39 038 261	113 101 038	1 397	66 500 000
Alan L. Grant	—	—	—	12 637 754	14 102 950	—	7 935 367
African Fruit Co.	5 700	5 412	6 088 827	—	6 511 586	1 125	n.a.
B. F. Goodrich	14 416	13 000	16 142 374	1 383 265	18 588 438	1 242	20 000 000
Salala Rubber Corp.	5 133	5 133	7 266 869	—	6 135 402	1 416	8 000 000
Liberian Agric. Co.	19 186	18 164	19 507 403	383 383	18 963 686	1 074	24 800 000
Totals	140 290	98 954	128 108 297	53 441 653	182 452 550		

Source: Rubber Planters' Association

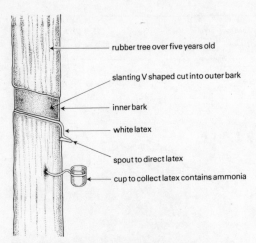

Fig. 65   Tapping a rubber tree

rubber tree over five years old

slanting V shaped cut into outer bark

inner bark

white latex

spout to direct latex

cup to collect latex contains ammonia

hectares belong to Liberian farmers themselves. Unfortunately they produced less than 29% of Liberia's total of 80 million kilogrammes of rubber in 1980. This was due partly to inefficient small farms, absentee landlords, inexperienced managers and poor standard trees. Yields were lower as well: 590 kilograms per hectare.

The biggest company plantation of all is that of Firestone Tyre Company, whose headquarters are in the U.S.A. The plantation is situated near Harbel, which is not far from Monrovia, and is shown in the photograph. It is well over 34 000 hectares in extent and produces nearly twice as much rubber as all the other plantations put together, as shown in the table.

There are about 12 million rubber trees, Hevea Braziliensis, on the plantation, which employs about 15 000 tappers. There are hundreds of nearby small farmers who also sell their rubber to Firestone. Near the border with Sierra Leone is another Firestone plantation: rather smaller at 4500 hectares.

Harbel is so big that there are many villages dotted all over its area; each one being responsible for part of the plantation. There are schools, churches, hospitals, television centres and other social services: all provided by the company. From each village the tappers go out every day. Some even live in huts away from the village. A skilled tapper can tap about 400 trees each morning but he must be very careful not to actually damage the tree.

At each factory the milky liquid known as *latex* is put into a tank of water when it arrives. To this

mixture a certain amount of acetic acid is added which turns the latex into a spongy coagulated mass known as coagulent rubber. This is then rolled into flat sheets which squeezes out a lot of the moisture and then dried on racks in a smoking shed: the smoke coming from smouldering chippings on the floor. To achieve *crepe* rubber the coagulent rubber is rolled between two rollers moving at different speeds and then air dried.

Question and answer session

1   What do the tappers do? This is a very skilled job. The tapper makes a slanting cut in the bark of the tree's trunk. Each cut is 'v' shaped and the milky white latex bleeds from the bark and runs down the groove into a cup which the tapper has fixed below the slanting cut, as shown in Fig. 65. He taps every morning and collects every afternoon. After the same trees have been tapped for six months they are then given a long rest and other trees take their turn.

A Firestone rubber plantation in Liberia
What is the man doing?   What else will happen?

LIBERIA — Balance of Trade ($m.)

	1976	1977	1978	1979	1980	1981
Exports	457.0	447.5	486.4	536.6	600.6	529.2
Imports	399.2	463.5	480.4	506.5	534.7	477.4
Surplus	57.8	−16.0	6.0	30.1	65.9	51.8

LIBERIA — Value of Major Exports ($m.)

Iron ore	331.6	273.5	274.3	290.0	310.2
Rubber	53.3	59.1	69.1	87.8	102.2
Logs	34.6	29.3	46.7	50.1	65.3
Diamonds	16.6	21.4	30.3	39.6	33.5
Coffee	4.5	6.6	43.0	25.3	27.1

2   What future is there for natural rubber? All the rubber producing countries think there is a great future. They think the successful challenge of synthetic rubber, made from petroleum, has been killed off by the current shortage and very high price of oil. A further indication is that radial car tyres, for which natural rubber is preferred, are becoming more and more important at the expense of crossply types. There is so much confidence in Ivory Coast that there are plans for a new tyre factory, run by the Michelin company.

3   How important is rubber to Liberia? The statistics are shown in the table above. 35% of the wage earners in Liberia, are employed by the rubber industry, in one way or another. What would they do if rubber failed?

Group tasks

1   Study the table on Page 77 showing rubber production in Liberia.
a) Place the rubber companies in order of merit by looking at their exports.
b) What is the order according to acreage?
c) Which one probably does not grow rubber
d) Draw a bar graph for the companies' exports. Use a scale of 1 mm = 1 million pounds.
e) Round all the export figures up or down to the nearest 100 000 pounds. Of the total exports what percentage came from Firestone's operations?

2   a) Multiply all the acreages by 0.40. This will give you the areas in hectares.

b) Find out what you should do to change pounds into kilograms. Work out the companies' projections for 1978 in kilograms.

3   Study Liberia's *main* exports, as shown in the table above.
a) Draw a long bar 10 cms by 2 cms. Divide it according to the percentages that each commodity achieves of the total export figure. Label each division.
b) What percentage is rubber of the whole? Study Liberia's balance of trade above.
c) Draw a twin line graph to demonstrate how Liberia's exports have performed in relation to imports between 1976 – 1981. Label it 'BALANCE OF TRADE'.
d) What percentage of the total exports is made up by rubber?

4   Think of some other uses for rubber. Make a diagram similar to the one for sugar. (Page 70)

Viticulture

Most of the plantation crops that we have studied or mentioned so far are crops of the inter-tropical regions of Africa. Plantation agriculture is, however, carried on outside these latitudes. One such crop is the vine, the cultivation of which is known as *viticulture*. The vine is a crop of the Mediterranean lands, although it is cultivated in many other countries such as Germany and Austria which do not have Mediterranean climates. Certainly the vine is cultivated in all the Mediterranean climate areas of Africa; as indeed it is in all lands which experience that sort of climate.

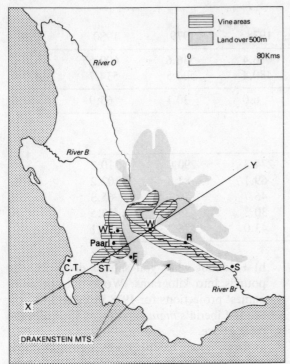

Fig. 66 Areas of vine cultivation in South Africa

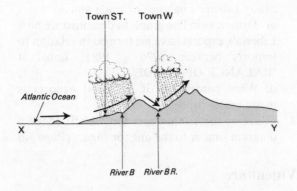

Fig. 67 Section across the vine growing area of South Africa

In many ways the vine is a perfect crop: equally suited to all scales of agriculture, from plantation style to quite small farms. Even 10 or 20 hectares will provide quite a good income. The South African wine producing region lies in a very small area just inland from Cape Town in the south-west tip: the only region south of the Equator with a Mediterranean climate. There the average size farm is 150 – 200 hectares, not really big enough to have individual wineries (factories which produce

A terraced vineyard in South Africa Notice the use of contours.
Why is contour cultivation necessary in viticulture?

wine). However the benefits of large scale, plantation-type farming are not lost because of this; because all farmers who grow the grape belong to a huge co-operative known as the Ko-operatiewe Wijnbonwers Vereniging. Their wineries are dotted all over the vine growing areas in main towns like Paarl. In this way the benefits of large scale production are available to farms of less than plantation size. An added virtue is the fact that the state is only remotely involved and the farmers own their own land, whether big or small, quite unlike the para statal settlement schemes where the farmers sometimes have to grow what they are told and often do not own their land.

There are many vineyards (grape farms) in the south-west Cape area of South Africa. They are found on the flat valley land of the Great Berge and Breede Rivers, as shown in Fig. 66. On the lower slopes of the nearby mountains the land is terraced in order to grow the grapes.

There are two basic vine areas in south-west Cape; one needing quite a lot of irrigation and the other not very much, explained in Fig. 67. The vine lands in the Paarl – Stellenbosch area receive good winter rains and so little irrigation is necessary; but over the mountains in the Worcester region, some areas lie in a rain shadow and there is insufficient rain: less than 350 mm. There the waters of the River Breede are very important.

Most grape vines will grow uncontrollably if left to themselves, but it is convenient that they should be kept as small bushes by means of an annual pruning in the winter when there are no leaves. The vines are usually less than 2 metres high and are planted in long neat rows about 2 metres apart in all directions. In this way the grapes' quality is maintained and they are easily picked. Each year the vines produce grapes which grow together in little clusters. Some are green and some are red or even dark blue; with anything between 5 – 20 grapes to a bunch.

Vines take a lot of nutrient out of the soil which must be annually replenished by means of cover crops like rye. These are sown after the harvest, grown during the winter and early spring and then ploughed in, together with fertilizers, during early spring. The humus content of the soil is maintained in this way; and, most important indeed, the soil is protected from erosion by winter rain-wash. Also in connection with this many farms keep both a herd of dairy cattle and some pigs. Their manure is a valuable fertilizer and the milk and meat bring a welcome, though small, regular income throughout the year.

Once the growing season is in full swing, weeding and spraying are essential for reasons we have discussed on other pages. The growing season is the dry season and so in those areas where winter rain is low irrigation becomes necessary. The method shown first in the sugar section is most popular; and the water is drawn from the main rivers or one of their tributaries. Irrigation finishes in January just before the picking starts.

Some grapes have quite a high sugar content. These are sold in the big towns or exported to Europe. They are known as table grapes. Others, the later ones picked in February and early March, do not have quite so much sugar and are used to make wine. Wines vary from 'sweet' to 'dry', the dry wines having a very low sugar content indeed. Some are a deep red colour while others are light and are known as rosé. Some may have only a faint yellowy colour and are known as white wines. Needless to say they are made from the green grapes. All the regular labourers live, with their families, on the farms; but in the picking season much extra help is needed and is hired from the nearby towns and villages. The seasonal workers are mostly women, and they join the families of the regular labourers in this work. Basket after basket of grapes is loaded onto a succession of lorries which are piled high with the

Picking the grapes Notice how many there are on a bunch.

grapes. As they make their way to the wineries of Paarl or Stellenbosch they leave a trail of grape juice on the roads. The grapes are crushed by their own weight and the juice often causes vehicles to skid and crash.

At the wineries the grapes are unloaded into great screw presses which crush the grapes and extract the juices: thousands upon thousands of gallons of it. It is left to ferment for many days and, as a result, alcohol is formed. When fermentation has finished the wine is put into huge

Transferring wine to barrels

barrels to await bottling. Sometimes it is exported in bottles and sometimes in the barrels from Cape Town. Some of the wine is used to make brandy, by distilling the alcohol from the wine and storing it for many years in big barrels. In 1979 South Africa produced 2% of the world's wine. Zimbabwe also has a wine industry. The latest winery is at Mukuyu near Marandellas and Wadze. The winery uses grapes from the nearby Mateppe vineyard which has 2000 vines at present. It also processes grapes from the Mazoe Valley.

Several other African countries produce grapes. There are vineyards in Egypt, Ethiopia, Algeria, Tunisia and Morocco.

Question and answer session

1 Do grape farms (vineyards) only produce grapes? No. They produce other fruits as well which are also suited to the Mediterranean climate. They also produce fruits like apricots and peaches which are used in the jam and canning industries. In North Africa they also grow large quantities of olives, which are a staple food of the Mediterranean countries and which also produce a valuable vegetable oil.
2 Do the North African countries make their own wine? Yes, but not much of it is exported in bottles. France buys most of it to mix and blend with some of her own wine. North Africa's people do not drink much of their own wine as most of them are Muslims whose religion forbids the consumption of alcohol.
3 How was the vine brought to South Africa? The Dutch, who first colonized the area in the early seventeenth century, brought in the first vines; but the industry received its greatest impetus when the Huguenots from France, refugees from religious persecution in their homeland, came to settle in South West Cape in the eighteenth century.

Group tasks

1 Copy the map shown in Fig. 66, and name the towns and rivers. Include on the map arrows which show wind direction in July – August and also is December – July. Use different colours.
2 Where is the rain shadow area on Fig. 67?

3 Is there another plantation crop produced in your country: or one which is produced under both large scale and small farm conditions? If so try to visit the farm or plantation. Find out all you can about it. How is it grown? What work is done throughout the year? How many people work there? Is fertilization needed and when? What is the *local* climate? Is irrigation necessary? Who buys the crop? Draw a map to show where it is.

Sisal

Sisal is a fibre crop which, in Africa, is grown almost exclusively in Tanzania and Kenya. Indeed for many years it was Tanzania's leading cash crop and topped its list of exports, but now it occupies fourth place; although even today, Mexico and Tanzania between them produce at least half of the world's supply. Sisal was introduced to Tanzania in 1892, brought by the Germans from Mexico when they colonized Tanganyika, as it was then called.

Sisal is a very adaptable crop in that it can grow in most soils, even quite poor ones, and also in near drought conditions for year after year. It grows better with rainfall of over 750 mm but it can manage on amounts as little as 500 mm. It can, in fact, grow where most other crops are unsuccessful. In both Tanzania and Kenya huge areas of the drier parts of the coastal plain are

A field of sisal See the long flowering pole.
What is the tree in the middle distance?

devoted to it. But there are equally large areas found inland and at much greater altitudes. However, they all have one thing in common; there is fairly easy access to a transport system particularly railways, as shown in Fig. 68. Sisal must be exported as only a limited amount can be used locally. Thus we find that the vast majority of sisal lands have a good rail connection to an export outlet like Mombasa, Tanga or Mtwara.

Sisal is a large plant with long sword-shaped spiky leaves. It is these leaves which contain the long fibrous strands enclosed by the juicy green flesh, as shown in the photograph. It flowers once only in its lifetime and produces during that time approximately 250 leaves. These are cut off, beginning at the base of the plant, as they become big enough. Again we come back to the great problem of inter-tropical crops: labour. As with

most others, sisal plantations need a large supply of workers who are not very well paid. Moreover, sisal cutting is hard, very hard work.

Question and answer session

1 How is sisal grown? When the plant flowers it throws up a long central pole-like stem which has sprays of flowers branching off at the top. A fruit forms after flowering which is known as a bulbil. There are many of these and they are gathered up and sown in a nursery on the plantation. Later, as small four or five leafed plants, they are planted out in the fields at the rate of 5000 per hectare. They grow for a total of three years before cutting is permitted and can reach nearly 2 metres in height. Cutting can be carried out at lengthy intervals for

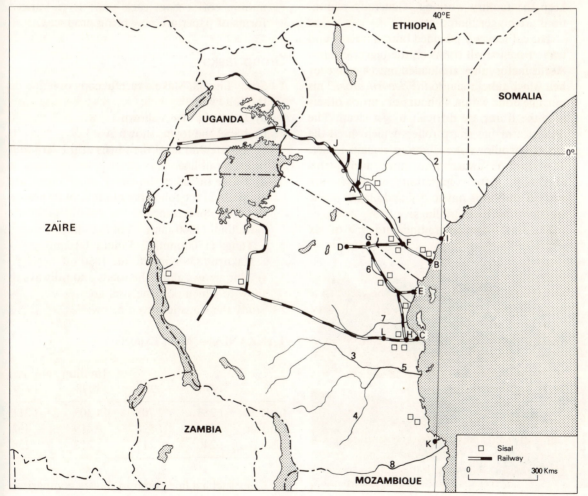

Fig. 68   Sisal growing areas in Kenya and Tanzania

another six years or until the maximum number of leaves have developed.

2 How often is harvesting carried out? Different fields are cut at different times in order to ensure that the factory is in use throughout the year. Yields work out at about 25 to 35 tonnes per hectare, but this is drastically reduced by processing when the final count is approximately two kilograms of fibre from every 50 kilograms of leaf.

3 Is processing the leaf difficult? No, but is is very expensive because of the machinery involved. Thus, to make sure a factory is economical it must work throughout the year; which means the plantations have to be very large indeed. The minimum size of a sisal plantation is approximately 1600 – 2000 hectares, because anything smaller could not keep the factory working. Generally plantations are bigger than that.

The cut leaves are loaded onto a tractor and trailer: even small trains on the bigger estates. At the factory they are loaded onto a conveyor belt which takes them to the *decorticator*. This must be done within 48 hours of cutting otherwise the fibres arc difficult to get clean. The decorticator has sharp rollers which shred the leaves but allows the fibres to remain intact. The floor is awash with juice during this operation. After separation the fibres are washed and hung out to dry and bleach in the sun upon long wire railings.

The final stage is grading into one of six

grades, after which it is packed into bales each weighing approximately 250 kilograms, and sent to ports such as Mombasa for export.

4 Why has sisal suffered recently? It has had to compete with man-made materials like polythene and nylon which are also used to make bags and ropes: two of sisal's main uses. In many areas along the coast sisal growing has been restricted and the land given over to dairy farming and market gardening. The increased tourist trade has made this a more profitable proposition: particularly in Kenya. Nevertheless, great efforts are being made to encourage the manufacture of sisal, particularly in Tanzania. The production of twine is increasing, gaily coloured mats, carpets, and baskets are being made and the Tanzania Bag Corporation at Moshi is producing over 3 million coffee bags each year. Even various forms of paper are now being produced.

Group tasks

1 Study Fig. 68. Make a careful copy of it and do the following.
a) Label the rivers shown 1 – 8.
b) Label the towns shown A – L.
c) Locate and label the towns at the terminus of each rail line.
d) Name the lakes shown.
e) Write in the following rainfall totals next to the town concerning.

   Malindi (1000 mm)   Voi (525 mm)
   Tanga (1800 mm)   Lindi (900 mm)
   Nakuru (850 mm altitude 1850 m)

f) Put arrows along the roads and railways to show to which port the sisal goes.

2 Study the statistics given below:

TANZANIA — Main Exports

				(million shillings)
	1976	1977	1978	1979
Coffee	1 283	1 708	1 303	1 211
Cotton	614	528	419	492
Sisal	240	217	218	258

Construct a 4 line graph to show a comparison of the values of Tanzania's 3 main exports between 1976 and 1979.

Sisal drying in the sun in Angola The sun has bleached it white.

6 Large scale irrigation

Water is to agriculture as petrol is to motor cars: the one cannot work without the other. No matter how fertile soils are, they can produce nothing of value unless water, sufficient water, is available. Nowhere is this illustrated more dramatically than deep in the Libyan desert where the oil drillers found vast artesian stores of water; enough, it is calculated, to last 500 years. Now on oilfields like the one at Serir — See Chapter 11 — hundreds of hectares of alfalfa form islands of green in the parched yellow desert. The alfalfa supports many thousands of sheep, where none could live before. Many vegetables are grown here for the oilfield workers. Given water even the desert soils can produce food and sustain life. But it is not in the worst deserts that the greatest hope lies: they are empty of all but a few people who crowd around, and travel between, the scattered oases.

The greatest need, the greatest hopes and, so far, the greatest developments in the field of irrigation are found in the tropical continental — semi-desert margins of Africa. It is in these areas, seemingly becoming drier year by year, that thousands of people live out a grim existence based on the annual arrival of the rains *which sometimes do not come*. These are the nomads, the semi-nomads, who follow the rains with their cattle, goats, sheep and camels. These are the subsistence farmers of the Sahel whose families are rarely free from hunger. They are the people who scratch an existence from the soil exposed by receding flood water near streams and rivers, and who face starvation if the rivers do not flood in the first place. It is to these regions, to these people, that a combination of their own efforts, state and international aid and great private investments has brought the greatest developments. It has not been easy because all these projects require vast amounts of money; and money, no matter what anyone says, is always in short supply.

To illustrate the contrast between an insufficient, irregular water supply and a reliable, controlled supply, let us look at two regions in Ethiopia.

The Plain of Death

This is an arid region, along the valley of the River Omo which drains into Lake Turkana in Kenya, as shown in Figs. 69 and 70. The plain is over 3000 square kilometres in extent and is bordered on all sides by rivers; all tributaries of the Omo itself. Within this enclosed region is a narrow range of mountains: the Mursi Mountains from which the *seasonal* River Elma flows. Communications are difficult and the only means of crossing the rivers is by dug-out canoe in the flood season, or by wading in the dry season. Both methods are dangerous; particularly the dry method as crocodiles are numerous. Thus both the region and the Mursi tribe, about 6000 of them, are very isolated indeed.

The Mursi people have many problems, not the least of which is a rainfall of less than 375 mm a year. They are pastoralists of a semi-nomadic kind but they cannot raise enough cattle to support themselves. The problem is worsening, and now they have fewer than 1 cow per person to support themselves. The reasons for this are threefold. First the cattle are unable to get enough food and also frequently suffer from rinderpest. Secondly the grass on the stony plain away from the rivers is insufficient for all year round grazing. Thirdly the Hammar, a fierce tribe to the east, often raid and kill both men and their cattle. Because of this the cattle often have to be taken to the dense bushlands near the Omo where the ever increasing population of tsetse fly do their deadly work.

A purely pastoral way of life in semi-arid regions requires from 4 – 6 cattle to support one person; and so the Mursi, being short of cattle, have had to become cultivators as well, but even this has been difficult. The women and girls cultivate the exposed fertile alluvial flats of the

Omo after the September – October floods have receded. During the rainy season for this area, March and April, they practise a shifting cultivation in the bush belt away from the river. Thus they get two crops of millet, maize and beans each year: IF the floods and rains do not fail. At the same time the men and boys take the cattle and wander the plains in search of grazing; moving eastwards to the Elma which usually has some water in it.

Thus the tribe is separated for many months of every year: the men and boys living on milk and

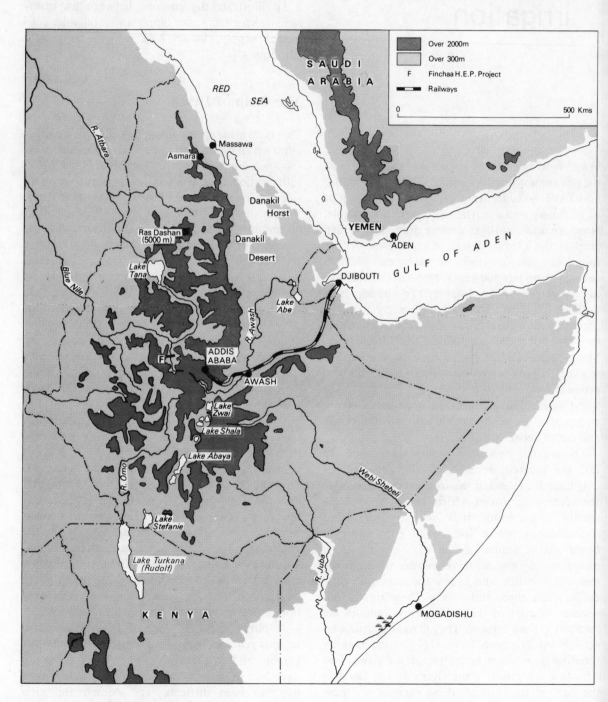

Fig. 69 Northern Ethiopia

blood and sleeping rough, while the women, girls and old people stay in the villages along the Omo, cultivating the land and living on the cereals they grow. Only during the rainy season and a month or so afterwards, from April to September, can the tribes people live together; and then only in temporary shelters on the edge of the bush belt, of the type shown in Fig. 71.

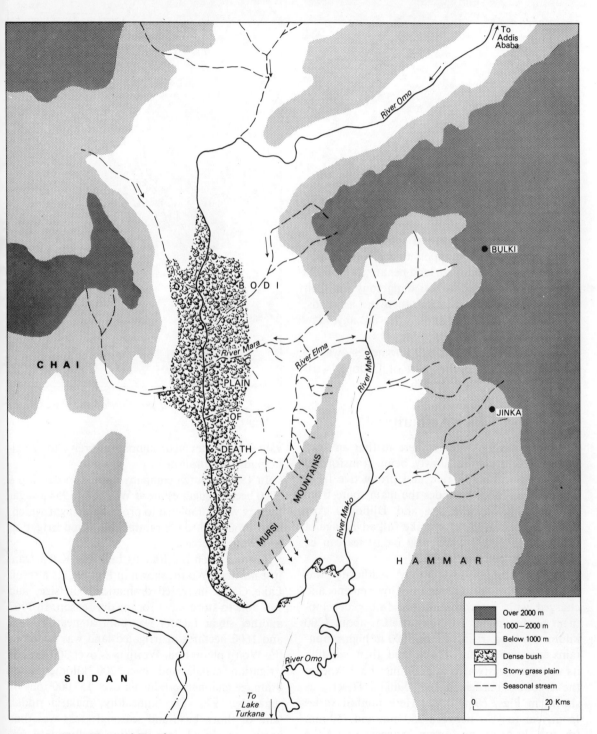

Fig. 70   *The Plain of Death*

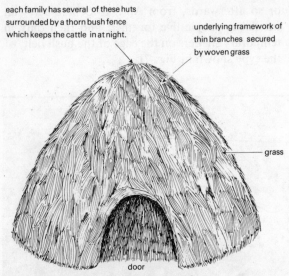

each family has several of these huts surrounded by a thorn bush fence which keeps the cattle in at night.

underlying framework of thin branches secured by woven grass

grass

door

Fig. 71   A temporary homestead

So here we have a pastoral people who cannot raise enough cows to support themselves. To survive they have to cultivate land next to, or near the rivers, but that land is too dangerous for their cattle. There is no education, there are no roads, no medical facilities and little, if any, law enforcement.

How different it all is 640 kilometres away to the north-east in another part of Ethiopia's rift valley, along the River Awash.

The Awash Valley Authority

The story is very different here in that an arid, inhospitable region is slowly being transformed into an agriculturally rich and productive land. The Awash Valley provides the main route from Addis Ababa to the sea and Djibouti. Any development can therefore take full advantage of transport facilities, while new industries can be based on agricultural produce.

In 1962 the Awash Valley Authority was established by the Ethiopian Government and charged with co-ordinating the future development of the valley. The river itself is about 1200 kilometres long, rising in the 3000 m high mountains west of Addis Ababa and then winding its way north-eastwards to drain into Lake Abe on the Djibouti border in the Danakil Desert, as shown in Figs. 69 and 72. Here rainfall varies from year to year between 250 mm and 750 mm (mostly closer to the former in recent years) the

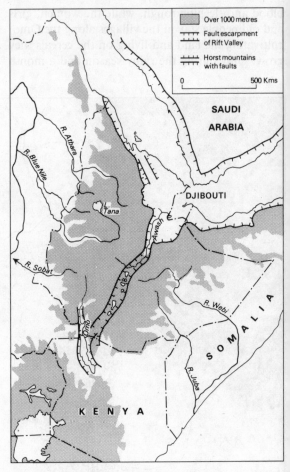

Over 1000 metres

Fault escarpment of Rift Valley

Horst mountains with faults

0   500 Kms

SAUDI ARABIA

DJIBOUTI

L. Tana

R. Atbara

R. Blue Nile

R. Sobat

Awash

Omo

R. Webi

R. Juba

S O M A L I A

K E N Y A

Fig. 72   The physical position of the Awash Valley

valley was devoted almost entirely to semi-nomadic pastoralism.

In 1951 a Dutch company started to develop a 5000 hectare sugar estate at Wonji. In 1954 a sugar factory was completed to process the sugar which, until 1960, had to use rainfall and flood irrigation as a water source.

Then in 1960 the Italians built the Koka Dam just north of Wonji, shown in Fig. 73. As a result Lake Galila increased dramatically in size, and was able to store water for the dry season. In 1962 another sugar factory was built at nearby Shoa and 1600 hectares of irrigated land was added to the Wonji plantation. Wonji uses over 300 kms of irrigation canals and over 200 kilometres of drainage channels producing over 157 000 tons of sugar by 1978. This unhealthy, malaria ridden land of thorn bush and seasonal grass was thus partly converted into highly productive land.

Lake Galila, Ethiopia

Twenty thousand people live in newly built villages on the Wonji and Metahara estates; each village having schools, medical and leisure facilities. There is a modern hospital at Wonji. At Metahara, begun in 1965 and also irrigated by Lake Galila water, there is another 11 000 hectare estate; and a sugar factory which produces 50 000 tonnes of white sugar a year.

A new scheme was planned to increase the irrigated area by another 13 000 hectares. This involves a diversion of more water into Lake Galila so the water will flow by gravity. The Malka-Amibara is another irrigation project started by the A.V.A. Since 1970 it has increased its area producing cotton, maize, tobacco and vegetables to well over 2000 hectares. Extra water from Galila and the Kesem Dam will increase the irrigated area to 14 000 hectares. In part of this scheme, over 200 Afars and their families have been settled round a 400 acre training farm and are being taught irrigation farming of cotton and maize. The A.V.A. gives assistance for housing, seeds, pest control and the cost of water.

Another major irrigation scheme on the Awash, is found at Tendaho, deep in the Danakil Desert to the north of Lake Abe. There, a British Company has a 10 000 hectare cotton plantation between Dubti and Dit Bahari which, in turn, is surrounded by small farmers who also grow cotton and sell it to the estate; by 1979 42 000 tonnes was produced. A huge agricultural project in progress in the middle Awash Valley, has placed 7500 hectares of new land under cultivation and developed existing farms.

Koka Dam stores water in Lake Galila, it

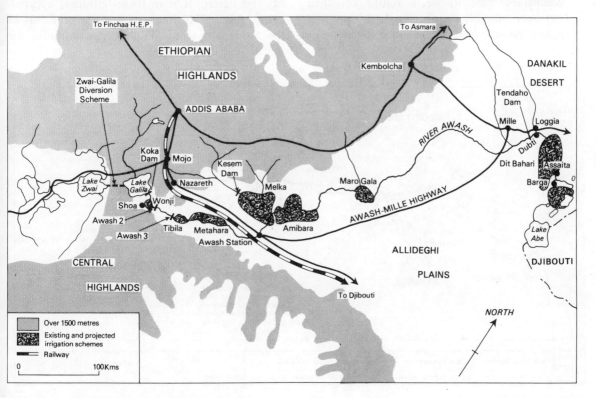

Fig. 73   Awash Valley Development Area

produces electricity. This power, added to that produced at two further H.E.P. stations at Awash II and III, supplies many new industries in towns like Mojo and Nazareth. These include the processing of cotton, tobacco, sugar and the making of paper from bagasse. So, for some of the 100 000 or so Afar tribesmen, irrigation has brought a higher standard of living than before and eliminated frequent near starvation. For others recurring drought continues to take its toll on man and beast: until, perhaps, increased water supplies allow proper attempts at settled ranching to take place. There is a hope of this here in the future, but there is little hope of it happening in remote regions like the Plain of Death.

Question and answer session

1   Why is the Plain of Death so neglected?
The reasons are very simple. It would be just as easy to irrigate as the Awash Valley. *But*, a major consideration is transport. Irrigation and growing things are the least difficult jobs of a very hard task. These projects are expensive. Money is scarce. People, countries, companies want to see a return for their money: preferably a profit. To do this produce has to be sold. To sell produce it has to be competitive in price, and this means an efficient transport system. Remote places like the Plain of Death do not have such a facility; and so development money is spent first where rewards will come relatively quickly. Unfortunately the remotest places are invariably the last to receive help.

2   Why is the Danakil area so dry? It lies in a large rain shadow. Winds are either from the north-east or south-west. Either way they cross high mountains and most rain that falls from these winds does so on the mountains. Exactly the same applies to the Plain of Death only not quite so badly.

Irrigation on the Senegal River

Let us move almost 6500 kilometres westwards, to another arid zone close to the Atlantic coast of Mauretania and Senegal. Here, along the River Senegal itself, which is the boundary between Mauretania and Senegal, an annual rainfall of 400 mm is the exception rather than the rule. Only a few kilometres to the north, perhaps a hundred, lies the desert. It is in these latitudes, approximately 14 – 17°N, that the greatest problems of the Sahel are seen. Within these latitudes the

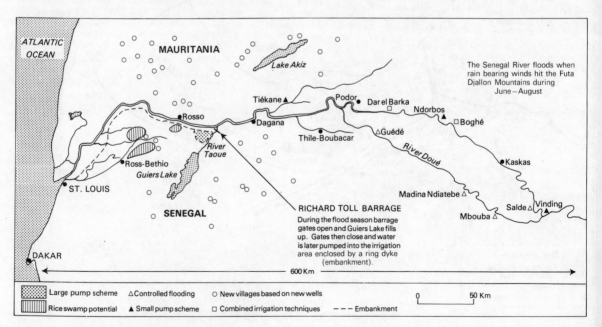

Fig. 74   Irrigation on the Senegal River

transition zone between the tropical continental lands and the desert occurs and sadly there appears to be a noticeable move southwards in recent years. People who, in the past have just managed to survive, are now unable to do so.

Senegal has become more fortunate than most countries whose lands lie partly in these latitudes. She has the Senegal River, many of the tributaries which flow into it and almost all the irrigable delta lands, as shown in Fig. 74. For hundreds of years, rivers which flow through these latitudes have been used for seasonal irrigation. As the annual floods receded large areas were cultivated on alluvial flats refertilised by the annual deposits of silt and alluvium. This is still carried on, the lands which are used for this being known as 'Fadama' lands. Along the Senegal subsistence crops include sweet potatoes, cucurbits, maize, tomatoes and beans. These are grown on the 'Falo' lands (the lower valley slopes). On the flat valley floors closest to the rivers, guinea corn (sorghum) and rice are produced. These areas are known as the 'Oualo' and are the first to be flooded and last to dry out. See Fig. 75.

However, more modern methods are gradually being used, typified by the increasing number of small diesel engine pump irrigation schemes. One of the first of these was at Guédé on the River Doué, see Fig. 74. There, about 420 families, each on about 2 hectares of land, grow rice, millet, sorghum and beans. Their cattle feed on the harvested land and help refertilise the soil every year. A 17 kilometre long dyke surrounds the irrigated area and pumps are used to augment flood water.

These are small-scale examples but a much bigger scheme is found at the head of the Senegal Delta where the River Taoue joins the Senegal.

The Richard Toll Scheme

Before the scheme was put into operation water would rush up the Taoue to fill Lake Guiers when the Senegal experienced its annual flood. As soon as this happened the people would hasten to build a great earthen dam to prevent the water in the lake flowing back into the Senegal when the floods receded. This dam also prevented tidal sea water from entering the Taoue during the dry season.

Then, in 1948, a permanent dam was built across the Taoue. It had gates which could open to allow the Senegal's flood waters into the Taoue and Lake Guiers, and then shut to serve the same purpose as the old annually-built earthworks.

The irrigated lands of Richard Toll on the Senegal River

1 What indications are there of a river in its lower course?
2 Is this area arid or humid? Use evidence from the photo for your answer.

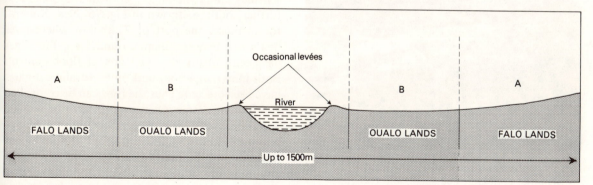

Fig. 75 Senegal valley areas

Five thousand hectares of flat land inside the confluence of the Senegal and Taoue were enclosed by a long ring dyke and over 100 kilometres of irrigation canals were dug to cover the area. A much greater length of drainage channel was cut and a pumping system installed. So when it was needed, water was pumped out of Lake Guiers and into the dyke-enclosed lands to flow by gravity to all corners of the scheme area.

The scheme has provided work and an increased standard of living to the many people who live at the new settlement of Richard Toll on the Senegal's banks. The major crop in the early 1970s was rice and yields of 14 000 tonnes were achieved: nearly 3 tonnes per hectare. Experiments with the mechanical cultivation of sugar cane were also carried out.

It has not been easy however. Strangely the delta soils are not particularly fertile, and so much fertilizer has to be used. The soils also have a tendency towards great salinity: possibly the result of annual flooding combined with a high evaporation rate and poor natural drainage. The drainage channels included in the scheme have only barely done the job required of them. And so, instead of being self sufficient in rice, Senegal still has to import it: rice accounting for 7% of her total imports.

Further west from Richard Toll the delta itself is undergoing development. The Delta Scheme is designed to exploit the vast areas of flat land there, which could easily be turned over to perennial irrigation. From Ross Bethio north to the Senegal, five new villages have been built and about 3500 farmers have been settled on 11 000 hectares of land protected by dykes. Ross Bethio is the headquarters of the scheme. The scheme ensures that land is mechanically prepared for the farmers, but all weeding and harvesting has to be done by them. The farmers also receive financial assistance towards seed, fertiliser and drainage costs.

The irrigation water is free if it doesn't have to be pumped. Once again however, there are problems with saline soils, poor drainage and hundreds of thousands of quelea birds, who are almost as effective as locusts in the damage that they do. They will have to be controlled. All these projects have problems; but perhaps the new plans for the Senegal river will solve them within the next few years.

Two dams are to be built, which will ensure perennial irrigation of over 400 000 hectares in the Senegal valley in Mauretania, Senegal and Mali: an area known commonly as the 'Futa Toro'. The first dam is in the delta at Diama which is near Rosso. This was started in early 1979; and then, later on in 1980 the other dam was begun at Mantale, south east of Kayes in Mali. As well as providing irrigation water the dams will control and conserve the river's floodwater. This flood control, together with the aid of a new navigation channel, will also provide year round navigation between Kayes and the delta lands on a river which, in the dry season, is sometimes reduced to a trickle. Watch your newspapers for news of this; and other exciting projects on the River Niger in Nigeria.

Irrigation on the Niger

There are already some very extensive irrigation schemes along the Niger; both in the Sahel and further south, as shown in Fig. 76. Near Kabara, for instance, the port of Timbuktu where river boats run between Bamako and Gao, the Niger has been embanked to give greater flood control. Both inlet (irrigation) and outlet (drainage) gates have been erected. Thus the flow can be controlled and drainage maintained over an area of 160 000 hectares of fertile land where rice is the main crop. Around Lake Faguibine to the north-west of Kabara, and the many small lakes to the south, large areas are irrigated by annual flooding which is being increasingly brought under control. These

Part of the Senegal delta Notice the many distributaries both large and small, and how flat deltaic land is.

areas are all part of the lower point of the old delta of the Niger. This was created millions of years ago when the Niger used to flow into a huge Chad-type lake which existed at that time.

The upper part of the old delta lands around Markala, Macina and Mupti normally remained dry: but in 1947 the annual flooding of these distributary valley lands was made possible by the building of the Sansanding Barrage across the Niger near Markala. It raised the level of the Niger behind it by about 4 metres and permitted new irrigation canals, supplied by the newly built Macina Canal, to supply those dry distributary lands of the upper delta. Less than 100 000 hectares have come under irrigation, growing cotton, rice and sugar. A sugar factory has been built, and cotton seed oil is used in the manufacture of soap. The waste from this and the rice supports a pig rearing industry.

Question and answer session

1 Are these the only irrigation projects in the Sahel? No. Two dams are to be built in northern Ghana. One will be at Afife and will produce 800 hectares for rice and vegetables. The other is the Vea – Tono project which will have, when it is completed, well over 3000 hectares of irrigated land and many large ponds in which fish will be 'farmed'.

2 Why are there not more such schemes? Time and money are the basic problems. Developing countries do not have much money to spare and so much of it comes from two sources: foreign assistance and multi-national companies who want a return for their investment. The smaller foreign aid schemes usually benefit the local people both financially and in raising living standards. Those where foreign investment is involved also benefit the local people to a great extent, but they also increase the country's economy and the companies profits. Every government has to calculate which is best for all concerned and the negotiations take time.

Group tasks

1 Always make sure that you have access to a national daily newspaper. They often have

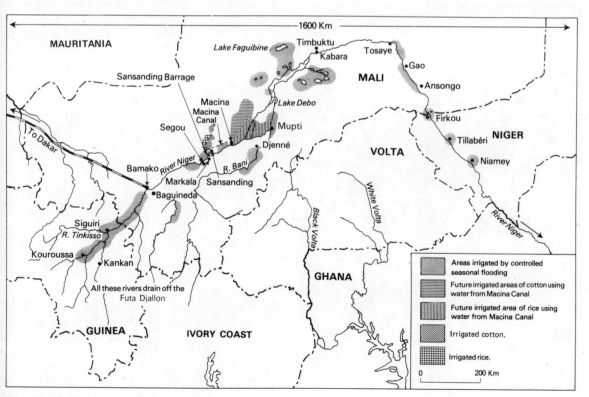

Fig. 76 Irrigation on the upper River Niger

93

maps and information on projects like these. Collect the articles and maps and insert them in the relevant parts of your exercise books. They will keep you up-to-date. Always share your discoveries with your class.

2 Study Fig. 77. Use Figs. 74 and 76 and your atlas to do the following:

   a) Make a sketch or tracing of Fig. 77.

   b) Label rivers A – F and towns 1 – 7.

   c) Label the highland region shown.

   d) Label the two barrages or dams shown at B1 and B2.

   e) Label, using an arrow if necessary, Lakes Guiers and Faguibine.

   f) Label the countries.

3 Is there an irrigation scheme, big or small, in your country? Make sure you study it carefully.

Irrigation along the Nile

Nowhere in Africa have the advantages of really large irrigation projects been better shown than along the River Nile. See Fig. 78. It was probably in the Nile Valley that man first became a cultivator, using the life-giving waters to bring success to his efforts.

Year after year the Nile would flood as the waters of the Blue and White Nile converged on each other, creating a pressure of water that the rivers' banks could not contain. The flood waters of the Blue Nile and Atbara covered the flat land of the valley, bringing with them an annual load of rich and fertile silt to revitalise the land. This annual rush of water from the Blue Nile causes a sort of dam at Khartoum; and, for a month or so each year, holds up the White Nile's water. As a result the White Nile rises high in the southern Sudan at this time, and thousands of square kilometres become covered with water. A great, vast papyrus swamp has formed which is known as the Sudd: an area, until now, entirely useless to man in terms of agricultural productivity. When the Blue Nile subsides this vast amount of stored water is released, and brings a further flood to the lower Nile Valley.

From the time man started growing his food he has attempted to extend his growing season by irrigation. Some of the methods invented two

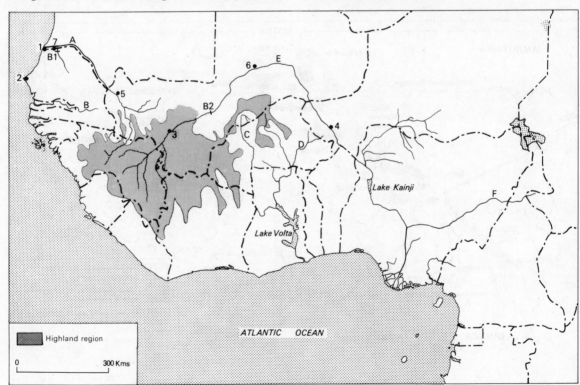

Fig. 77 The Senegal and Niger Basins

94

thousands years ago and more, are still in use today, see in Fig. 79. Inefficient though they are, they are still vitally necessary in places. They gave a small degree of control over the use of the Nile's waters. These methods spread across northern Africa over the succeeding centuries. A further degree of control was added by digging what are known as inundation canals: canals dug from the sides of rivers which lead to the fields.

The really modern method of irrigation is to build a dam and create a man-made lake behind it.

The dam at Sennar on the Blue Nile

This saves water for use in the dry season, which would otherwise run uselessly out to sea. Perennial canals, as shown in Fig. 80, can channel water from the man-made reservoir at any time of the year.

The great Aswan Dam is a famous example of this method, but a much older example is found further south in the Sudan. There the Sennar Dam provides water for the Gezira Irrigation Scheme; at 800 000 hectares the largest farm under one management in the world.

The Gezira Scheme

The scheme is situated between the Blue Nile and the White Nile, north of Sennar but south of Khartoum. The British thought of the idea back in 1904 and the first experimental crops were produced in 1911. The Sennar Dam was built in 1925 and gradually the area has developed into its present size. The Sudan Government nationalised it in 1950 and set up the Sudan Gezira Board to manage it, which it does to this day. The area farmed was doubled in size in 1962, when the Managil extension was completed. It is difficult to imagine anywhere else in the world more suitable for irrigation than Gezira. Between the two rivers are millions of hectares of very flat land, extending as far as the eye can see, which also slope gently *away* from the Blue Nile *towards* the White Nile. Thus both irrigation and drainage can be done cheaply by using *gravity* flow. Irrigation costs here are the lowest in the world, with only a minimum of pumping necessary during the low water season on the Blue Nile. The completion of the Roseires Dam in 1966 further ensured adequate water supplies: with plenty to spare for elsewhere.

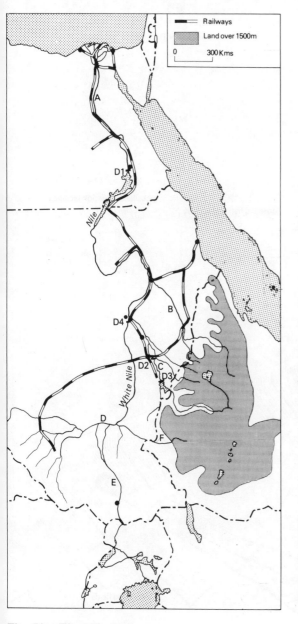

Fig. 78   The Nile Basin

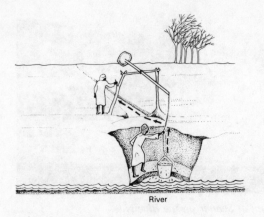

The Shaduf

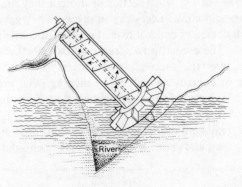

The Archimedean Screw or Tambour

Fig. 79 Ancient methods of irrigation

Perennial irrigation from a dam like Sennar or Rosieres

possible fishing industry

possible recreation facilities

power station

man-made lake

perennial canals

irrigated fields

Fig. 80 Perennial irrigation

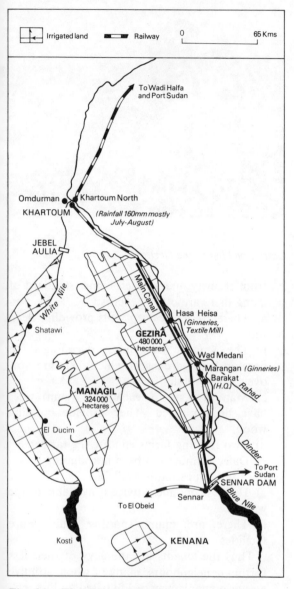

Fig. 81   The Gezira Scheme

There are two main irrigation canals. One is the Main canal and the other, the Managil, supplies the 1962 extension. From them thousands of kilometres of smaller channels developed on a rectangular system of gradually decreasing size, carry water throughout the whole scheme. The scheme is doubly fortunate in that the land is well above the water table and so water-logging never occurs; something which is as bad as no water at all. A further advantage is that the clay content of the soil is quite high, and so when the canals were filled with water they became impervious and needed no water-proof lining.

There were other advantages. The climate, given the irrigation, was ideal for cotton, which was intended to be the main cash crop. Because of the area's aridity there was no expensive clearing of bush or forest land, and, most important, the large supply of labour required did not have to be moved in from elsewhere; they were already there, scratching an uneasy living from their parched soils and skinny cattle. All that was necessary was to re-arrange them, each to a consolidated block of land which was rent free and secure, as long as they worked satisfactorily.

The people took some persuading to change their traditional way of life, but were convinced when they saw the improvement that a regular supply of water brought to their staple food: dura, a form of sorghum. Each tenant received up to 16 hectares of rectangular shaped land which was ample to grow food and, the real reason for the scheme, cotton. This cotton is sold for them by the Gezira Board; and so, not only is their food supply assured, they also have a good cash income. Furthermore, not only do the people benefit but Sudan's economy does as well.

Question and answer session

1   Surely there have been problems at Gezira? Yes, indeed there have. Two diseases, black-arm and leafcurl, nearly ruined the scheme in 1934. Blackarm is a bacterial disease spread by wind and rain. Leafcurl is a virus disease spread by the white fly. The boll worm and leaf hopper are other menaces. They all harm the cotton and expensive spraying is necessary to keep them under control.

There is also a rhizome-like weed called Seid which competes with crops for the soil's nutrition and has to be kept under control by very deep ploughing.

There are problems with the irrigation canals as well. They naturally keep silting up as irrigation water deposits its suspension material in them. Regular dredging of the canals is necessary. Then there are the water weeds. With so much water and Sudan's hot climate they would soon choke the canals if they were not regularly cleared. Finally, as is almost inevitable in these schemes, bilharzia is a serious problem.

2 How is the scheme organised? It is organised at three levels involving partnership, co-operation and control. First, the Sudan Government provides the land and is responsible for its irrigation. Secondly the tenants have to work the land and produce the crops; in return for which they live rent free and receive cash for their crops. Thirdly the Sudan Gezira Board, a cross between a para statal and a cooperative, processes and sells the crop, supplies seed, fertilizers, field advisers and inspectors; looks after the light railway system, farm machinery and vehicles and the distribution of profits.

3 How is the 'income' shared? The income depends on the price received for the cotton. After expenses have been deducted it is distributed as follows:
a) 36% to the Government.
b) 50% to the tenants.
c) 4% to village councils and social services.
d) 10% to the Sudan Gezira Board.

4 What crops are grown? The main cash crop is cotton. In 1976 over 210 000 hectares of land were sown with it: rather more than in 1975. Gezira usually supplies 70 – 75% of Sudan's total crop. Other crops in 1976 included groundnuts (100 000 hectares), maize (6000 hectares), dura (125 000 hectares), lubia, a bean for both food and cattle fodder, (50 000 hectares).

A very complicated 8 year rotation system was followed which involved at least 4 fallow years to allow the soil to recover its nitrogen content and to cut down on food for pests. However, with new ideas on fertilisation and the introduction of more leguminous crops to replace nitrogen and provide more cattle food, this practice has diminished in recent years.

5 Where is the cotton processed and how is it exported? A light railway system delivers the cotton to at least 10 ginneries on the scheme, which work 24 hours a day during the picking season. They are at Hasaheisa, Manangan and Barakat, shown in Fig. 81. Sudan's exported cotton leaves by way of Port Sudan via the railway from Khartoum.

6 What are the benefits of the Gezira Scheme? On a national scale Sudan's economy has benefited but the real importance lies with the benefits to the people of the scheme. Apart

Cotton picking in the Gezira

from security and a much higher standard of living there are other benefits:
a) There are many deep wells providing clean water.
b) The tenants have been encouraged to develop fruit gardens of which there are now over 275 in total.
c) Many forests of eucalyptus (gum) trees have been planted. They provide building wood.
d) Two training farms educate the farmers.
e) Dairy farming has been introduced.
f) Adult education is available.
g) Home economics advice is available to the women.
h) There are many sporting and leisure facilities.

Thus the tenants are the envy of their less fortunate neighbours, many of whom still live a semi-nomadic way of life based on livestock and shifting agriculture.

7 Are there any other schemes like this in the Sudan? Yes. The Kenana Sugar Scheme commenced in 1975. By 1982 84 000 feddans were under irrigation and produced 230 000 tonnes of sugar. By 1985 the target of 330 000 tonnes could be achieved. Pumping stations supply White Nile water from near Kosti to a main canal and a network of feeders. There are villages, schools, clinics and a main town. Workers and their families now number 75 000. The factory alone employs 1500 people. Burning the bagasse powers the factory and will also soon provide electricity

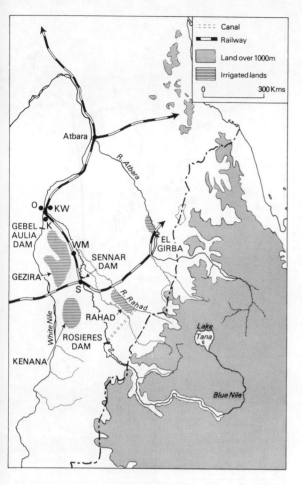

Fig. 82   Developments in the Sudan

for the whole estate and pumping operations. An animal food factory, yeast and citric acid supplies, a bottling plant, fast timber growth and self sufficiency in food are aims for the future. Another scheme, also shown in Fig. 82, of similar size is on the River Rahad which always dries up around November. A barrage has been built which will store the flood waters. These will not be enough in the dry season and so a canal is being built from the lake behind the Roseires Dam on the Blue Nile. Two and a half metres deep, it will top up the Rahad's reservoir during the dry season. A huge pumping station will move the water from Roseires to 120 000 hectares of land in the Rahad Valley. There will be sixty new villages housing 13 000 tenants and their families who will each have 10 hectares of land to work. The Rahad Corporation will perform

the same sort of function as the Gezira Board and similar benefits of regular food, good housing, schools, medical facilities and a cash income will come to thousands more people. Cotton and groundnuts will be the cash crops and dura, maize and vegetables will provide the food.

The Jonglei Canal

The Dinka Herdsmen of southern Sudan graze their herds to the south of Malakal as far as the Zaïre-Uganda borders. They know and want no other life. Today a huge bucket wheel excavator digs relentlessly away; and, inevitably, will alter their life style.

The Jonglei Canal is being cut to bypass the White Nile between Bor and Malakal; a distance of 225 miles (360 kilometres) and costing £1 million per mile.

The equatorial lakes supply the Nile and the Sudd, but evaporation in the Sudd prevents half the Nile's flow from going further north. Egypt and Sudan need that water to irrigate new areas to provide food and cash crops for their increasing population. The Jonglei should be finished by 1986, taking a quarter of the Nile's flow into the White Nile at Malakal.

Hopefully plans are afoot to control any future exceptional floods. All that extra water descending on the Jebel Aulia Dam and Khartoum could do a lot of damage; particularly if the Blue Nile is also exceptionally full and impeding the White Nile's flow. See page 95.

Benefits:
1 Fishing Cooperatives will be introduced throughout the area. A target of 100 000 tonnes of tilapia and perch has been set.
2 Fishing methods will be improved.
3 Solar fish driers will be provided.
4 There will be a fish market at Bor.
5 The road, parallel to the canal, will improve communications.
6 The UNFAO is already preparing the Dinka people to improve subsistence agriculture (sorghum) cash crops (tobacco) livestock, water supplies, health and education.
7 The canal will prevent water drainage off the eastern plains into the Nile. This will extend the grazing period on these plains.

8 The water table in the Sudd will be slightly lower, thus increasing the extent of inhabitable areas. Agriculture and grazing will benefit.

9 A commercial aspect to Dinka cattle herding can be introduced.

A Warning

The desert is jealous and grasping. It hates losing. It loves winning. Inadequate and unreliable rainfall are its basic weapons BUT, sometimes it has an important and thoughtless ally: MANKIND.

Throughout the old White Nile irrigation scheme south of the Jebel Aulia Dam and its surrounding rain fed farm lands supported by wells, see Fig. 81, the desert is fighting back because

i) of labour shortages.

ii) of cattle ruining crops on their way to wells.

iii) fertilizers often arrive too late to be effective.

iv) of very late payment to farmers who then cannot pay their workers to do essential early preparation.

v) sometimes irrigation water is sold illegally to private farmers, leaving insufficient for the official areas.

vi) diesel pumps at wells have failed because of poor maintenance and lack of fuel.

vii) cattle herders have deliberately invaded irrigated cotton fields with their animals.

viii) of a drain of skilled workers to better paid areas like Kenana.

ix) of poor transport facilities.

x) of too many animals grazing too little grass.

And so the desert creeps back. If it can happen once it can happen again and again all over the marginal lands. When irrigation arrives the battle is only half won or, from the desert's point of view, only half lost.

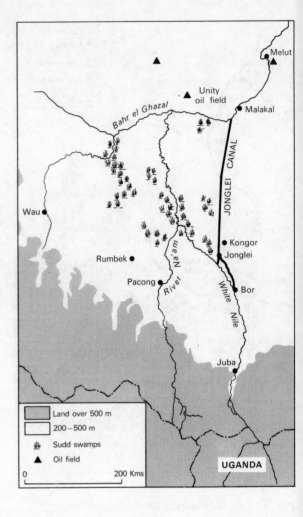

Fig. 83   The Jonglei Canal

These are three more examples of the progress that irrigation is bringing to Sudan. Watch your newspapers for new developments.

SUDAN —Exports by Commodity (Value £S million)

	1974	1975	1976	1977	1978	1979
Cotton	43.3	70.2	97.8	133.2	106.5	152.8
Groundnuts	18.6	34.3	39.0	26.1	20.7	9.9
Gum Arabic	14.3	7.4	11.3	12.6	13.9	18.2
Sesame Seed	16.5	11.9	17.3	16.9	19.1	6.2
Cake and Meal	2.2	4.1	n.a.	2.1	1.3	1.3

Group tasks

1 Study Fig. 78 and an atlas. Make a large copy of Fig. 78. On it, add the following:
a) Label rivers A to F and all the lakes shown.
b) Label the towns shown by dots and dams D1 to D4.
c) Label the highlands shown. Shade in and label the Nubia Mountains.
d) Put in arrows to show the route of Sudan's exports.
e) Shade in and label with 'G' the area of the Gezira.
f) Label all the countries.

2 Study the export figures for Sudan shown in the table below.
a) Place Sudan's exports for 1978 in order of value.
b) Does this order change in 1979?
c) Which export crop performed worst of all between 1975 and 1978?
d) How much did the export value of cotton increase between 1978 and 1979?
e) Which crop's performance was worst in 1979 compared with 1978?
f) Which crop's performance was best in 1975 compared with 1974?

7 Multi-purpose river development

One of the first great multi-purpose river development schemes in the world was started in 1933 in the Tennessee Valley region of the U.S.A. Having been reduced to a flood-prone, erosion-devastated wilderness by uncontrolled deforestation and widespread shifting agriculture it has since been reclaimed. By controlling the rivers and making them work for man, instead of against him, the wider aims were made possible. It was the forerunner of many such schemes, both big and small; several of which have become famous on the African continent.

The control of Africa's rivers is, arguably, of greater lasting importance than the discovery of oil or precious metals. The rivers will be there long after these have gone; and so will the benefits they bring when they are controlled. Water can provide power for industry and it can make crops grow where none grew before. Rivers can provide this water, but sometimes they do not. Often they nearly dry up and then at other times they flood uncontrollably. The water rushes uselessly out to sea, leaving dry lands without crops, industry without power and countries remain poor. Water can provide even more because fish grow in rivers and, being a source of protein, are a valuable food. In many countries people suffer from a protein deficiency because meat is too expensive. A fishing industry could supply this need; but fish cannot live in any quantity in rivers which sometimes dry up. Many countries would benefit greatly from an efficient and regular riverine transport system; but boats and barges can only sail on rivers which have no rapids and which do not dry up. Large and valuable deposits of minerals remain unexploited because there is no power supply available.

'A large dam and the man-made lake behind it can provide the answer to most, if not all, of these problems.'

That is what multi-purpose river development is all about, whether it is in Africa or elsewhere. The hydro-electricity which is produced by these dams tends to receive most publicity, but many of the other results are also of great importance. River development does not bring only benefits, but problems as well; however, generally speaking the good things tend to outweigh the new problems that may arise.

Africa has tremendous potential for river development, including H.E.P. The Aswan Dam is one of the better known examples and will be dealt with in more detail later, together with Lake Nasser, the man-made lake which has grown up behind it.

Most of the potential lies south of the Sahara where many large rivers flow through the very narrow gorges they have cut as they plunge off the multi-stepped high plateau regions on their way to the sea. The River Zaïre must have the greatest potential of them all, if you include the many huge tributaries which flow into it from north and south.

It is best that the market for hydro electricity should not be too far away from the dam site because a considerable percentage of the power generated is dissipated and lost if it has to be transmitted over long distances. However, this is not essential if a site is excellent for building a dam and for the creation of a man-made lake behind it. It is even less important, as we shall see, if the reasons for building the dam are based on political considerations as well as economics.

First of all then, let us look briefly at one or two of the less well known examples of river control; examples which may, perhaps, receive greater recognition in a year or two's time.

The River Zaïre has the greatest potential of all Africa's rivers and one of the first of its projects is to be found at Le Marinel in Shaba province; where the N'Zilo Dam produces power for the copper mines from the headwaters of the River Lualaba as shown in Fig. 84. The lake, which is now nearly 100 kilometres long, provides fish for nearby towns like Kolwezi. The Inga Dam shown on page 103 now produces 1200 megawatts from

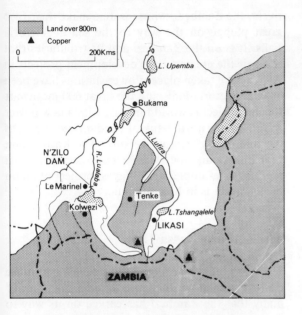

Fig. 84   N'Zilo Dam on the River Zaïre

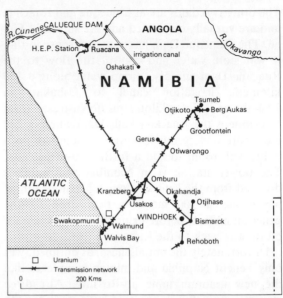

Fig. 86   Calueque Dam on the River Cunene

the rushing waters of the Inga Falls near Matadi for the power hungry region between Kinshasa and the coast. Soon the second phase will be finished, while another dam in the Kisangani Falls region will supply Kisangani and its growing industries with a further 350 megawatts.

Further south on the Angola-Namibia border is the River Kunene where a combined H.E.P. and irrigation scheme is being built. Financed by South Africa it has, unfortunately, suffered many interruptions because of civil war in Angola and the struggle for independence in Namibia. The River Cunene (Kunene in Namibia) has tremendous hydro electric capacity and, all told, it is planned to build seventeen dams along its length which will produce 2400 megawatts. As well as the power, the irrigation potential for both countries is enormous. However, the plans so far call for three dams. One, a long way up stream at Gove is just a storage dam and was completed in 1973.

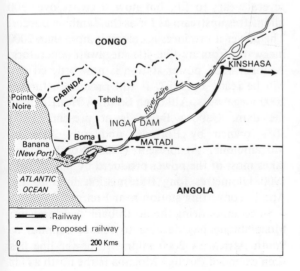

Fig. 85   Inga Dam on the River Zaïre

The Inga Dam near Matadi   It will produce power for Zaïre.

The other two dams are at Calueque and Ruacana and are virtually completed and are shown in Fig. 86. The Calueque Dam has a dual purpose in that it will store water and control the flow to the Ruacana Dam and also pump water along a 130 kilometre irrigation canal to Oshakati in Ovamboland. Forty kilometres downstream from Calueque is the Ruacana Falls Dam where a 240 megawatt underground power station has been built, with room to add a further 80 megawatts. The power station is in Namibia and water is diverted from the Kunene along a headrace tunnel which has a 100 metre vertical drop to the generating plant, before being led into the tailrace on its way back to the Kunene.

Unfortunately the initial phase, as outlined, will only benefit Namibia and mining complexes like the new uranium mine at Rossing. Already a transmission network has been built ready for the new power. Once peace comes to this troubled area however, the completed project will bring great benefits to all concerned.

The River Cunene rises on the high plateau region of Angola: the Bie Plateau. So also do some of the tributaries of one of Africa's greatest

Kariba Dam Notice the arch construction.
1 In which direction are we looking?
2 Pinpoint the headrace and the tailrace.
3 Where do you think the power station is?

rivers, the Zambezi, whose waters make their first great plunge on the way to the sea at Victoria Falls. It is on the Zambezi and its tributaries that some of the greatest river development projects in Africa have taken place. Power stations have been built at Victoria Falls and the great 600 megawatt Kariba project is world famous, with a new power station on the north bank of the dam site as well as the one on the Zimbabwe side. The Kafue Dam near Lusaka and the Shire River project in Malawi are further examples. The biggest project of all on the Zambezi is in Mozambique.

The Cabora Bassa Dam

This dam located in Fig. 87 has been built at the downstream end of the Quebrabasa Gorge, one of many that the Zambezi has carved on its way to the sea. It is an ideal site for a dam. The gorge sides are of hard, resistant rock which is well able to support the side foundations of the dam. The gorge is narrow and thus easily blocked.

The dam was started in 1969 and the first phase was finished six years later in March 1975. It is 160 metres high and 300 metres long at the top and is a typical example of an *arch dam*: a dam which does not depend on huge bulk for its strength. The stresses and strains are contained by the design: a curve which, facing upstream, deflects the force and weight of the water to either side of the dam where its foundations are firmly embedded into the gorge side. The man-made lake behind it took several years to fill, but now stretches over 300 kilometres upstream as far as the Zambian border. The power it produces is colossal: more than 2000 megwatts from its five 408 megawatt generators. A north bank power station is now ordered and will be ready by 1987. It will produce a further 2000 megawatts. Although South Africa financed the dam, Cabora Bassa is at present (1983) 80% owned by Portugal and only 20% by Mozambique. At present (1983) South Africa takes most of the power produced by way of twin 1900 kilometres long transmission lines to the Apollo converting station near Pretoria.

Since announcing the north bank development, Mozambique has decided to reduce supplies to South Africa. A 2000 kilometre power line has been extended through Mocuba in the north as far as Nampula. It is now ready to power a new

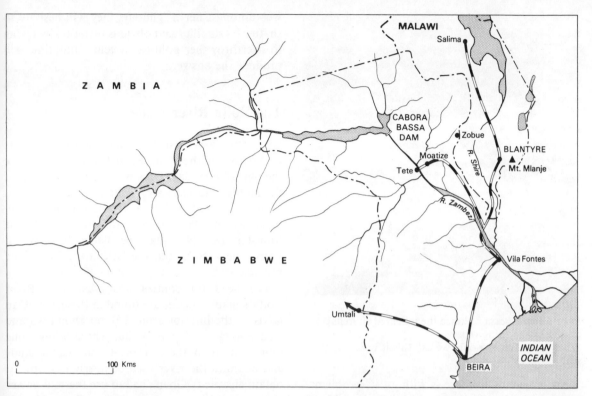

Fig. 87   Cabora Bassa Dam

aluminium industry, iron and steel near Moatize, textile production, cashew nut factories, and the homes of Mozambique people themselves.

The dam has also brought agricultural benefits. Most of the whole region's rainfall comes between November and April. The Zambezi flooded uncontrollably. During the other months there was often only a trickle of water along parts of its course. Soon, the Mpenda Uncua scheme which is 40 kilometres below Cabora Bassa and two other dams further downstream will ensure more power, flood control and reliable navigation facilities as far upstream as Tete.

Agricultural losses from flooding have been reduced and irrigation supplies new cotton, sugar and rice developments. Piped water will supply cattle and afforestation projects near Malawi.

Minerals should soon be exploited. The coal mines at Moatize can be expanded, there are iron ore reserves capable of yielding 1 million tonnes a year and perhaps the bauxite on Mount Mlanje in Malawi can be exploited. The 170 square kilometres man-made lake will provide the basis for a fishing industry which could supply the region with its needs for protein.

The gorge site of Cabora Bassa
What makes it suitable for an arch dam?

Lake Cabora Bassa Notice the indented shoreline caused by the rising water.
What sort of coast would we call this if it was by the sea?

No project of this size is without its problems. The land to be flooded by the lake had 25 000 people living on it. They had to be resettled and this has been done around Moatize and Zobue, on land which will come under irrigation.

Cabora Bassa was a political dam, built by the South Africans and Portuguese to perpetuate their hold on the region. The Cunene Dam and Oxbow have similar aims. The money that migrant workers send home from South Africa, forming a major part of the income for Mozambique and Malawi, also had this aim. South Africa hopes that by weaving a vast interdependent economic web amongst her neighbours they will hesitate to shatter its stability and obvious benefits, by trying to overthrow her political system. Only time will produce the answer.

The Volta River Project

One of the very first multi-purpose river projects in Africa was the Volta River Project. Ever since the old colonial days back in the 1920's control of the highly seasonal River Volta at Akosombo has been considered desirable. It was not until independence in 1957 however, that the then Prime Minister Dr. Nkrumah persuaded the World Bank, the U.S.A. and the U.K. to invest in the project.

The need for control was great. The River Volta's many sources are found in the dry plateau lands of the interior around Bobo Dioulasso and Ouagadougu in Upper Volta. There is only one rainy season in these tropical continental lands and at times the river used to nearly dry up. To obtain electricity Ghana had to use thermal power stations which necessitated spending valuable foreign exchange on oil imports. The dam was started in 1963 and opened three years later. It was built at the village of Akosombo, about 100 kilometres from the sea where the valley was at its

The Volta dams
Make a sketch of this picture and label:
(1) power dam (2) the rock fill dam (3) the flood control dams (4) the power house (5) the penstocks (6) the headrace (7) the tailrace

Kariba power lines
What erosion process can we see in the foreground?

narrowest as shown in Fig. 88. Like the Aswan Dam it is a *rock fill* dam. About 8 000 000 cubic metres of rock and rubble were used in its construction, all of which is lined with thick layers of concrete. It is 134 metres high and 426 metres wide at the base of the main dam. The complex includes a power dam and station on the west bank and a flood control dam and saddle dam on the east bank. The saddle dam plugged a further gap not covered by the main dam when the waters rose.

Six huge pipes known as *penstocks* lead water from the headrace down into six turbines, each capable of producing 150 megawatts when power production reached its maximum in 1979. From the generators water is led through the tailrace back into the Volta and so to the sea.

Lake Volta is the man-made lake which has risen behind the dam. In the rainy season the lake rises and the gates of the flood control dam have to be opened to stop water flowing over the top.

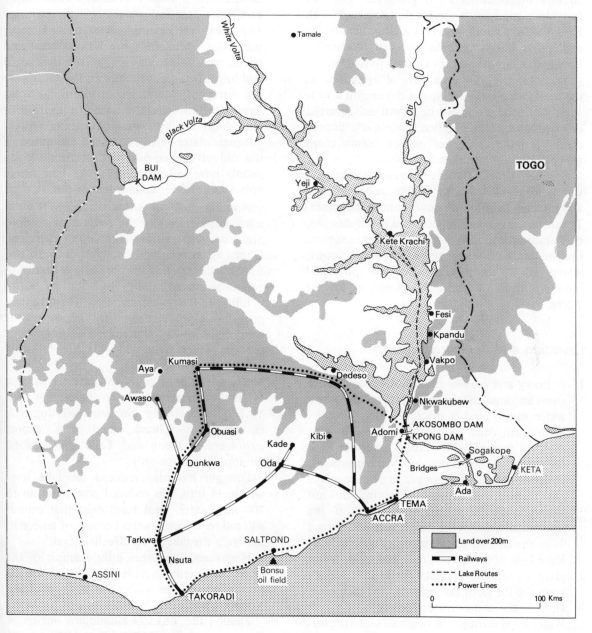

Fig. 88   The Volta River Project

During the dry season the flood control gates remain closed most of the time and water only goes through the penstocks. In this way the 8500 square kilometre lake is kept as full as possible throughout the year.

The dam has brought many benefits to Ghana and her people. There is a large fishing industry run by the Battor tribespeople who live round the lake. The annual yield has now settled to about 40 000 tonnes: a valuable source of protein for a country with such tsetse fly problems. The lake provides a good north – south shipping route with Kete Krachi, Kpandu and Akosombo three of the main ports. Lake cargoes include fish, foodstuffs, firewood, charcoal and, of course, passengers.

The lake also provides a form of irrigation. As the level falls a little during the dry season a wide variety of food crops can be grown on the moist exposed soils. This practice, known as 'drawn-down' farming, produces out of season crops which fetch high prices in the towns.

Another benefit is the increased electricity supply which has risen by 1200%, reducing costs and bringing light to millions of Ghanaian homes. The increased power has permitted new industries, encouraged the modernization of old ones such as saw milling and helped to reduce mining costs. Above all it has powered the new port and industrial town of Tema 27 kilometres east of Accra.

Question and answer session

1   Is heavy and regular rainfall necessary where dams are situated? Obviously there has to be a water supply and it must be fairly reliable. With small dams like some of those in East Africa it is essential that there is regular rainfall, otherwise no power would be produced. However, with the bigger projects, once a lake has formed, variations in rainfall do not matter quite so much; particularly if the 'catchment area' of the dam is very widespread as in the case of the Zambezi, Zaïre or Nile. Rain falls at different times and in different places over these vast river basins so it doesn't matter if the rains fail over part of each area.

2   How do the dams produce power?
Water is led through the penstocks into the turbines. The water's power drives the turbines which in turn drive the generators which produce the electricity. The size of the turbines and generators depends entirely on the force of the water (the head) built up behind the dam.

3   Has the Volta Dam created any problems?
Yes. The worst one concerns the resettlement of the 80 000 people who lived in the 700 villages drowned by the lake waters. Fifty two new townships were created around or near the lake. Each family was provided with a basic house, about 2 hectares of land, a water supply and some practical assistance with farming. The new settlements have proved most successful where the move was minimal and people were able to stay within their own tribal and linguistic areas so that social systems were not disrupted. Major moves to strange areas have been less successful owing to insufficient land, local hostility, strange surroundings, inadequate water supplies and the disruption of the old village co-operative systems. Many people have left settlements like Fesi where only 19 out of 53 families remain.

Another problem is that of east-west communications. Despite the bridges at Adomi, Sogakope and the trans-lake shipping services, Ghana is, at present, effectively cut into two by the lake which is thus proving a barrier to communication.

Bilharzia is another problem. The lake now provides approximately 7000 kilometres of calm shallow water shoreline: ideal conditions for the water snail which is the *bilharzia vector*.

Since 1980 other problems have arisen. The original preferential price agreement for VALCO's electricity has annoyed domestic customers in Ghana, and also export customers in Benin and Togo who pay 50 million dollars annually.

Drought has also reduced the lake level which, in turn, has reduced power output to 700 megawatts. Real fears exist that output will fall to 450 megawatts because of a need to maintain the lake at an effective level.

Here then, is another grim example of the effects of unreliable rainfall in the Sahel areas to the north: the source of most of Lake Volta's water.

Finally, the VALCO aluminium smelter at Tema uses, in fact, 65% of Volta's power and

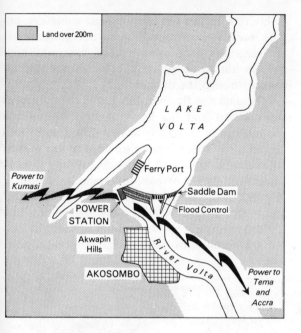

Fig. 89   Akosombo Dam

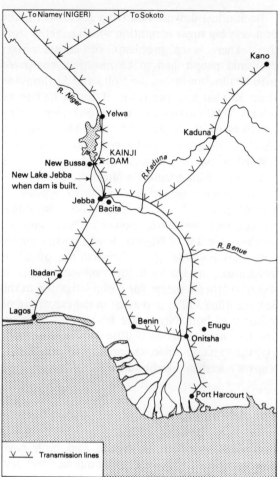

Fig. 90   The Kainji Dam

did not even use Ghana's own bauxite in 1983. Worse still, VALCO say they may have to close two pot-lines, see Fig. 129, because of this reduced supply.

4   Are there any other river projects in Ghana? Yes. The Bui Gorge Dam on the Black Volta provides irrigation water for the Black Volta Valley. There is however another development in progress near Akosombo.

The Kpong Project

Forty kilometres downstream from Akosombo, at the town of Kpong, a new dam shown in Figs. 88 and 89 is being built to use the discharged waters of Lake Volta.

It became necessary because VALCO aluminium smelter intended to introduce a fifth 'pot-line' and needed another 100 megawatts of power. Also Ghana sells electricity to Togo and Benin.

The Kpong Dam will produce 140 megawatts a year and will provide irrigation water for 8000 hectares of land: vitally necessary under Ghana's new 'Operation Feed Yourself and Your Industries' campaign.

The Kainji Dam

Six hundred and fifty miles north east of the Volta Dam is another great project on the River Niger which is shortly to be enlarged. Opened in 1969 it lies on the Niger about 550 kilometres north of Lagos in a remote, thinly populated and very poor part of Nigeria. It has 12 generators and produces 960 megawatts which are used at present in the southern grid towns. The dam is 66 metres high and 55 metres long and has produced a man-made lake behind it, known as Kainji Reservoir which is 130 kilometres long, and 1300 square kilometres supporting a 10 000 tonne per year fishing industry. There is now a much greater degree of flood control together with irrigation facilities.

Bacita, just downstream from Jebba, is the site of a very big sugar plantation which benefits from this. There were problems of course. Sixty thousand people had to be resettled, compared with 80 thousand from the Volta and 51 thousand from Kariba; and the town of Bussa had to be rebuilt 70 kilometres west of the old town. Yelwa has to be protected by a 7.5 metre high wall, but some flooding occurred nevertheless. It is now a flourishing port at the southern end of the riverine trade route with Niamey in Niger.

New extensions are widening the spread of Kainji's power. The Kainji-Niamey-Sokoto transmission line now carries power to Niger and the north-west states of Nigeria. It will make tremendous cuts possible in the importation of oil in those areas, needed for thermal power stations. It will also provide power for pump irrigation in the Sokoto-Rima Valley and assist in the expansion of industry in both Niger and north-west Nigeria. The new dam at Jebba will further increase both irrigation and power for the north west and Benin, Nigeria's western neighbour.

The Aswan Dam

There are two dams at Aswan and both have power stations. The first was built in 1903 but was, at first, only intended to provide some sort of flood control. It was totally inadequate but it was not until 1956/57 that its successor was begun. Placed 25 kilometres south of Aswan, the dam had two main purposes: to produce large quantities of hydro electricity and to store massive amounts of water for irrigation purposes. Both these aims have been fulfilled in abundance.

The Aswan High Dam was completed in 1970 and only in recent years has the lake finally achieved its present size. The dam's statistics are staggering. It is 3600 metres long and 111 metres high. At the top it is 40 metres wide while its base is almost a kilometre wide. It is so strong that only a nuclear bomb, or perhaps an exceptional earthquake, could destroy it. Behind the dam is Lake Nasser which is 500 kilometres long, reaching back nearly 150 kilometres into Sudan. Up and down the lake fishing, cargo and passenger vessels are to be seen everywhere.

The dam has twelve giant turbines whose generators can produce 2100 megawatts of power.

Only 1000 megawatts are produced at present, but the need for more will arise in future years. Beneath the dam a waterproof base was built which almost completely prevents seepage of water through the bottom.

The dam was finished only just in time. Egypt is 96% desert and her approximately 42 millions population is increasing at over 2% a year. This population, which will be doubled by the end of the century, almost all live along the 10 – 11 kilometre wide strip of cultivable land as shown in Fig. 92. More food was necessary and without a controlled irrigation supply this was impossible. Added to this Egypt was, and still is, losing at least 10 000 hectares of land to building each year.

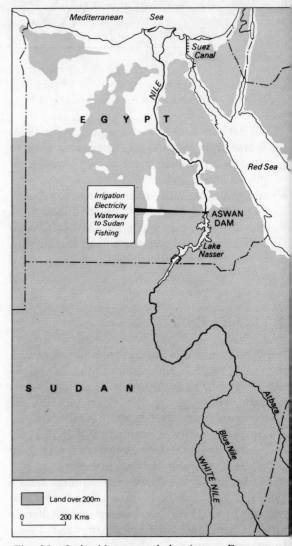

Fig. 91   Lake Nasser and the Aswan Dam

When the Nile flooded, cultivation was delayed and most of the water ended up, wastefully, in the Mediterranean. Egypt has little or no coal and so had to use a lot of her limited oil production for powering thermal power stations. This was expensive. She needed to expand her industries quickly, but without power this was not possible. The dam was desperately needed and thanks to Russian money and expertise, and Egyptian labour, it was completed.

Problems

As usual there have been problems, but most are minor ones compared with the benefits. For instance, now that the Nile no longer floods, the farm lands along its banks no longer receive the annual fertlisation received from silt carried in suspension and deposited when the floods subsided. This was a problem at first, but now literally limitless supplies of phosphates have been found between the Kharga and Dakhla Oases and are processed at the new Aswan fertilizer plant: powered of course by Aswan's electricity.

Deprived of its annual delivery of 150 million tonnes of silt, the Nile Delta is now suffering quite serious erosion. It is losing up to 30 metres a year to the sea. Barriers may have to be built to prevent sea water pushing back into the delta farm lands. Now that the silt no longer arrives offshore the sardine fishing industry has seriously declined. Unfortunately Lake Nasser's fishing industry has not yet developed sufficiently to replace this lost food source.

A more worrying problem has arisen since 1980 to which, so far, there has been no answer. Drainage is not as efficient as it could be; particularly in the New Valley and other depression schemes. Even along the Nile it could be better. Because of this the high evaporation rate is leaving increasing saline deposits in the soil. This is not helped by the slightly increasing salinity of Lake Nasser's water itself: once again because of evaporation. An estimated annual loss of 15 cubic kilometres of the lake waters leaves an ever increasing content of precipitated salts. Drainage, therefore, has to be improved to wash these salts away.

Since 1970, as Lake Nasser gradually rose to assume its present-day shape and size, agriculture in Egypt has been transformed. Already 900 000

hectares of the Nile valley land have perennial irrigation, where before only inundation irrigation was available. As a result double, even triple, cropping is possible. What is more, now that water and fertilizers are permanently available, multi-cropping is possible.

It is a common sight to see bright green berseem (a type of clover) growing through the harvested

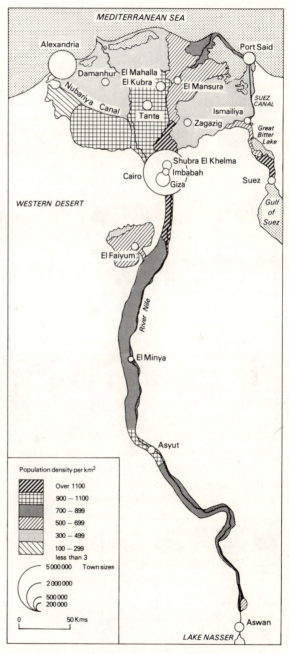

Fig. 92 Population density in Egypt

111

stubble of a wheat field, sure of irrigation through the long hot summer. The rice lands of the delta have now increased to over 400 000 hectares from which at least two crops a year can be obtained. The power from the dam also permits electric pumps to deliver water to farm lands above, and away from, the narrow valley floor. At least fourteen schemes where land is being reclaimed from the desert are already in operation dependant upon Aswan's power and water. Two of these are The New Valley Project and Tahrir Province Scheme.

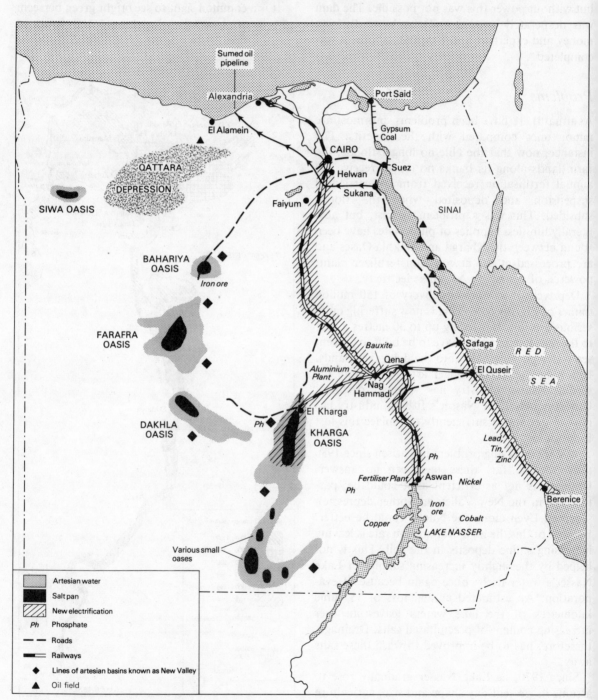

Fig. 93   Post-Aswan developments in Egypt

The New Valley Project shown in Fig. 93 is a long term project and will take many years. It will be developed along the line of oases in the Western Desert which runs almost parallel to the Nile. Beneath them are vast artesian reservoirs of good groundwater which, it is hoped, will help reclaim 600 000 hectares all told: the flatter areas most suitable for irrigation. They will be in oases like Kharga, Dakhla, Farafra, Bahariya and Siwa. Pilot schemes already exist at Kharga and Dakhla oases, where over 20 000 hectares have been reclaimed and roughly one hundred thousand people resettled. Aswan's power enables the water to be pumped up from over 900 metres below ground level and distributed to the cultivated land. The new villages have social and health services, new roads, factories which process dates, make bricks and also cement. El Kharga is the centre for this stage of the development.

Tahrir Province is another reclamation scheme just west of the delta between Cairo and Alexandria. The southern sector is almost as low as the delta and irrigation from the Nile is quite easy, although the soils are difficult to improve. In the northern sector soils are more responsive to fertilisation. The Nubariya canal brings water which is pumped up by electricity to the scheme's level. Over 3 million hectares have been reclaimed and there are now seven villages with a total of 25 000 people. As the scheme is extended only young, healthy married men are selected. The work is hard, even irrigation and drainage ditches being dug by hand. Each family is allotted two hectares of land, a simple house, some cattle and poultry. The land is farmed in large blocks and each man has a share in each block. Most of the farm work is done by hand as the schemes are labour intensive. However, cropping of large wheat fields is done by the co-operative's combine harvester. Crop spraying is also mechanized. A section of the reclaimed land is shown in Fig. 94.

Here, there is a triennial crop rotation for arable crops which consist of berseem, maize or wheat and then cotton. The co-operatives organise fertilizers, pesticides, irrigation and marketing and there is always advice from trained agricultural supervisors.

The change is amazing. The land is shared and cultivated by all. Profits are also shared. Huge fields of arable crops alternate with orchards full of plums, large vineyards and olive groves. Evergreen trees line the roads and vegetables and flowers grow in personal gardens. For all this, together with the other schemes, the waters of the Nile are responsible and Aswan's power helped make it possible.

The Orange River Scheme

This widespread scheme is under construction in Cape Province in South Africa. The Orange and its tributaries rise in the high Drakensberg system in the east of the country, but flows through lands that become progressively drier to the west. In fact there are a periods in the winter when no water flows through the mouth of the Orange; yet during the wet summer so much water is wasted in the sea. With that water goes an annual load of silt which is enough to cover over 9500 hectares of land a metre deep. This is because unprotected soil is washed into the Orange system by the summer rains. If this loss could be controlled by fixing the soils of the valley land with irrigated crops and

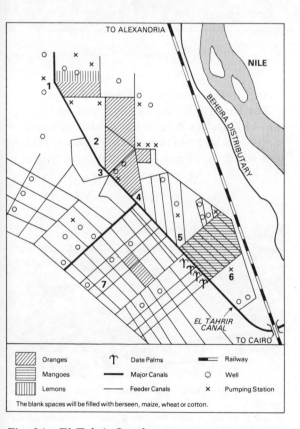

Fig. 94   El Tahrir South

113

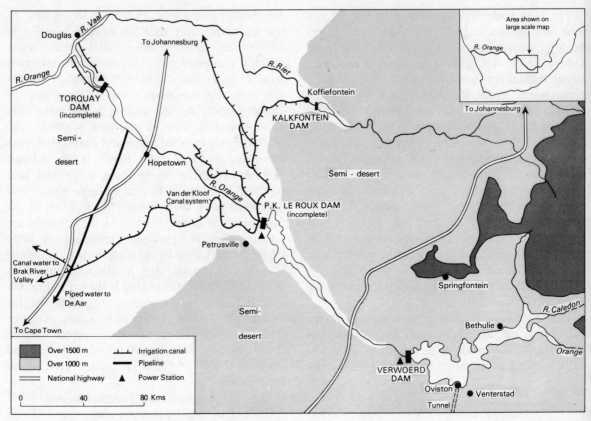

Fig. 95   The Orange River Scheme

pasture, great benefits would result. As South Africa's population is increasing by over 350 000 each year greater food production and more jobs in industry would be a good thing.

This is what the Orange River Project is designed to encourage. It started in 1962; and when it is finished in the 1990's there will be much improved flood control, more water for people and industry, 230 megawatts more hydro electric power for homes and industry, more fish in the man-made lakes and 305 000 more hectares of valley land under irrigation, whose soils will be stabilised and not lost in the Atlantic Ocean.

The core of the whole project is a series of dams along the Orange and its tributary the Caledon. They are, or will be, sited between the already completed Welbedacht Dam on the Caledon south east of Dewetsdorp and the confluence of the Orange and Vaal near Douglas. The other main dams are the Hendrik Verwoerd Dam which has now been completed, the P.K. Le Roux Dam near Petrusville and the Torquay Dam just 40 kilo-

metres from the confluence with the Vaal.

The Hendrik Verwoerd Dam is 55 metres high and 1100 metres long. It has already provided its man-made lake which is nearly 90 kilometres long and which holds nearly 6 billion cubic metres of

The Verwoerd Dam: part of the Orange River Project.
What does the picture tell you about rainfall amounts in this area?

114

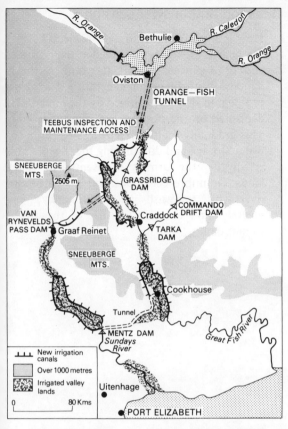

Fig. 96   Great Fish and Sunday River Valleys

the Sunday River near Graaf Reinet, while at Cookhouse on the Great Fish, another scheme will transfer more water to the Sunday by means of a 13 kilometre long tunnel and canal system. This water will be stored by the Mentz Dam, shown in the map above.

All told the project will have 20 H.E.P. stations and many dams like those smaller ones on the Great Fish and Sunday Rivers as well as the three big ones. The fertile valley lands of the semi-desert regions of the Great Karoo and central Cape Province will become productive, giving increased supplies of beef, dairy produce, deciduous and citrus fruit, cereals, cotton, vines and legumes.

The Lesotho Highlands Water Project: Oxbow

This great project could supply Transvaal industry with water and Lesotho with money and electricity by 1994. Agreements have still to be reached on water prices and water control but compromises are very likely. Five dams will be built — see Fig. 97 — across Lesotho's southward flowing rivers.

water. The other two dams will provide irrigation water to the arid valley lands which stretch in a wide arc to the north west. The Van der Kloof Canal system will flow from the P.K. Le Roux Dam which was opened late in 1977 with a capacity of 220 megawatts. Valleys of seasonal rivers as far away as the Brak will receive water from this dam by canal when the project is complete.

The irrigation water will also go south as shown in Fig. 96 to the Great Fish and Sunday Rivers. Because of the plateau and mountains in the Sneeuberge range of hills, a great tunnel is now being built. Almost 83 kilometres long, with a diameter of 5.4 metres, it goes from Oviston on the shores of the Hendrik Verwoerd Reservoir, under the escarpment to the headwaters of the Great Fish River where it will be stored by the Grassridge Dam. The water will not require pumping along the tunnel because it dips by about 4 centimetres in every kilometre on its way to the Great Fish. A further tunnel will take the water to

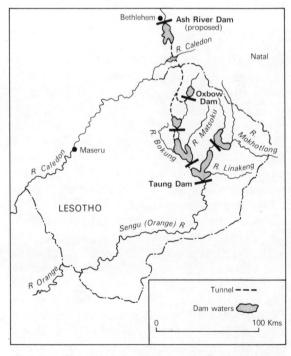

Fig. 97   The Lesotho Highlands Water Project

Water will be pumped and tunnelled to Bethlehem at 3000 million litres a day. All being well it will start in 1987. Study your newspapers for more news.

Group tasks

1 If there is a multi-purpose river project in your country try to visit it. Certainly find out all you can about it. Compare its size and scope with the ones in this chapter.
2 Prepare and undertake a formal debate on the following motion
   'This class believes that the Volta Project was more trouble than it was worth.'

Question and answer session

1 How is silt a problem to dam projects?
   Silt guards are always installed at the headrace end of a power station. It would seriously damage the turbines and generators. It is also a problem in that it is trapped by the dam and is deposited on the floor of the man-made lake. This gradually builds up leaving less room for water storage and diminishing the 'head'. This is why careful farming is essential in valley lands. On unprotected land soil is washed into rivers by rainwash and, ultimately, can severely limit the effective life of the downstream dam.

8 Pastoralism

The land is Africa's greatest natural resource. It provides both food for man and also for man's domestic animals. The most important of these are cattle. Millions of Africa's people keep cattle in numbers varying from one to many hundreds; and even larger numbers of people depend on cattle and their products for part of their daily food. These are the town and city dwellers who expect meat in the butchers' shops and dairy products in their grocery shops.

Africa is traditionally a cattle raising continent and yet cattle are not easy to raise there. Two things make life difficult for the cattle owner. One is drought and the other is disease. To a certain extent each is connected with the other.

Drought means that grass becomes scarce, and if grass is scarce cattle are unable to eat well. Well fed cattle have some protection from disease but half starved cattle have none at all. The worst disease of all is brought by the *tsetse fly* and affects all cattle, not just the half starved ones. The tsetse's bite causes a disease known as *Trypanosomyasis* in humans as well as cattle. In East Africa it is known as Nagana when it affects cattle. In humans it is sometimes called sleeping sickness. Both cattle and humans become extremely tired, they have no energy and lose a considerable amount of weight. They often die.

The tsetse fly thrives within tropical Africa wherever there are warm or hot, damp conditions. They welcome the shade of forests and thick bushland. There are wide expanses of such areas within the tropics and in them successful cattle raising is almost impossible.

The tsetse fly cannot live in dry areas and so there are none in the desert and semi-desert lands. Not only are they too dry, there is also not enough shade. But, if it is impossible for the tsetse fly in these areas, it is also extremely difficult to keep cattle there. The tsetse fly cannot live in cool conditions which is why there are none to be found outside the tropics. There are also many areas within the tropics which are too cold for them. There are few, if any, above 1500 metres and it is in these areas that we find some of Africa's best cattle lands.

Let us see where cattle can be kept successfully in Africa. Look also at the natural vegetation map in your atlas. Once you have eliminated the tsetse lands shown also in Fig. 98 and the deserts there is

The tsetse fly

A Zebu cow suffering from sleeping sickness

117

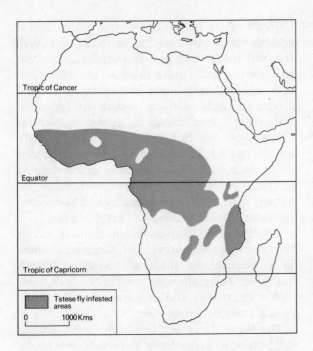

Fig. 98 ~ The extent of the tsetse fly in Africa

Tstese fly infested areas

0   1000 Kms

not much left is there? Remember also that plateau Africa is only suitable below about 2750 metres, above that altitude it is often too cold for both man and beast.

There are three basic environments in which cattle may be kept successfully in Africa, but in two of them the problems are much greater than the other. The three environments are:
a) The low grass savanna and semi-deserts where grass comes with the rains and dies in the dry cool season. There are no tsetse flies.
b) The higher cooler wetter lands where there is rain and grass throughout the year and there are no tsetse flies.
c) The bush and wooded savanna lands where the tsetse can live and where grazing is available for much of the year.

You may wonder about c) so let us have a brief look at those areas first, as it is these areas which offer the greatest hope for development. Plainly, cattle and tsetse flies cannot live together; and so the tsetse flies must be eliminated: an expensive and laborious process, but possible nevertheless. The tsetse likes shade so most of the bush and trees must be cleared. But the bush and wooded savanna lands are the home of vast numbers of Africa's wild animals which, in fact, carry the disease Trypanosomyasis and from which the

tsetse carries the disease of cattle and humans. So the animals must also be removed and prevented from coming back.

Successful experiments in Uganda in the Ankole and Bunyoro districts have shown that if wide strips of land around the cleared grazing lands are settled and cultivated, the return of wild animals to these grazing lands will be prevented. Spraying the remaining trees from *beneath* also makes sure that the tsetse cannot use its favourite shady habitat. It is also essential that there is a good animal health service with sufficient veterinary surgeons. This is possible, but is extremely hard work and expensive; which means that only limited areas can be cleared and settled at a time. Uganda and Kenya are in the forefront of this sort of clearance and thus have valuable experience to offer in the field of pastoral development. As the century draws to its close and Africa's population will have doubled since the 1960's, more and more developments of this nature will have to take place to exploit this vast potential.

The low grass savanna and semi-desert lands

There is a great belt of this type of land which extends right across North Africa between the tsetse regions to the south and the desert lands to the north. See both Fig. 98 and your natural vegetation map. There are large areas in eastern Africa from Somalia southwards into Tanzania. Zambia has large areas of these lands and Botswana and Namibia also have large areas of such lands.

Healthy cattle on rangeland over 1500 metres

Although conditions are difficult, cattle are very important indeed and for a certain type of people the cattle form the basis of a complete existence in two different ways. Semi-nomadic pastoralism is one of them.

The cattle owners have to walk long distances and so cannot have a really permanent home for themselves. Long distances have to be covered because of the continuous need to search for both water and grass. The grass only grows after the rains and so this type of pastoralism means that the tribespeople and their cattle follow the rains. Sometimes the rains fail as they did in the early and mid 1970's in the north African lands, so grass cannot be found and the cattle begin to starve. They produce little milk when this occurs, and so the people who depend on them for food and drink also begin to starve. Many of these semi-nomads cultivate a little land during their lengthier stop-overs in the rainy season, or just afterwards. If the rains fail they cannot even do that.

There is another problem, self created, experienced by some of these tribes. They also keep goats, and a pattern emerges whereby vast herds of cattle overgraze the land and cut up the soil with their sharp hooves, leaving it at the mercy of wind and rainwash. The goats follow behind, eating the grass roots and stripping bushes of their leaves, thus completing the devastation. All this is compounded by the fact that watering places are few and far between, and so vast herds tend to concentrate at them. Healthy cattle mix with diseased cattle with the result that disease is spread. This is a particular problem in East Africa where the traditionalist Maasai, Karamojong, Samburu and Turkana wander with their herds.

Although this is rather an unhappy picture changes have been occurring in the last ten to fifteen years. They are accelerating, and gradually the emphasis is beginning to shift towards *quality* rather than *quantity*, regular sales and money in the bank rather than vast skinny herds and no money, stable ranching techniques rather than indiscriminate wandering, a greater degree of health care rather than an acceptance of a certain percentage of mortality. Let us look at one such tribe who travel great distances on a north-south axis in West Africa.

The Fulani

Like the Maasai of Kenya and Tanzania, the Fulani do not bother too much about political boundaries as shown in Fig. 99. They wander across borders, from Senegal to Chad and Cameroon, as the need for grazing dictates. As long as they meet the strict animal hygiene and dipping requirements and possess the necessary clearance certificates to this effect, they are not interfered with by the authorities through whose districts they pass. Of course, any one group of Fulani does not wander the length and breadth of

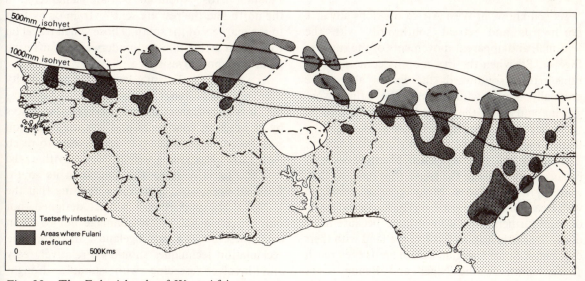

Fig. 99   The Fulani lands of West Africa

119

The problems of too many cattle in the Sahel
1   What evidence suggests these cattle are ill fed?
2   This is Senegal. What period of the year is it? Give
    reasons for your answer.

West Africa. Each group restricts its wanderings
within certain fairly flexible limits.

The Fulani live in the drier savanna lands some
of which are almost semi-desert in places. Grass is
often in short supply, water holes are very few and
sometimes there is no rain for seven months; more
if the rains fail badly. The constant search for
grazing involves sending men out on horseback to
search far and wide and to then return to guide the
cattle to the new grass. Storm clouds in the far
distance one day could mean a little grass will
grow a few days later. The horsemen have to find
it.

As you know, in West Africa the rains advance
northwards and retreat southwards with the
seasonal, and apparent movements of the sun, see
Fig. 41. So when the dry months come and the
rains retreat southwards the Fulani also move
gradually south with them. They find what
grazing and water they can, but they have to be
very careful as the further south they go the
further they get into permanent tsetse fly country.
Their cattle must be kept clear of any woodland
because that is where the tsetse flies lurk; so they
graze by the roadsides, often ignoring grassland
with trees. Often they graze on the harvested fields
of local farmers, who do not mind because in so
doing the cattle help to fertilize the land with their
droppings. Some Nigerian Fulani herds even reach
as far south as the Niger and Benue rivers
before retreating north with the advancing rains.

This is a sort of *transhumance* by latitude rather
than by altitude.

The rains bring grass back to the northlands
where, of course, there are no tsetse fly. The tsetse
fly does in fact advance northwards with the rains,
but only as far as thick tree or bush cover lasts.
Beyond that it cannot go. The rainy season is the
worst time of the year for the Fulani as they are
almost permanently soaked to the skin, there is
mud everywhere and hyenas attack the cattle
which then stampede.

Sometimes the whole group stays for a few
weeks in the home village; but normally they will
not stay long in one place. After four or five days
they move on, with their tents and equipment on
the backs of their animals. During the course of a
year they can cover anything up to 350 kilometres
in their wanderings. The men and young boys look
after the cattle: a very tiring task in the dry season
when wells have to be used for watering the cattle.
Each cow is given about 5 bowls of water in the
morning and in the evening, so to water the whole
herd twice a day is a long and arduous task.

During the year the Fulani sell quite a lot of
their cattle, together with milk and butter, in the
months when grazing is good. With this money
they buy maize meal to augment their diet. They
also grow limited amounts of millet and beans on
land near their home village, tended by the women
or fitter ones among the elderly.

Each year in Nigeria alone, about 750 000 cattle
are sold. This represents about 10% of the
Fulani's herds. About 400 000 are slaughtered in
the north and the rest are sent by train or by foot
to the markets of the south. Those which travel on
foot often arrive thin and underweight, suffering
from trypanosomyasis.

At present the Fulani's land carrying capacity
averages out at about one beast for six hectares;
but, it is feared, this capacity is exceeded in places
by as much as four times and is a major reason
why Fulani cattle take up to seven years to reach
their rather low killing weight. Not only that, the
overgrazing is assisting the Sahara in its southward advance, so it is hardly surprising that the
U.N.E.P. is supporting a project designed, not
only to put a halt to this damage but to claim
back these devastated rangelands. In theory the
reclamation techniques should be relatively easy
and involve reseeding with suitable drought
resistant grasses, plus an education programme

which spreads the gospel of proper range management. In practice it is not easy, as money is needed in large quantities and education takes time.

A start has been made at Katsina near the Nigerian border with Niger. Ranches have been set up, permanent watering places built, cross-breeding has started and pasture is being improved. Land carrying capacity allied with paddocking is being practised and cotton seed waste and groundnut leaves are being processed into high protein cattle food. On this scheme, cattle are being fattened and then killed: to be sent south in a refrigerated state, not sent on foot to catch trypanosomyasis on the way. Not surprisingly the Fulani cattle sales have given rise to a tremendously important trade in hides and skins, many of which are being increasingly used in the northern towns' manufacturing industries.

A much simpler form of transhumance is practised on the fadama lands by the people, some of whom are Fulani, who live around Lake Chad, particularly on the west and south-west shores. In the wet season they move away from the lake and then back again for the dry season, when part of their grazing is supplied by the harvested fields of sorghum.

Here an unavoidable fact presents itself; not only to the Fulani, but to all semi-nomadic pastoralists. The 20th century is passing them by, and soon they could become, because of their lack of education and the basic instability of their permanently mobile life-style, an old fashioned, disenfranchised, embittered, unhealthy and socially divisive series of minority groups. For people with such a proud history of independence and self sufficiency this would be tragic. They would be wise to take advantage of every attempt to stabilize and educate them before the 21st century, allied with scientific farming methods, condemns them to a fragmented life of poverty and cultural starvation in ever diminishing areas or pockets of existence.

Ranching

The best way of raising cattle is on a ranch within a certain defined area. The range land is managed in such a way that overgrazing is eliminated and grazing or supplementary food is always available. With United Nations or governmental help semi-nomads in many countries are being encouraged to settle down to this method.

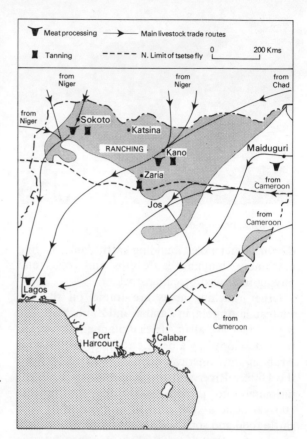

Fig. 100   Cattle in Nigeria

Water holes are created and grazing is controlled by dividing the ranch, which may be up to 50 000 hectares, into a series of fenced off sections known as paddocks. There are never too many cattle and they are moved from paddock to paddock, in such a way as to ensure that once a paddock has been grazed it has time to fully recover its grass cover before being used again. In the dry season extra food is given to the cattle, and throughout the year they are dipped every week to eliminate tick-borne diseases. Areas with ranches like these are found in the Laikipia Plateau region of Kenya. Others have been developed in the Maasai country between Nairobi and the Tanzania border.

There, Group Ranches have been formed with thirty to forty families owning a ranch big enough to support them and their cattle. One at Poka, has 12 000 hectares supporting a herd of 2000 cattle: a land carrying ratio of 6 hectares per beast. For ranches like these, government loans and credits are necessary for improvements like fencing,

A Tanzanian cattle dip

digging water holes, building earth dams, buying machinery, building cattle dips and roads and buying improved breeding stock.

Other ranching areas are found on the Bie Plateau in Angola, in Zambia and Zimbabwe. The biggest ranch of all in Africa is planned for Sudan, to be developed by a private company with Saudi Arabian and American capital. Situated between the Dinder River and the Blue Nile it is hoped, ultimately, to provide 3000 jobs and process 100 000 cattle a year; as well as growing its own cattle food and some cash crops by using Roseires Dam water. Part of a 400 000 hectare project, it is intended to assist nomads to settle down on 150 livestock ranches, as well as about 1000 small irrigated arable farms.

Botswana is a country which, until the recent discovery and exploitation of diamond pipes and copper-nickel deposits, was entirely dependent on cattle and cattle products for export earnings. With foreign assistance, some of it from the European Economic Community, a ranch training

A cattle drive in Botswana

scheme has been introduced. Demonstration ranches have been built to which farmers can go with their own cattle to learn modern methods. They are taught the principles of paddock grazing, how to build simple dams and cattle dips, and the need for their regular use. Above all they are taught that quality is more important than quantity and that regular sales can not only produce an income, but will help protect their land from overgrazing.

Botswana has always sent most of her meat to the United Kingdom via South African Railways. This is done from the Lobatse abbattoir, the biggest in Africa and as modern as any in Europe. In 1979 Botswana sold 16 000 tonnes of beef to Britain and, until 1976, supplied 80% of Zambia's beef requirements. She also exports 900 tonnes a month to Angola.

Zambia is an example of a country whose pastoralism is still largely traditional. She has a cattle population of approximately 2.2 million, of which 1.9 million belong to traditional pastoralists who place great value on numbers and rarely ever sell. Of the rest 260 000 belong to commercial farmers, while about 44 000 belong to State ranches which are trying to pass on modern methods and ideas to the traditionalists.

It is in Zambia that, arguably, the greatest feat of land reclamation in the whole of Africa is possible. It was proved before 1900 when, under the leadership of King Lewarika of the Lozi people, simple canals were dug throughout the flood plain margins of the Upper Zambezi region of Bulozi. Parts of this huge, annually flooded area were thus drained for food production and grazing. Unfortunately this system fell into disrepair, for reasons too numerous and complicated to recount here. Since then, there has been an annual transhumance away from the flooded plains in the rainy season and back to the river in the dry season. See Fig. 101 for the extent of the flooding. Money (the old old story) and the will to cooperate and succeed could transform this region into the agricultural and ranching success story of all time in Africa. A series of dams, a few hundred kilometres of simply built canals, together with an international Zambezi River Authority could largely control these floods to everyone's mutual benefit and greatly diminish South Africa's economic influence on the Zambezi Valley countries.

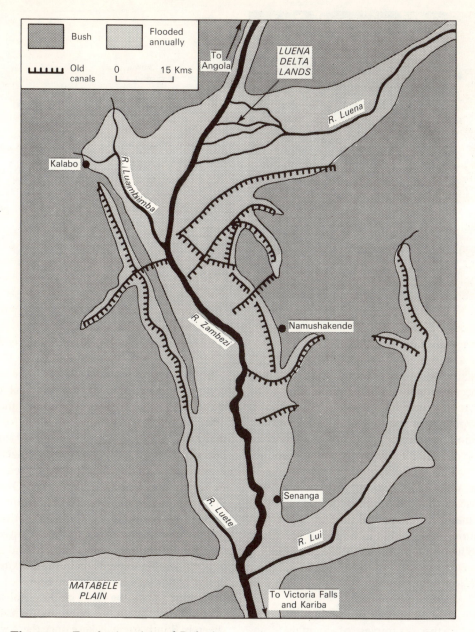

Fig. 101   The upper Zambezi region of Bulozi

The higher cattle lands

These are free from the tsetse fly because of the lower temperatures experienced. Not only that, greater altitude also gives rise to rather more rain and so grass tends to be much richer. These lands are particularly good for dairy farming as the rich grass permits the cows to produce a lot of milk; some of which can be processed into butter, cheese and cream.

One of the more important dairy farming countries in Africa is Kenya, whose highland regions close to Nairobi have several hundred thousands of dairy cattle. There are many in Tanzania's northern highlands, on the slopes of Kilimanjaro and Meru, and in both the Zambian and Zaïre copper belts. Dairying is widespread on the plateau lands of Transvaal where the huge industrial based population buys all that is produced.

Part of the modern Lobatse abbatoir

Fig. 102   *Distribution of cattle in South Africa*

Some dairy farms are found in dry lands, perhaps because there is a large population to be supplied. In dry areas a great deal of water is required from rivers and wells; both for irrigating grassland and for the cattle to drink, as dairy cows need a lot of water to enable them to produce milk.

Another great dairy farming area is Natal on South Africa's east coast where there is plenty of rain and many rivers. Along the valley bottoms rich nutritious grass grows in abundance, to feed one of the highest densities of cattle in Africa.

Sheep

Sheep are further examples of animals domesticated for man's use since recorded history. Their meat is good to eat. In some ways they have more advantages than cattle; their skins can be used for clothes it is true, but so also can their wool. A cow has only one skin but a sheep will produce wool year after year. Some sheep are kept mainly for meat but most are kept for their wool. There is another advantage which sheep hold over cattle: they need less water, a fact illustrated by Figs. 102 and 103. Each map shows the 500 mm isohyet (rainfall line). West of that line there is less than 500 mm rainfall; to the east there is more.

South Africa has more sheep than any other country in Africa. The two principal breeds of sheep in that country are Afrikander and Merino. The fat-tailed Afrikander is raised for its meat while the Merino is possibly the most famous wool bearing sheep of all. Vast herds graze the great grasslands of the Karoos, the central Cape Province areas and the southern Orange Free State. Spreading out far into the distance they can be seen perpetrating the damage to the land for which they are notorious: the excessively close cropping of the grass. This has led, and is leading, to considerable soil erosion in the dry almost semi-desert conditions of the Karoos.

Because of this the range land cannot support so many sheep. There are now less than 40 million sheep in South Africa where once there were about 50 million. Although sheep can manage on less water than cattle they still require a daily quantity. If they go short of water their numbers inevitably decline, so several hard droughts in recent years have taken a heavy toll; helped by diminishing grazing and wild animals. However, improved methods of disease prevention like regular dipping and additives to manufactured foods have helped to keep problems like blow flies, worms and scab under control.

Large organisations also exist to which sheep farmers can go for advice. The National Wool

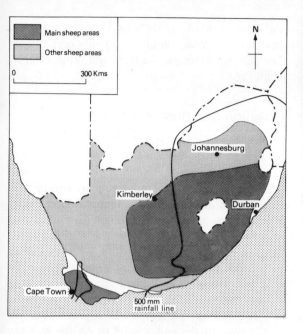

Fig. 103 Distribution of sheep in South Africa

Sheep shearing in South Africa These sheep are Merinos

Merino rams

Growers Association and the National Ram Breeders Association are two such organisations, while the Grootfontein College of Agriculture provides an excellent education for young sheep farmers.

Another breed of sheep is the Karakul, whose skin is highly prized for clothing manufacture and which can survive, like the Afrikander, in drier conditions than the Merino. Their skins are extremely valuable but only if the lambs are killed within a few days of birth. Most are found in the dry regions, but not too far away from the Orange and its tributaries between Bloemfontein and Upington.

South Africa is not the only country in Africa which has many sheep, although she has more than any of the others. The Arab countries also have many sheep because mutton is a very popular meat with the people. Most are kept along North Africa's coasts where rainfall is a little more generous; but there are also large herds in the desert, based on the oases. Numbers have increased since the prospecting and drilling for oil began; because together with the oil, large artesian reserves of water have been found which permit the cultivation of fodder crops and thus an increased sheep population. See Chapter 11.

There is one other advantage which sheep have over cattle; and that is their greater resistance to the tsetse fly. Therefore many farmers in equatorial west and east Africa have a few sheep on lands which are well drained so that foot rot does not become a problem.

Goats

Goats are probably the hardiest of all man's domestic animals; and, from an all round point of view, provide the widest range of benefits. Unlike the sheep they produce a lot of milk and their meat is very good to eat. Their skins can be used to make clothes and also water containers in the less developed areas. Their hair can be woven into a very hard wearing cloth. They need less water than the hardiest of sheep; and they can eat almost

Afrikander sheep

anything which grows. Goats can survive where sheep and cattle would die.

But these animals can seriously damage the land. Often kept by the semi-nomadic pastoralists, they follow the cattle and consume anything which the cattle leave, even eating grass roots and leaves and shoots of bushes. If they are kept in large quantities no vegetation can survive their onslaught; and, together with the cattle, they soon produce near desert conditions with soil erosion from wind (deflation) and rainwash.

Goats, like cattle and sheep, are only dangerous to the land if they are kept in too great numbers. There are many parts of Africa, particularly the wetter equatorial lands, where they do no damage. They do not suffer from the tsetse fly, their milk

and meat provide protein and they are a great benefit to the many families who only keep four or five of them amongst the trees and crops of their small farms.

Question and answer session

1   What is transhumance?
    This involves the seasonal movement of cattle and their owners in search of grazing. In North West Europe it is a movement of altitude: up to mountain pastures in summer, while fodder crops are grown on the valley farmlands and down to stalls for the winter and stored food.

    In Africa it is more often a movement of latitude to follow the rains which produce the grass. However, a limited amount of altitude movement is seen in East Africa's rift valley. The Maasai's permanent homes are often on the tops of the valley sides or on the benches formed by step faulting. They move down to the valley every year when rain falls in order to rest their rangelands higher up.

2   What is land carrying capacity?
    This is the number of cattle that a given area of land can feed without permanent damage to the pasture. Alternatively it is the length of time that a given area of land can feed a larger number of cattle before suffering irreparable damage. Once this capacity has been established, together with its recovery period, it should not be exceeded.

9 Africa's forests: a case of survival

Africa has thousands of square kilometres of forest land ranging from the rain forests of the Equator through rich savanna woodlands, vast man-made forests and the strange trees of the Mediterranean lands. Trees are one of nature's richest gifts to Africa. Singly or in forests they are beautiful: far too beautiful to be massacred without a thought for the future.

The trouble is that trees are very useful. They are used for building, for making furniture, boats and, above all, for making paper.

Trees are more than just beautiful and useful. A country which is deprived of its trees can become almost a desert, particularly if that country is close to a desert margin. Examples include Algeria or even Kenya.

Wood is the most important cooking fuel in Africa and is used as it is or in the shape of charcoal. Paraffin and gas are important but their price has risen so much in recent years that many people find them too expensive. It has been estimated that for every person in Africa a tonne of wood is used for cooking every year. That is a lot of trees for Africa to lose year after year if they are not being replaced.

It has been proved, time and time again, that if a land loses its trees it will very soon begin to lose its soil. The roots help hold the soil in place and their branches and leaves slow down the force of the rain and wind. Without them the rain and the wind can quickly remove the fertile top soil. Below the top soil there is not much humus and so little or nothing will grow; and erosion will become worse. This is happening in many parts of Africa.

Some people believe that really big forests help bring rainfall to a country. Their leaves pass moisture into the air by transpiration, which in turn is transformed into rain by convection. Without trees in numbers like this it certainly would not happen. Without trees and forests there would be no wood for building, none for furniture or paper, charcoal would disappear, food could not be cooked, soil erosion would accelerate and the desert would advance. You think this is over-stating the case? Then read what happened in the Tennessee Valley in the U.S.A. Perhaps you can see it beginning in your country.

There are only two ways to prevent this. Trees must be replaced if they are cut down, a practice known as *reafforestation*. New forests must be planted where none existed before: *afforestation*. Forests must not be cut down faster than new ones can grow, so for every tree cut down **at least** one more should be planted. The Algerians call it *defence and restoration* of the soil. They are working very hard at using their forests wisely as

Gullying: the result of careless land use

The great Usutu Forest with a wood pulp mill

127

we shall see later. Nevertheless, in Africa in 1983, for every hectare of replanted forest, 14 hectares were lost. This is a recipe for total disaster. For instance, by 1990 Nigeria may have to import wood to maintain her processing industries. First of all however, let us move to southern Africa where, in Swaziland, great efforts are being made to renew the forests of yesteryear. High in her western mountains there were once many great forests which were thoughtlessly cut down for fuel and the provision of more farmland. Overgrazing and the heavy rainfall (1000 mm – 2250 mm) of the Drakensbergs did not take long to do their work and great erosion occurred. But, since 1940, much reafforestation and afforestation has taken

place. There are now three vast coniferous forests in this hilly and mountainous region shown in Fig. 104. The first was started in the Piggs Peak area of north-west Swaziland, and today there are over 32 000 hectares of man-made forest in that area.

Further south, near Mbabane, the Great Usutu Forest was begun in 1950. Today it exceeds 40 000 hectares in all directions around Bhunya. It is one of the largest man-made forests in the world. The most recent addition is the Nhlangano Forest in the south west. Between them the Swazi Government and the Commonwealth Development Corporation have largely financed these projects. Today Swaziland's man-made forests of pine and eucalyptus exceed 100 000 hectares.

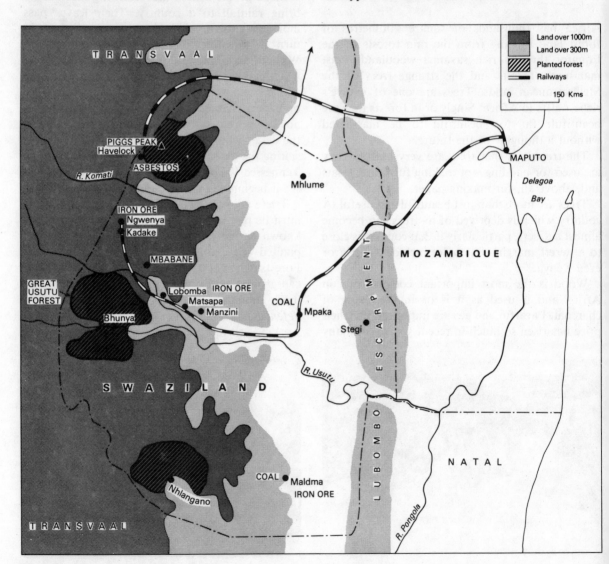

Fig. 104   The forests of Swaziland

One of the most important points about soft-wood trees in tropical and sub-tropical areas with good rainfall is their growth rate. Maturity is reached in about fifteen years, at least three times quicker than pulpwood conifers in Sweden, Russia and Canada. As soon as a 'stand' of trees is cleared the land is cleared and replanted.

Four saw mills were built and now produce sawn and planed timber, block-board, pit props and telegraph poles. In 1959 a large pulp mill was built at Bhunya on the River Usutu; financed by the C.D.C. and Courtaulds. It produces over 140 000 tonnes of pulp a year for the export market. At Mbabane's new industrial estate a furniture industry has become very successful indeed.

Tree cutting is done largely by mechanical saws, and horses and tractors drag the logs to the main service roads where they are loaded on to huge lorries for transport to Bhunya or a sawmill.

The most important thing of all is that the carefully planned rotation system of reafforestation ensures that Swaziland's timber supplies will be maintained, and possibly increased, and the soil is being defended and restored.

Swaziland is a small country and her part of the Drakensbergs is also small, but all over those windward slopes there are many similar forests in South Africa. Wattle is very important indeed in Natal's upland regions and is used mostly for wood pulp. Its bark also yields a valuable extract which is widely used in the 'tanning' of hides and skins. Another valuable forest region in South Africa, known as the Knysna Forests, is situated around the town of Knysna. Here, thoughtless cutting almost ruined the forests; and trees such as stinkwood (furniture) and yellow wood (building) have nearly gone. To save the forests the government has closed them to the timber cutters for the next two hundred years. Large areas of conifers are being planted to take their place in the furniture and building industry.

Tropical hardwoods

The most valuable woods for making furniture are the hardwoods which are found all over the African equatorial lowlands from Zaïre to Guinea. They grow where temperatures are always high and where rainfall is regular and heavy.

The hardwoods are extremely difficult to cut and take away. They are so big and heavy and they only grow singly, not in groups like coniferous trees. Another tree of the same type might be several hundred metres away. The forests are thick and dense and rough roads have to be carved out of the undergrowth. Rainfall is often torrential and vehicles frequently get bogged down in the mud.

In Nigeria the greatest hardwood forests are found in the Benin region. There are plenty of waterways in the delta lands and the logs are floated downstream to the coast to timber ports like Sapele, a few kilometres to the south. Some of the wood is processed at Sapele which has saw mills and a plywood factory.

When the logs have been cut they are pulled away to either a collection point or a river. In Ghana they are either railed to Samreboi, a timber

A felled hardwood tree in Ghana's forests Trees like this cannot be replaced in less than 100 years. Yet it only takes a few minutes to cut one down.
1   What does the photograph tell you about the numbers of trees like this?
2   What is happening in this picture?

129

industry town, or to Takoradi where they are placed in the harbour to await export. This also happens at Abidjan in the Ivory Coast.

Hardwoods like mahogany (red in colour) and ebony (black) will float, but some are so dense and hard they would sink if put into water. Ironwood is one such wood and so this has to be moved by road or rail. Sometimes the forests are hundreds of kilometres from the coast and so road and rail are again necessary; as for instance in Congo, whose only big port is Pointe Noire. In fact in Congo, ruthless cutting has reduced the coastal forest areas to an unproductive savannah. Wisdom is prevailing however. The Ministry for Water and Forestry Development is coordinating a sensible plan for the inland forests. New roads have been built and the Congo-Ocean railway given a new heavy duty track. The Office Congolais des Forêts et du Reboisement (Congo's department for forests and re-afforestation) is organising a replanting programme. A new eucalyptus (gum tree) plantation will begin supplying a new paper mill at Pointe Noire in 1985. Remember softwoods grow very quickly within the rain fed tropics.

Gabon provides another example. Her great forest lands lie in the basin of the River Ogooué as shown in Fig. 105 and the timber was floated down the main river and its tributaries for export from Port Gentil. The timber is now exhausted and the timber companies want to move further inland to the 20 million hectares of untouched forest. Here the river will not help as it is too long and winding. The answer to this has been to construct a new port called Owendo, just north of Libreville, and a new railway to feed it which reached Booue in 1983. This railway will serve a fourfold purpose:

a) It will make possible the exploitation of all the hardwoods of the Ogooué basin.

b) The feeder roads which serve it will now open the devastated forest areas to agriculture.

c) A later branch line to Franceville will make export of uranium and manganese easier and should be finished by 1987. At present it is sent to the Congo by a 76 kilometre overhead cable railway for export from Pointe Noire.

d) A further branch line will open the northern forests and permit a rich iron ore field at Belinga to be developed but not before 1990.

As a result of exploitation so far, all natural stands of okoume, an extremely valuable light coloured wood which grows nowhere else, have been exhausted. It is now being grown on a plantation scale in reafforested areas. The trees

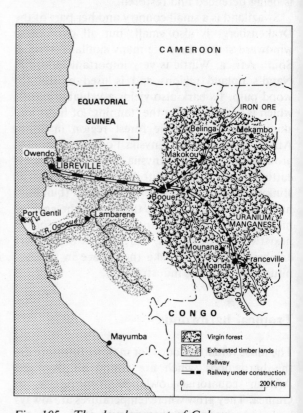

Fig. 105 *The development of Gabon*

Takoradi harbour: logs awaiting export

1 To which country does the central ship belong?
2 What evidence suggests that winds were not strong when this picture was taken?

take sixty years to mature and the damage will take many decades to repair; but at least it is a start.

The problem with hardwoods is the very long time new trees take to mature: at least 65 to 70 years in most cases and over 100 in others. Yet they can be cut down in less than half an hour. The result is that most of these types of trees are lost forever. Eucalyptus trees are planted instead as they grow in about 12 to 15 years.

Liberia has a reafforestation programme, but in a nearby country, Ivory Coast, it is almost too late. Ivory Coast is possibly the fastest developing country in Africa and the timber industry has played its part in this. So much so that it is estimated that by 1985 to 90 Ivory Coast's forests will be completely exhausted of its major trees. This is not all. Using the timber companies roads 'get rich quick' small farmers have moved into these fertile (temporarily) areas, cleared the remaining vegetation and planted it with cocoa, coffee and bananas. Not bothering with expensive fertilization, they clear more land when yields decline, leaving the exhausted soils to the mercy of erosion processes like rainwash and the wind.

It is a very difficult dilemma. Timber and its products are the third largest item in terms of value of Ivorian exports, occupying 16% of the total in 1979. But in 1972 timber was the second largest export with 23% of the total. The decline in its importance is there for all to see and is illustrated in Fig. 106. No defence or restoration was carried out in colonial times and even since independence only 3500 hectares a year have been replanted. There is even illegal cutting in the national parks. However, new efforts are to be made, including the replanting of hardwoods. In the main, replanting will be done with eucalyptus. These trees, plus the remains of the original forests, will serve a new pulp mill which is shortly to be built.

An effect on Ivory Coast's climate is already being seen. Without the protective covering of the forest, rain water evaporates more quickly, there is much greater run-off into the swift seaward flowing rivers and soil goes as well. There is less transpiration and thus less rainfall in the northern forest zone. The balance has been disturbed and it is all helping the slight but inexorable southward advance of the savanna lands: and no-one needs to be told what is advancing behind them.

In Cameroon positive efforts are being made to

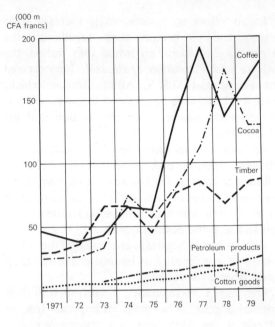

Fig. 106 Exports from Ivory Coast

preserve the rain forests. Although that country's wood processing industry is increasing and now, in 1983, stands at over 50% of the total annual cut, preservation plans are proceeding. The Government has created its first National Rain Forest Park at Korup. Six more will be created, of which those at Djar and Pangar Djerem will be next. See Fig. 143. These are encouraging examples of another measure which could help save tropical Africa's forests, soils, agriculture and some of its wild life.

The fight against the desert

The desert is still a long way from Ivory Coast, but in Algeria it is ever present and occupies over 80% of her land surface as shown in Fig. 107. Only in the north are forests possible and then only if great care is taken. Remember, the Mediterranean climate does not make growth easy.

Before independence came to Algeria her forests had suffered as they had been ravaged both for fuel and charcoal. Further, because the best land had been denied to the local people they had moved into the hills and mountains. They cleared the forested slopes to grow their crops and graze their cattle, leaving unprotected soil which was rapidly eroded.

In an effort to restore, even increase their forests and to protect their farmlands, the Algerians embarked on what they called the *defence and restoration of the soil*. They created the Forest and D.R.S. Administration which, from 1967 onwards has trained foresters, carried out research, organised reafforestation and afforestation.

As well as the forest service, thousands of students, soldiers and civil servants have planted millions of trees in the last few years. They hope eventually to restore about 5 million hectares to forest growth which they hope will stabilize the soil and stop the desert's advance.

To help in this Algeria is encouraging the use of her own large supplies of natural gas rather than wood, to use for cooking.

They have been replanting the forests with their original species. The most widespread tree in Algeria is the Alep Pine, a softwood which is found all over the High Plateau and the Aures Mountains. Replanting has been so successful that the Alep Pine is now fully supplying the factories at Telagh, Djelfa and Batna, shown in Fig. 108 which produce hardboard and wood panels made of reconstituted sawdust. Apart from these, the only other products made from Algerian wood so far, are packing cases and pit props.

Alep Pines in Algeria Notice the terraced hillside.

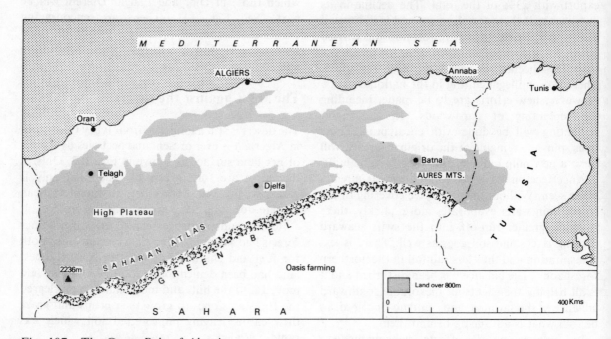

Fig. 107 The Green Belt of Algeria

132

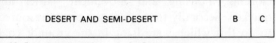

| DESERT AND SEMI-DESERT | B | C |

B Mediterranean vegetation   C Grass steppe

Fig. 108 Natural regions of Algeria

The famous cork oaks of the coastal lands are near extinction because of excessive harvesting and no renewal. Used in the wine industry and heat insulation, they can only be harvested about ten times. After all, a tree depends on its bark for life. Take its bark and it dies. Continued replanting is essential, and only now is it being done.

The most famous tree is the cedar, highly valued in the furniture industry and now only seen in the higher mountain lands. They are slow growing and will take many years to renew.

The hardiest of all North African trees are the Juniper and Green Oak, both of which are able to grow in drier conditions than any of the others. These and the Alep Pine are leading the fight against desertification in Algeria. Huge areas have been planted in the High Plateau; some of which are designed to act as windbreaks to protect farmland.

Orchards of peaches, apricots and olives are also being planted wherever possible. They help stabilize the soil and their fruit also brings a financial return. They are often planted in long rows along contours with grazing belts of permanent grass between them.

Since 1970 planting of both orchard and forest trees has proceeded at the rate of at least 25 000 hectares a year and is increasing yearly. Two further trees which have figured in this are the ever present eucalyptus (what an adaptable tree it is) and the poplar.

We can see then that trees are one of nature's greatest natural resources. In some countries there are so many that they seem inexhaustible and are freely and ruthlessly removed. In other countries, countries like Algeria, the damage caused by reckless cutting is only too apparent. What is equally apparent is that repairing the damage is a long and expensive process.

Question and answer session

1 Isn't fire dangerous in the Mediterranean summer?
Yes, it is. To guard against this wide fire belts have been created in Algeria. These are strips of cleared land between forest sections which deprive fires of anything to burn. Look-out towers are dotted throughout the forests and there are many trained fire fighting units on call.

2 Many saplings must be needed for replanting. How are they obtained?
In Algeria there are nurseries which provide these. Each year they provide at least 200 million forest saplings and 6 million orchard saplings. In any forest service nurseries will be created to supply these.

3 Where is the fight against the desert most serious in Algeria?
On the southern borders of the Saharan Atlas. There, one of the most exciting projects of all is in progress; the Green Barrier is being built from the Tunisian to the Moroccan border and is shown in Fig. 107. The National Youth Service is in charge of this mammoth task in which a belt of trees about two kilometres wide is being planted along the whole length of over 1000 kilometres. It is eventually hoped to plant 150 000 hectares a year. Among the more important aims of the project are the following:
a) to halt the desert advance.
b) to stop erosion in the High Plateau.
c) to produce more wood for planned cutting.
d) to protect agriculture and help its expansion in the Saharan Atlas and on the High Plateau.
e) to provide even more than the present 30 000 jobs already existing in the Forest Service.

Group tasks

1 Make sure you know where the forests are in your country, who is responsible for them and how they are being looked after.

2 Which trees grow most successfully in your district? Try to plant some in a corner of your school grounds.

3 Conduct a survey amongst your friends. What is the cooking fuel used in their homes? Express your findings as percentages of the whole in one long bar graph.

10 The development of industries

Africa is not an industrial continent, having only one such region which compares in scale and scope with great industrial regions like the Ruhr, Pittsburgh and the Great Lakes or the Donetz Basin in Russia. For the rest, there are smaller pockets of industry, intended in the main to serve the country in which they are situated.

Until recently, since World War Two perhaps, Africa's resource base was solely the land. The majority of Africa's people were and still are, pastoralists, or cultivators, or both. Values, philosophies, life styles were all rooted in the land and its varying degrees of fruitfulness.

Modern industry was for the temperate lands where, in Britain, it was first developed in the late 1700's. The spread of industry occurred on a horizontal basis at first; along the temperate latitudes to east and west, into North America, Europe and Asia. By the 1900's it had moved, on a small scale, into the southern temperate latitudes, but still on a horizontal plane, to places like southeast Australia, the River Plate Republics and, to a lesser extent, the south coast of Africa. However also by then, a sleeping giant was beginning to stir in South Africa.

Industry can only develop on a really large scale under a very special set of circumstances. Without them, large scale development of industry is just not possible; and neither is the accumulation of great wealth which a wide industrial base inevitably brings. A glance at the great industrial countries of the world will show the circumstances under which industry can grow.

First of all there is the need for machines to make the production of life's basic needs, food, clothing, housing and movement, easier and quicker. Secondly there were the power resources to do this which were lying in the ground: coal. Thirdly there was the other basic raw material with which to work: iron ore. These three factors are what the development of large scale industry, both heavy and light, is all about. There are many others of course, but without at least two of the three we have outlined, great industrialization is unlikely.

A further look at some of the great industrial nations will show that the local iron ore has long since been exhausted. But that doesn't matter as the industries are established. They might expand, but they won't actually be moved. The necessary raw materials, like metalliferous ores, will just be transported in from elsewhere. As long as a satisfactory power base remains, so will the industry. Having discussed the basic requirements for large scale industrial development, and before looking at industry elsewhere in Africa, let us now look in greater detail at Africa's one great example of such development: the sleeping giant we mentioned earlier, which brings to South Africa much of her great wealth and power.

Johannesburg and the Rand

The heart of South African industry today lies on what has become known as the Rand, short for Witwatersrand, that gold rich strip which stretches east-west across much of southern Transvaal. It was to these goldfields in 1886 that people came in their thousands to dig for the precious metal. Eventually the mines came under the control of a few big firms, who alone could afford the tremendous cost of the mechanisation needed to extract the gold from its ore. The people stayed on as employees of the gold mine companies; and from this beginning the great industrial area known as the Rand grew to its present huge extent.

The power source! Long before gold had been discovered vast quantities of coal had been found. It was just waiting for a job to do. That job was to provide the power for smelting and refining gold.

If the Rand is the heart of South African industry then Johannesburg is the heart of the Rand: a great sprawling colossus of a city, more than 275 square kilometres in area. It is the focal point, the central place; and smaller towns and industrial areas are spread out on all sides of it, principally to the east, south and west. They almost all had their origins in gold mining but have since expanded the nature of their industries to:

a) meet the needs of the ever increasing population of southern Transvaal

b) take full advantage of the new mineral discoveries which have been made and which need industries to process and manufacture goods from them.

Gold ingots in a Pretoria bank

An aerial view of Johannesburg
What evidence suggests that the sun was overhead when the picture was taken?

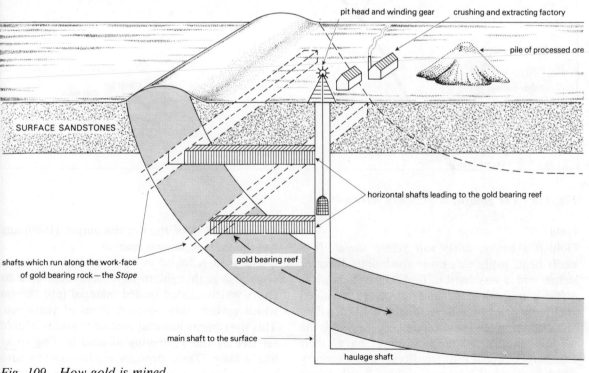

pit head and winding gear

crushing and extracting factory

pile of processed ore

SURFACE SANDSTONES

horizontal shafts leading to the gold bearing reef

shafts which run along the work-face of gold bearing rock — the *Stope*

gold bearing reef

main shaft to the surface

haulage shaft

Fig. 109   How gold is mined

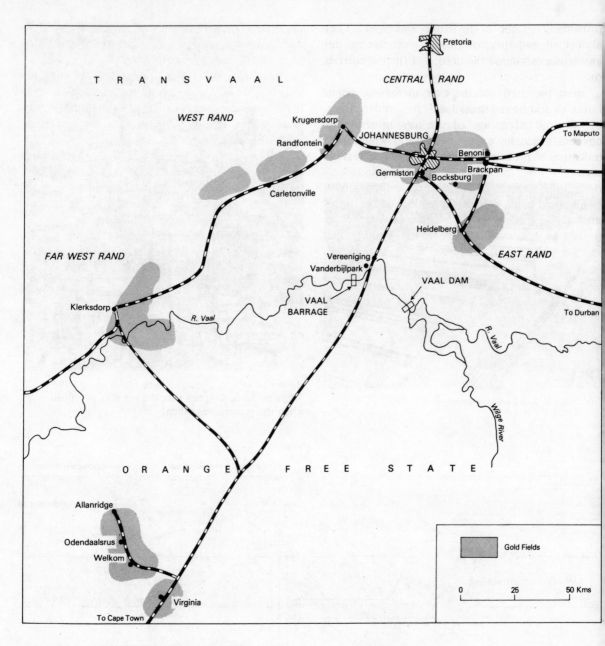

Fig. 110   The goldfields of South Africa

Gold

Gold is a heavy, fairly soft yellow metal. It is easily bent, easily cut, easily made into different shapes and is very hard to find. Once found, it is difficult to both mine and refine. It is valued greatly by man. Men have fought, robbed, killed and died for gold. They still do because gold is the world's money. Countries may have their currencies but gold is international; and a country which has a lot of it is very wealthy. South Africa

has about 56% of the world's output (1980) and has the greatest known reserves.

The gold is found in layers of rock known as *reefs* and is thought to have been deposited by rivers which carried eroded material into the sea which covered this region millions of years ago. This river-borne material contained grains of gold set free by the weathering of gold bearing rocks like granite. These deposits are thought to have been metamorphosed by great pressure and then folded and uplifted by the earth's movements. The edge of the deposits was exposed later by erosion and the reef discovered. The rock in the reefs is called *banket* and it is this which is mined.

.The method of mining as shown in Fig. 109 is much the same as that used for underground copper ore, except that the work face where the banket is blasted is called the *Stope*. By stages the banket, which has been brought to the surface, is crushed to a fine powdery dust which is then mixed with water in large precipitation tanks until it is a liquid mud or slime. Cyanide is added to this mixture and dissolves the gold content to form potassium gold cyanide. The actual liquid is then run off and zinc dust is added which precipitates

the gold. The gold is removed, smelted to refine and remove the impurities and then cast into ingots at Germiston in the Rand.

The goldfields shown in Fig. 110 are divided into four basic areas within the Rand region; but there is another very rich area in the Orange Free State centred around Odendaalsrus. Between them they produce almost all of South Africa's gold which, apart from being cast into ingots and stored in deep underground vaults, is used mainly in the jewelry and gold craft industries.

Uranium
This metal holds an ever increasing influence over man's affairs in the world today. It occurs with

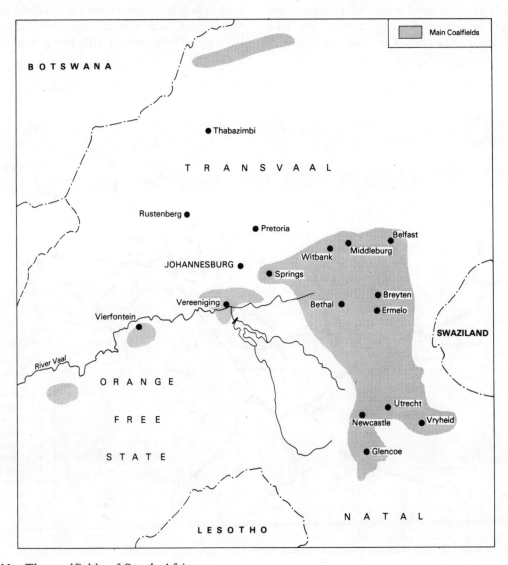

Fig. 111   The coalfields of South Africa

137

the gold deposits in South Africa and is extracted from the residual mud and slime, at only a little extra expense, once the machinery to do it has been installed. It is even being extracted from the yellow-white slag heaps of old processed gold ore. Sulphuric acid which is an essential ingredient of the extraction process is a by-product of the refining of copper: a mineral of which South Africa luckily has two large deposits.

South Africa produced 6000 tonnes of uranium in 1980. Most of it, 99.7%, comes from the gold mines but the great increase it is hoped will come from the Rossing mine in Namibia: an area which she hopes to be able to control despite possible independence.

So gold gave the Rand industrial region its start: but there was more to it than that. We have already mentioned coal. This was the source of

power. There is so much coal that accurate estimates of the reserves are almost impossible. One estimate has it that South Africa has 20% of the world's known reserves, and most of that is in the Rand region or close to it as shown in Fig. 111. South Africa has so much coal that she is now able to export almost 150 000 tonnes of it a day from her new port at Richards Bay, 150 kilometres north east of Durban in a widened and deepened lagoon which was formerly enclosed by longshore drift. Six trains a day, each carrying about 25 000 tonnes of coal will move along the new railway line from the eastern Rand coalfields.

The Rand's good fortune did not finish with just gold and coal. Plentiful deposits of iron ore were also discovered within the coalfield areas at Middleburg, near Glencoe and Newcastle and at Pretoria. These are all still being worked, but

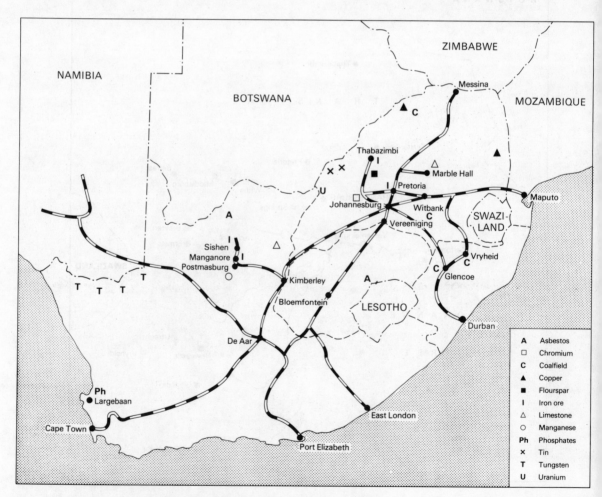

Fig. 112   Other non-precious mineral resources of South Africa

South Africa's best deposits are found at Thabazimbi which is about 275 kilometres north west of the Rand. A railway was built and the ore now moves into the Rand iron and steel mills at Pretoria, Johannesburg, Witbank, Vereeniging and Vanderbijl Park.

With the Thabazimbi deposits and those at Sishen and Manganore, South Africa has 6% of the world's known iron ores containing 60% or more of iron: an estimated 5 billion tonnes.

With such amounts of coal and iron ore an iron and steel industry was inevitable. Even the limestone needed to produce iron and steel is available in huge quantities from sources that are nearby.

One thing further is vital for all mining and industrial processes: *water*. Now this is something which is in very short supply in South Africa; yet the Rand was fortunate. The border between Transvaal and Orange Free State is the Vaal River, which has been dammed in two places: the Vaal

Dam and the Vaal Barrage. The Rand – Pretoria – Vereeniging iron and steel mills use at least 900 million litres of water a day. To help make a tonne of steel at least 9000 litres of water is needed so the previous figure is hardly surprising.

Major towns and their manufactured goods

Johannesburg and district
Because of its surrounding mineral resources and subsequent industrial development and population increase, Johannesburg is now a major route centre for road, rail and air traffic. It is also the commercial and financial centre of South Africa. It has every service industry that a huge conurbation requires. The iron and steel industry supplies the manufactures of railway wagons, mining machinery, vehicles and farm machinery.

A line of furnaces at the ISCOR works in Vanderbijl Park near Vereeniging

Textiles and textile machinery are produced as well as clothing, electrical goods, chemicals, furniture and cement. One of the Rand's major ports is Maputo in newly independent Mozambique.

Pretoria
The administrative capital of South Africa, Pretoria has a large iron and steel industry based on Thabazimbi iron ore and Witbank coking coal. Her other industries include glass, cement, cables and motor engineering.

Vereeniging and Vanderbijl Park
These combined towns make up a major coal mining, engineering and iron and steel centre. At Vanderbijl Park there is also a tin plate industry as well as the manufacture of copper and steel, and iron and steel alloys. At nearby Sasolburg oil is produced from coal.

Germiston
This town is the rail centre for the whole of the Rand and is the home of the Rand's gold refinery. It produces metal goods, chemicals, foods and textiles.

Springs
There are both gold and coal mines here. Industries include mining machinery, food processing, electrical goods, bicycles, printing machinery, steel alloys, glassware, paper and canned foods.

These are just a few of the towns of the Rand. There are very many more and they are all connected in one way or another with gold, iron and steel or coal.

Diamonds
The Rand is not really connected with diamond mining, apart from the nearby Premier Mine near Pretoria; but industries connected with diamonds are found in Johannesburg, where there are most of South Africa's diamond cutting factories plus a diamond research centre. Furthermore De Beers, the great company which controls diamond sales throughout the whole world, has its headquarters on the Rand. The first diamond was found near Hopetown in 1866, but the great deposits at Kimberley were not found until 1871. Diamonds are the hardest material known to man. They are a form of carbon and look like small pieces of ice. When cut they glitter and shine. They are very beautiful and, like gold, they are difficult to find, difficult to mine and difficult to recover from their parent rock.

Diamonds are formed beneath the ground by the great heat of subterranean volcanic activity. They are formed in the same sort of situation as the central pipe of a volcano. In some of these pipes there is blue rock and it is here that the diamonds are found. Because the first great deposits of diamonds were found in what came to

Diamonds from Kimberley

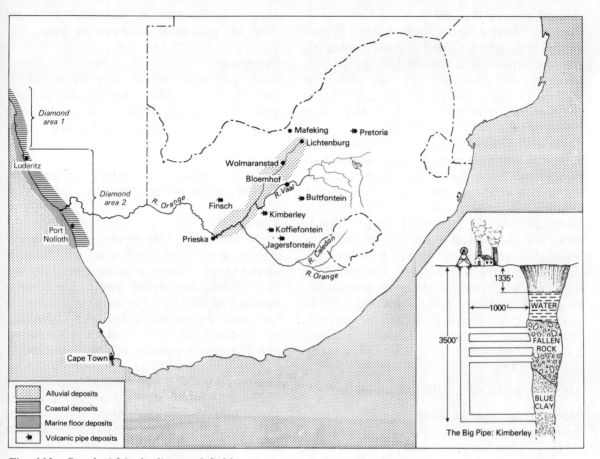

Fig. 113 South Africa's diamond fields

From all directions a complex transport system brings the raw materials
of industry from the rest of South Africa to the Rand factories

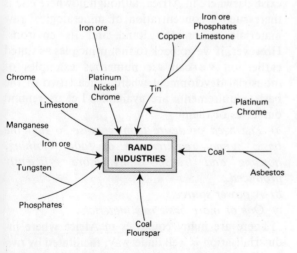

*Fig. 114 Diagrammatic sketch of the Rand's
sources of raw materials*

be called the 'Big Hole' at Kimberley, the blue
parent rock was called Kimberlite.

Since then many pipes have been found in
places as far apart as Pretoria, Bultfontein,
Jagersfontein and Koffiefontein. They all began
as open-cast mines but water and falling rock
made it dangerous below a certain depth and
mining had to be continued by the shaft method.
A vertical shaft is sunk 300 metres from the pipe
itself and then horizontal shafts at different levels
(cross drives) are dug into the pipe as shown in
Fig. 113. The ore is then blasted and lifted to the
surface.

The Finsch Mine is a more recent discovery, just
east of Postmasburg. It was opened in 1967 and is
mined mainly by open-cast methods.

Mention must be made of the largest diamond
treatment plant in the world, presently situated at
the Orapa mine and Letlhakana diamond mines in
Botswana.

Alluvial diamond deposits

These are found along the Vaal – Hartz – Orange valleys, in stream beds, dried up water courses and on river terraces. It is thought that the deposits were removed from their original pipe sites millions of years ago by the normal cycle of riverine and rainwash erosion which then deposited them in their present sites.

These deposits are also found along coastal margins in marine sands and gravels between Fort Nolloth and Walvis Bay. Twenty to thirty metres above sea level, the gem stones are richest between Oranjeminde and Luderitz. These deposits could be the result of longshore drift (see Figs. 3 and 4) of the estimated annual 90 million cubic metres of material delivered by the Orange River over the past 70 million years. See Fig. 113. This indicates a higher sea level in the past along this desert coast. Huge bucket wheel excavators remove up to 25 metres of this material to expose the diamond layers beneath. These are then carefully searched by gangs of men with large brushes and dustpans.

Other minerals available to the Rand

Johannesburg and the Rand have all the basic factors necessary for industrial development on a simple gold – iron and steel – coal basis, but within just a few hundred kilometres an even wider variety of metal ores is available, with a transport system which converges from each source to the Rand for manufacture as shown in Figs. 112 and 114.

Platinum

South Africa is the world's largest producer and exporter and has 83% of the world's known reserves, most of which are at the Rustenberg mine. Platinum is expensive to refine as the metal content is usually less than 3 grammes per tonne of ore. It is widely used in jewelry and as a catalyst in the purification of exhaust gases from internal combustion engines.

Chrome

South Africa is the world's second largest producer of this metal which is also mined at Rustenberg as well as at Lydenberg, Steeleport and Penge. The chemical industry uses it to make tanning materials, dyes, paints and in electroplating. The iron and steel industry also uses chrome for various alloys. The Rustenberg pro-duction is exported to Germany while the Lydenberg production is used on the Rand.

Manganese

South Africa is second only to Russia in production. Her exports represent 22% of world production. It is widely used in alloys with steel in Johannesburg, Vereeniging and Pretoria.

Nickel

This is also mined at Rustenberg and is another agent in the iron and steel industry.

Asbestos

South Africa has 14% of the world's asbestos reserves, some types of which are only found in South Africa: namely crocidilite and amosite. These fibrous crystals are used in fire-proofing materials of all sorts. The asbestos is mined at Barberton, Penge, Steeleporte and Lydenburg; and what isn't used in the Rand towns is exported, with Swaziland's asbestos, by way of Maputo.

These are not all the minerals readily available to the Rand industrial region, but they do give an idea of the abundant riches which have first given rise to, and then greatly expanded, the greatest and most comprehensive industrial development on the African continent to date.

Further developments

The necessary factors for industrial development exist elsewhere in Africa, although nowhere else is there such a concentration of mineralogical raw materials as on the Rand and its environs. However, if we go back to first principles as stated earlier on we can see numerous examples of industrial development where at least two of the basic requirements are available. Let us remind ourselves of them.

a) The need or desire to mechanise so that the basic human requirements of food, clothing, housing and transport are more efficiently produced.

b) A power source.

c) One or more basic raw materials.

There are many countries in Africa where industrialisation is well underway, facilitated by two or all of the above requirements. There are many more with great potential for industrialisation.

Ghana

A start on industrialisation has been made because the need and desire was there. The power source came with the Volta Dam, but there was initially a heavy price to pay for its construction, dealt with in more detail earlier. Ghana had to agree to the construction of a foreign-owned aluminium smelter before finance for the dam was forthcoming. The smelter is highly automated and only employs 2500 Ghanaians. It cannot use Ghana's own large supplies of bauxite because there is no plant to first produce the alumina. However, getting the power source was most important.

As a result, shown in Fig. 115 the industrial town of Tema was built up with this new activity,

Tema from the air showing the bauxite smelter in the foreground

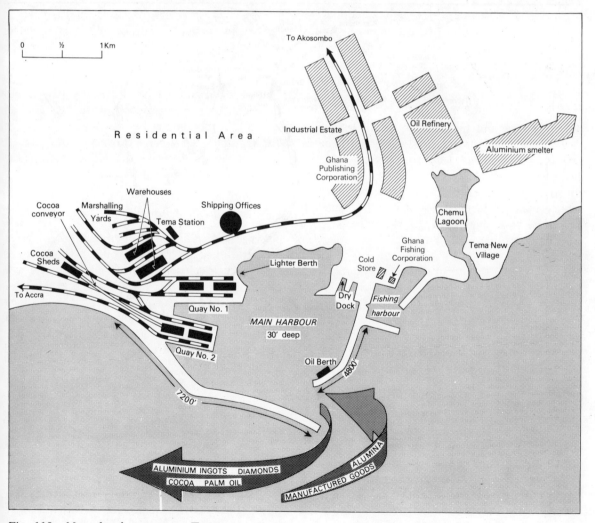

Fig. 115   New developments at Tema

143

to house the Valco Smelter, twenty seven kilometres east of Accra. The deep offshore waters facilitated ships' usage of the new port which also had to be built to allow ships from the West Indies and Guinea to bring the huge supplies of alumina needed. New road and rail facilities open out from Tema to the rest of Ghana and gradually a new industrial complex has grown and developed using the power from the dam. Already there is an oil refinery, a textile factory, concrete manufacture, vehicle assembly, fish processing, an electronics industry and chocolate manufacture. Paint, chemicals, steel building materials, furniture and fertilizer factories are also concentrated round the focus of Tema and its new port.

It is sad that internal problems and drought have recently retarded Ghana's industrial development. Her Aya, Awas and Kibi bauxite deposits still await development and home processing. Civil unrest, Akosombo's low power output and a world recession have made this impossible so far. Ghana has the wish to industralise, a basic raw material and some power. But do remember that without coal and iron ore really large development is difficult. Hope for the future lies in oil exploration. By 1983 the Bonsu field, discovered in 1977, was producing 4.5 million barrels daily: all used in Ghana. Optimistic exploration is currently taking place offshore at Assini, Axim and Keta. See Fig. 88. Who knows, oil could provide the power and raw material for a lift-off in Ghanaian industry.

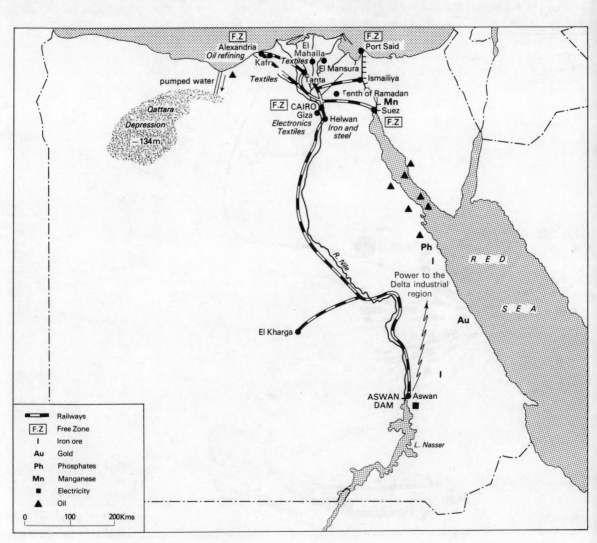

Fig. 116 *Industrial developments in Egypt*

Suez and the Nile Delta Lands

Egypt as a whole is the second biggest industrial country after South Africa and most of this development is found in lower Egypt.

Egypt has a very special problem, which becomes more acute as each year passes. It lies in the fact that Egypt will, in all probability, never be able to grow all her own food. Because of this she must develop and expand her industrial base so that exports from industry can pay for the import of food.

The building of the Aswan Dam provided the power for expansion and great developments have already taken place in the production of cement, iron and steel, fertilizers, oil refining, textiles, light and heavy engineering and electrical goods of all sorts. As yet these industrial products have not made much impact on Egypt's exports, 69% of which were made up of cotton (raw and manufactured) and crude oil in 1980. The new industries are however supplying the home market and saving on the cost of importing them from elsewhere. A huge home market is important in industrial development as it provides a reliable base from which to expand. Egypt's forty million people provide this base.

A flourishing electronics industry producing radios and television equipment is situated at Dar es Salaam, a suburb of Cairo. The iron and steel plant at Helwan shown in Fig. 116 has undergone expansion using iron ore from Aswan and the Bahariya Oasis. Power is supplied by Aswan.

The textile industry is very large and widespread. Its raw material is cotton, grown throughout the length and breadth of the Nile Valley. Helwan, Giza, El Mahalla el Kubra and Kafr el Dauwar are all towns with textile mills. Every year Egypt spins, weaves and prints more of her own cotton. Egypt exported 296.4 £E million worth of raw cotton in 1980. Could this be the sign that the textile industry is becoming so well established that Egypt can soon afford to grow less cotton, more food and still make money from textiles?

Tapping a blast furnace at Helwan, Egypt

Free Zones

Industry in the Suez and Delta lands is being encouraged in another way by the creation of Free Zones. Within these zones foreign companies may import raw materials and export finished products free of charge. Telephones, roads, railways and water will be supplied and industries pay rent for the land. Once these facilities are completed progress should be rapid.

Already the Port Said Zone has been established with facilities for food warehousing, general warehousing and manufacturing industry. Others will follow at Suez, Alexandria and Cairo. Many jobs will be created, particularly in the manufacture of component parts for industries in the Free Zones.

Typical of the increasing industrialisation in the lower delta lands is the appearance, now under construction, of a new industrial city called 'Tenth of Ramadan'. Situated 50 kilometres from Cairo on the Cairo-Ismailia road it will ultimately provide work and housing for some of Cairo's exploding population. This, together with the planned expansion of the canal ports of Port Said, Ismailia and Suez will take up most of Aswan's power and more besides. Thermal power stations are being built to bridge the gap, but an even more exciting possibility exists.

The Qattara Depression Project

The Qattara Depression, in the desert west of the delta, is approximately 19 500 square kilometres in area and, at its deepest point, 134 metres below sea level. Plans are now under way to construct ten man-made lakes at differing levels in the depression. Water will fall from one to the other, passing through power stations as it goes and generating great amounts of electricity.

The water for this will be pumped from the Mediterranean and will also support fish farming in each lake, not to mention the build up of evaporated salts in the lowest areas of the depression which could perhaps support a new sodium salt-based chemical industry.

Egypt has a population problem; but with the help of friendly countries, the significant advances in agriculture and industry which were initiated by the great Aswan Dam will be expanded still further to help keep pace with it.

Group tasks

1 Discuss with your friends the validity of the suggested three basic requirements for industrial development. Do you agree? What other factors do you think are important? Ask your teacher to advise you and to collate your findings for the benefit of all.
2 Discuss with your friends the possibilities of industrial development in Nigeria and Mauretania.
3 Watch your newspapers for reports on industry in your own and other African countries. Record them carefully.

Question and answer session

1 How is coke for smelting prepared from coal? Much of coal is carbon but there are too many impurities in it for use in a blast furnace. They have to be removed as they would mix with the molten liquid. This is done by heating the coal in huge metal containers known as retorts or coke ovens. There is no air in these retorts and thick clouds of yellow gas leave the coal as well as a black liquid called tar. What is left is coke. It is almost pure carbon, very light in weight and burns with a very fierce heat. There are many of these retorts on the Rand.
2 How are diamonds processed? After excavating, the rock is crushed and then mixed with water. The diamonds and other heavy material sink. This mixture is then crushed with rotating steel balls but the diamonds, of course, are not damaged. The mixture is then washed over trays which are covered in thick grease. As diamonds are water repellent they stay dry and stick to the grease while the rest is washed away. They are then recovered by hand.

11 Minerals and mines

Africa's mineral wealth is renowned both for its abundance and its variety, with fresh discoveries being made year after year. In many countries, particularly those just beginning to recover from the problems of establishing stability after independence, the mineral wealth is only just beginning to be discovered. In the empty desert and semi-desert countries there is probably vast undiscovered wealth waiting to be exploited: so also in the rugged mountains and dense forests. In many countries a mining industry has been established for so long that in some cases another sort of problem has to be faced: the mineral is running out. What is going to take its place in an economy accustomed to the financial returns of mineral export? Almost all the major minerals are found in Africa in commercial quantities; and in some cases, like cobalt (about 42%), bauxite (34%) and copper (17%), she has a significant share of the world's known reserves. As a start, let us look at the metal which is most commonly used in the world today.

An open-cast copper mine at Chingola Notice the terraced method of excavation.

The iron ore mines at Ngwenya, Swaziland Notice the ore being deposited prior to transport to the coast.

Iron ore

Iron has, possibly, more uses than any other metal. It is one of the most common ores and is found in vast quantities in every continent. It is certainly found in almost every country in Africa.

Because it is so common the great industrial nations can afford to pick and choose which ones they will buy. They choose only the richest ores because the refining and transport costs are high. Any ore with less than 50% metal content is usually left in the ground unless there are other sound reasons for exploiting it. Sometimes production ceases because the quality has declined. Swaziland has to face this problem.

Not far from the Piggs Peak forest at Bomvu Ridge iron ore was discovered. It lies in that part of the mountains known as the Ngwenya Mountains and is mined by open-cast methods. Reserves, when mining started in 1964, were estimated at 30 million tonnes of quite high grade (63%) ore. The iron ore field was so remote that a long railway (217 kilometre) had to be built from Kadake near Ngwenya to the Mozambique border near Goba, where a railway to Maputo already existed. The ore was rich and the expense was well worth it.

Japan wanted the ore so three ships, each with an ore carrying capacity of 77 500 tonnes, were built and new ore loading facilities were built at Maputo harbour. By 1971 production had reached 2 700 000 tonnes a year by working a 24 hour, three shift day.

Economic production is now a struggle and Ngwenya is facing serious problems with hundreds of people facing unemployment in 1982. There are, in fact, a further 300 000 000 tonnes of 30 – 35% iron ore, but who will want it? The transport costs would be too great without primary smelting and a factory to do that would cost an enormous amount of money, and raise the price of the ore so high that only a nearby market would make it worthwhile. The Rand Industrial Region, see Chapter 10, is very near but there is plenty of very good iron ore nearer than that of Swaziland. Swaziland's economy needs something to replace the iron ore revenue. Perhaps the great increase in irrigated farming in the Low Veld will help.

Swaziland exports pineapples, sugar and beef products. Perhaps the answer lies on the land. The land, the soil; they are always there if they are treated carefully and with respect.

From the south-east let us now move north-westwards to the burning deserts of Mauretania. Mauretania is almost empty; practically all desert except for the south which is a semi-arid sahelian area with an annual rainfall of, perhaps, 300 mm. North of this sahelian zone the desert is all powerful except for the odd oasis like Tidjikja and Atas-Chingueti. Along the coast and north into what used to be Spanish Sahara the cold Canary Current helps reinforce the desert conditions as mentioned in the climate chapter.

Before 1960 livestock products, gum arabic, dried fish and salt formed Mauretania's tiny exports. Since then however there has been a change.

The Kedia D'Idjil mountains, near the old border with Spanish Sahara were found to be largely composed of *haematite*, a type of iron ore. F'Derik is the main source of the reserves which are estimated to be 150 million tonnes of at least 60% ore: well worth exploiting. As in Swaziland a railway had to be constucted; only this one was 650 kilometres long across the desert from Zouerate to Nouadhibou. It was built during the days when Spanish Sahara existed and so had to skirt that country's borders. A 1900 metre long tunnel even had to be dug because a steep escarpment touched the border. The problems were great. Barchans had to be stabilized by spraying with heavy oil because otherwise they would have overun the railways lines. Saline sands erode metal rails and sleepers which have to be renewed every six or seven years. Wind action can also undermine sleepers' foundations.

As in Swaziland mining is by open-cast methods and two ore trains a day make the 16 hour journey to the coast. The trains are 2 kilometres long, have 200 seventy-five tonne capacity wagons and are pulled by 4 diesel locomotives at an average speed of 60 kph.

The other major problem is that of water. There is none at F'Derik and Zouerate, and it has to be railed from the Bou Lanouar Wells to the mines' headquarters at Zouerate; where, incidentally, the rain in 1968 was the first for 13 years.

The ore terminal is at Port Central where a 12 metre deep harbour with a low tidal range allows

Fig. 117   Iron ore production in Mauretania

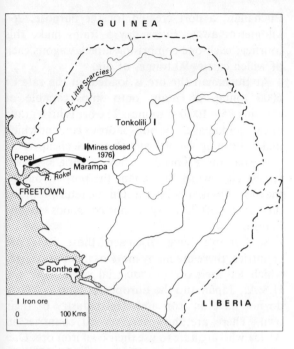

Fig. 118   Iron ore in Sierra Leone

and in 1981 Austria came to the rescue. She loaned $14 million to reopen the mines and guaranteed to buy 1 million tonnes of ore annually for 15 years. This trade begain in 1983, the proceeds of which will help pay off the loan.

There is plenty of iron ore elsewhere in Sierra Leone, particularly at Tonkolili where there are two types of ore. The surface ores are rich haematite but the really interesting ore lies below the haematite. This is magnetite and there is a possibility that the magnetite may be mined and not the haematite, which is more difficult to refine. Development is still awaited. Either a new railway or a pipeline which could carry crushed ore mixed with water must be built. The present world recession has so far prevented the expenditure of the necessary enormous amount of money.

Liberia is Sierra Leone's neighbour. She also has vast supplies of iron ore, even more than Sierra Leone, and is currently the world's tenth largest iron ore exporter. Her iron ore accounts

ships to come and go at any time. The loading equipment is modern and can put ore on a ship at the rate of 3000 tonnes an hour. Annual production rose to over 8 million tonnes with Britain, Western Europe and Japan taking most of it. But by 1983 production had fallen to 7 million tonnes because of a fall in orders and diminishing supplies. There is a new development at nearby Gwelb, starting in 1984, designed to maintain overall production at present levels. Unfortunately, because countries like Nigeria are now producing their own iron and steel the great industrial countries may find they have to reduce their production because of falling orders. They, in turn, will need less iron ore.

Because of her iron ore Mauretania's economy has been transformed and there is, at present, a favourable trade balance. See page 180. The question now arises, what happens if orders fall further or, in the long term, when the ore runs out?

One country where iron one mining HAD stopped was Sierra Leone. After 43 years, mining closed in 1976. Three thousand people lost their jobs. With their families this affected over 30 000 people all told. The mine closed because of a dispute between the owners and the state. There was still plenty of ore at the Marampa mines, see Fig. 118,

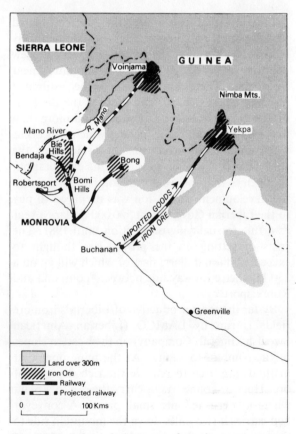

Fig. 119   Liberia's iron ore deposits

Loading iron ore at Buchanan

1 From where has this ore come and how did it get there?
2 How is the ore arriving on board?

for about 65% of her total export income and was worth 290 million dollars in 1979. This income is therefore tremendously important to the Liberian economy.

Liberia's total iron ore reserves were estimated to be about 1 billion tonnes of commercially worthwhile ore until the recent discovery of new deposits in the Wologisi Mountains near Voinjama. These have doubled the estimated reserves. These deposits and those in the Bie Hills on the border with Sierra Leone could more than make up for the loss of income which will occur when Bomi Hills iron runs out. However the colossal expense involved is delaying exploitation; so much so that the American company which has the development concession was prepared to pay to the Liberian Government 500 000 dollars a year as a fine for delaying production until 1981. The costs of setting up the project are thought to exceed 1 billion dollars, part of which will go on a 250 kilometre railway line between Voinjama and Robertsport.

By far the most productive of Liberia's iron ore fields is run by LAMCO (Liberian American Swedish Minerals Company) on the western slopes of the Nimba Mountains. At the mine open-cast methods are used to remove the rich deposits of ore. Huge 35 tonne trucks carry the ore to a plant where it is crushed into small pieces. A conveyor belt carries it two miles down the mountain side to the railhead at Yekepa where it is railed to

Buchanan, a port created for the purpose, 264 kilometres away. Every day 5 trains make this journey; each one comprising ninety wagons each of which carries 90 tonnes of ore.

At Buchanan the ore is loaded, at the rate of 6000 tonnes an hour, onto ships capable of carrying 75 – 100 000 tonnes. The ore is high grade at 65%; and has a low phosphorous content which makes refining simpler and therefore cheaper.

Yekpa, the railhead, is now Liberia's second largest city, while Buchanan, the port, is one of the most modern in Africa. On the return journey the trains often carry imported goods to the interior.

So far we have discussed those iron ore countries; there are many more of them of course, which sell their ore to industrial nations like the U.S.A., Japan and the European countries. They do not have an iron and steel industry of their own. There are, however, several countries in Africa who are able to use their own iron ore. One of these, the richest and most powerful of all at present, is South Africa. The ore mines at Thabazimbi supply the iron and steel industry of the Rand towns. See Chapter 10. She has no need to import other countries' ore. Another such country is Egypt whose iron ore mines near the Bahariya Oasis and Aswan supply the iron and steel works at the Cairo suburb of Helwan.

South of the Sahara, Africa's second greatest heavy industrial development has been and is taking place in Nigeria. Iron ore from Enugu and Itakpe near Lokoja supplies the new (1983) steel

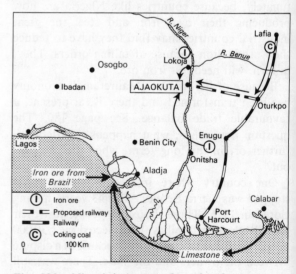

Fig. 120 Nigeria's iron and steel industry

A conveyor belt on the Nimba iron ore field

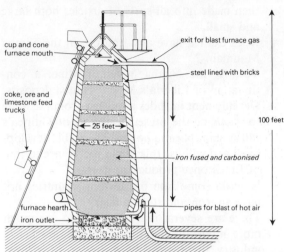

cup and cone
furnace mouth

coke, ore and
limestone feed
trucks

← 25 feet →

furnace hearth
iron outlet →

exit for blast furnace gas

steel lined with bricks

100 feet

iron fused and carbonised

pipes for blast of hot air

Fig. 121   A simplified section of a blast furnace

plant at Ajaokuta. Coal from Lafia and Enugu supplies the power. A new town and river port have also been built.

Three steel rolling mills at Oshogbo, Jos and Katsina are supplied by Ajaokuta and the new (1982) Aladja Steel Plant near Warri. See Figs. 120 and 135. Aladja is powered by 2 million cubic metres per hour of natural gas from nearby gas-oil fields. It uses Brazilian iron ore and 160 000 tonnes annually of collected Nigerian waste metal. The limestone comes from Calabar.

These projects will make Nigeria self sufficient in iron and steel production, although transport costs are colossal, e.g. Katsina is on the Niger border in Kaduna State. All this, together with the proposed new railway from Port Harcourt to Ajaokuta indicates a great leap forward in heavy industry based on our three principles. See page 139.

Tanzania also has the ingredients for an iron and steel industry with iron ore at Chunya and coal south of Tukuyu. The industry would be at Mbeya on the Tazara Railway and branch lines would feed the factory with the raw materials. The industry could supply Zambia, Mozambique, Kenya and Uganda with all its requirements. Once again expense is the problem.

Question and answer session

1   Does Swaziland have any other minerals?
    Yes. The first mineral exploited was chrysolite asbestos at the Havelock mine on the border with Transvaal. Communications were so bad that it had to be sent by a 20 kilometre aerial ropeway to Barberton in Transvaal. From there it is exported by way of Maputo. Soon, however, the asbestos could become too difficult, and thus too expensive to mine and production could cease. Two thousand men would lose their jobs and a hospital and school would fall into disuse.

    Swaziland also has a lot of coal which is found at Mpaka and Maloma. Reserves are thought to be over 300 million tonnes. The coal fires the power station at Stegi, but there is little other use for it at present.

2   Why is low grade iron ore more expensive to transport and process?
    Let us assume that iron ore costs X number of dollars per tonne to transport from A to B. 65% ore might yield 1300 kilograms of iron for the X number of dollars. 40% ore might only yield 800 kilograms of iron for the same price. Thus low grade ore is always more expensive: no matter which it is.

3   How is iron made?
    It is a fairly simple but very expensive process and large factories are needed which contain one or more blast furnaces. Finely ground iron ore, coke and limestone are poured into the blast furnace and the coke is lit. Hot air is blasted through the burning mixture and everything melts. The iron separates from the mixture, a process accelerated by the limestone, and sinks to the bottom of the blast furnace where it is run off into large containers. It is cooled into long bars which are

then made into all sorts of articles both large and small.

4 Does Guinea have any iron ore in the Nimba Mountains?

Yes. At the Nimba Mifergui Mine: a continuation of Liberia's Mount Nimba deposits. Development includes a railway from the mine to Kankan, the present railhead of Guinea's rail system. Nigeria has a share in this development and will use this ore in preference to that of Brazil once production starts.

5 Why do some iron ore owning countries not have an iron and steel industry?

There are several reasons, but two are much more important than the others. For any heavy industry there must be a source of power: preferably coking coal for iron and steel. Only Swaziland of the countries we have mentioned has coal. Secondly the iron has to be sold and so there must be a large market. Countries with small populations cannot meet this requirement. Not many countries have both these requirements *and* iron ore. Those that do are among the richest and most powerful in the world.

Copper

Copper is an extremely useful metal for several reasons: it does not break easily, it bends instead and is therefore easily moulded into many different shapes. Copper is a very good conductor of heat and an excellent conductor of electricity; in which industry its use is most widespread.

Once again it is the world's industrial nations who use most of it; and of these the U.S.A., U.S.S.R., and Canada produce their own. Of the rest, Europe and Japan are the major users and they buy almost all of Africa's copper: at a price which is, to all intents and purposes, decided by them.

The world's economy has been fluctuating widely in recent years; and so, therefore, have metal prices: copper in particular. In 1974 for instance it was £1400 a tonne, but in 1975 it dipped to well below £600: very much less than it costs to produce. Even in 1982, despite some increase in world prices, Africa's producers were still operating at a loss. To countries such as Zambia whose economies depend entirely on one major

commodity this is a disaster. In Zambia no new development has taken place. The Bwana Mkubwa mine actually faces closure. These grim facts only highlight the danger of monoproduction, whether it be a crop, a mineral or a manufactured product. If anything goes wrong there is no back up.

Africa depends a great deal on her copper exports. With the exception of oil it is her greatest export in terms of money; and of a 1974 total of nearly 1500 million tonnes it formed nearly 20% of the world's total output. Of this total Zambia (596 million tonnes) and Zaïre (460 million tonnes) produced about 79%. It is not surprising that Zambia and Zaïre are the world's second and third largest copper exporting countries behind Chile. Zaïre's share was due to be even greater when the

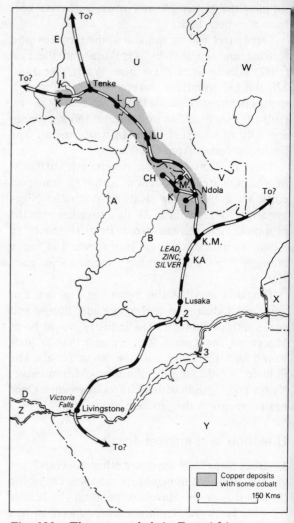

Fig. 122   *The copper belt in East Africa*

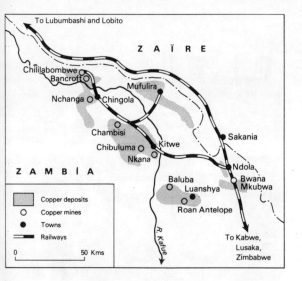

Fig. 123   Zambia's copper belt

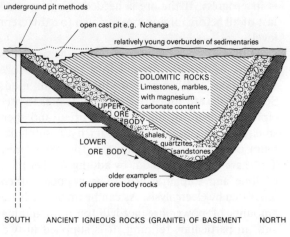

Fig. 124   How copper occurs in Zambia

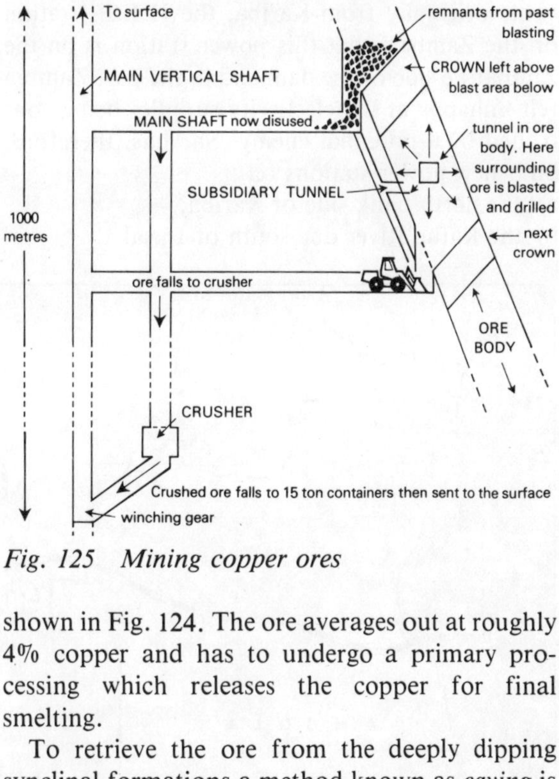

new development at Tenke-Fugurume came into production, but civil war in both Angola and Zaïre itself has seriously delayed it. When it does start the aims are for 130 000 tons of copper and 6500 tons of cobalt to be produced each year. Reserves are thought to exceed 51 million tons of 5.7% ore which could make Zaïre a much bigger producer than Zambia.

Other African countries which produce copper include Mauretania where production has temporarily ceased, as it has also at Kilembe in Uganda, because of the low world price. Of the smaller producers in Africa, South Africa has the largest production with large deposits at Messina on the border with Zimbabwe and at Phalaborwa, also in the Transvaal. As with iron ore South Africa uses all she produces. At present Zambia is the greatest producer in Africa as shown in Fig. 122.

Zambia's Copper Belt

Zambia's copper deposits are found in a 50 kilometre wide belt which extends from the Ndola-Luanshya area north-westwards to Bancroft. These deposits are continued into Zaïre through Lubumbashi, Likasi and almost to Le Marinel. The copper ores are found in folded marine sedimentary rocks deposited up to 600 million years ago, and they are mined at various centres throughout the belt. The ore lies in the synclinal part of the folds which means that both open-cast and underground mining methods are used as

Fig. 125   Mining copper ores

shown in Fig. 124. The ore averages out at roughly 4% copper and has to undergo a primary processing which releases the copper for final smelting.

To retrieve the ore from the deeply dipping synclinal formations a method known as *caving* is used as shown in Fig. 125. In this method horizontal shafts are dug from the main vertical shaft into the ore body. The ore is then blasted and falls into the horizontal shafts. Front loading machines take it and drop it into a vertical shaft at the bottom of which is a crusher. This reduces the size of the ore before it is sent to the surface. Back in the ore body a *crown* of ore is left above the blasting area to prevent total collapse while work

153

is in progress. If the ore is needed it is blown up last of all before mining moves down to a different level.

At the refineries both types of ore, the sulphides and the oxides, are ground to a powder before being mixed with water to form a thin mud. Sodium salts are added to the sulphide ores to precipitate copper sulphide. This is dried and then smelted. The addition of sodium hydrosulphide, palm oil and fuel oil precipitates the oxide ores. These are then leached out by adding further milk of lime and sulphuric acid. The copper is then separated by electrolysis. As can be imagined huge amounts of power are needed for both mining and, in particular, refining. It is supplied in two main forms, hydro electricity and coal.

Hydro electricity for the Zambian Copper Belt came originally from Kariba, the H.E.P. station on the Zambezi, but this power station is on the Zimbabwe side of the dam and in the past Zambia felt unhappy at her electricity supplies being controlled by a potential enemy. She has, therefore, built new power stations on

a) the north bank side of Kariba,

b) the Kafue River due south of Lusaka.

The refinery at Mufulira copper mine

Between them these dams supply the Copper Belt's needs. Some coal from Zambia's own coal mines at Mamba is also used, together with about 5000 tonnes of charcoal which is needed to control the oxygen content in the molten copper.

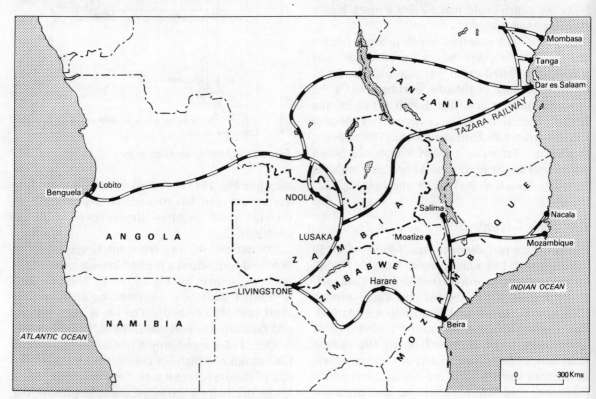

Fig. 126 Export routes for Zambian copper

Copper bars being loaded on to a Tanzanian truck

	1976	1977	1978	1979	1980	1981
Zambia	850	819	767	724	736	701
Zaire	444	453	473	400	459	505
South Africa	197	205	206	191	201	199
Zimbabwe	41	35	34	30	27	25
Namibia	43	49	38	42	39	39
Morocco	16	12	12	24	24	24
Other African countries	12	12	15	15	16	18
AFRICA TOTAL	1604	1585	1543	1424	1502	1511
WORLD TOTAL	6223	6315	6180	6721	6160	7149

Sources: *UN Monthly Bulletin of Statistics, June 1983*

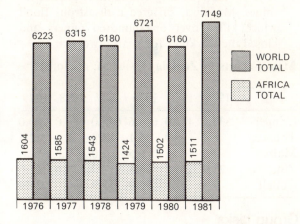

Fig. 127 Africa's copper production

Export problems: Landlocked!

Like several other countries in Africa, Zambia is landlocked. She is surrounded by other countries; has no coastline and, therefore, needs a reliable outlet to the sea for her copper exports; particularly as her whole economy depends on the money received for her copper. Thus political stability in the nearby countries is of great importance. For Zambia the quickest and most efficient outlet for her copper is through Zimbabwe to Beira in Mozambique. However, Zambia's contact with Rhodesia was very poor at times, and alternatives had to be found. Normally the Benguela railway could be used, but during the civil war this route was closed; stranding 26 000 tonnes of copper and 20 000 tonnes of lead and zinc. The road route to Salima in Malawi can be used only in the dry season. From there a little ore is railed to Beira and Nacala. Mombasa, the port best equipped to handle the copper, is used; but the route is complicated and so very little passes through Mombasa. At one stage, in the early 1970's, small amounts of ore were even sent by road to Mpulungu at the southern end of Lake Tanganyika, thence by boat to Kigoma and by rail to Dar es Salaam.

The problem was eased when the Tazara railway was opened in 1975. By the end of 1976 it was carrying a monthly 50 thousand tonnes of copper to the partially modernised port of Dar es Salaam and bringing the same amount of imports back to Zambia.

Sadly, although Zambia's import–export routes are partially eased, see Fig. 126, the world recession has struck. The price of copper has declined to such an extent that in 1982 Zambia earned nothing from her copper exports. Now tens of thousands of miners and their families live in the shadow of unemployment and Zambia has an unfavourable trade balance.

155

Question and answer session

1 Who owns Zambia's copper mines?
Zambia has a controlling interest in the mines which are partially owned and completely administered by ore company – Zambian Consolidated Copper Mines.

2 How does Zaïre export her copper?
Zaïre is worse off than Zambia. Eighty per cent of her export earnings come from copper and normally go to Lobito along the Benguela railway. She has no railway connection between the copper mines in Shaba province and her Atlantic Coast and has had to export through Port Elizabeth in South Africa via Zambia and Zimbabwe railways: a long and expensive journey.

3 What caused the large drop in Zambian copper exports in the year 1972?
One of Zambia's largest and most productive mines, Mufulira, suffered a disastrous flood which killed over one hundred miners and closed the workings for nearly two years.

Main Exports of Zambia (Kwachas: millions)

	1974	1975	1976	1977	1978	1979
Copper	838.0	472.0	688.6	645.0	598.0	900.0
Tobacco	6.2	5.0	5.1	5.8	3.4	2.5
Maize	7.3	1.4	0.5	2.0	7.8	n.a.
Zinc	25.2	20.3	26.5	17.9	17.6	27.0
Cobalt	7.9	7.1	15.9	15.3	36.6	25.4

Group tasks

1 Study your atlas and Fig. 123. Make a large copy of Fig. 122 and on it
a) Label *ALL* the towns which are shown by letters and also insert those which are named.
b) Label rivers A – E.
c) Label dams 1 – 3 and the two largest lakes shown.
d) Put a destination wherever it says To?
e) Label all the countries shown T – Z.
f) Indicate on your map the transmission of electricity from Victoria Falls, and two other places, to the Zambian Copper Belt.
2 Express the information shown in the twin bar graphs in Fig. 127 in some other graphic way.
3 i) Make a list of 6 very large and 6 very small articles in which iron or steel is used. Are any of them produced in your country?

ii) Discuss amongst your friends the biggest articles you know which are made completely from copper. What conclusions do you draw regarding the uses of copper?
4 Try to account for the drop in copper exports from Zambia in 1975, shown in the table above.

Bauxite

As mentioned earlier Africa has roughly 34% of the world's known reserves of bauxite and most of this is found in several countries in West Africa. Bauxite is derived from rocks which have a high alumina content and is the product of many thousands of years of chemical weathering, in areas which have experienced alternating heavy rainy seasons and very dry seasons. The result is a red clay-type rock which is rich in aluminium hydroxide and from which, after a very expensive process, is obtained aluminium.

Aluminium is certainly one of the most useful metals known to man and, because of this, is in great demand. It is a quite strong metal, although it can easily be moulded into different shapes; but its great value lies in the fact that it is very light. It can however be made as strong as steel by the addition of small quanities of other metals and is thus of great value in the aero-space industry.

The major problem with bauxite is that while it can be fairly easily reduced to alumina, (the chalky white powdery substance achieved by primary smelting) it needs colossal amounts of electricity for the final production of aluminium itself. So far the only electricity that has been cheap enough to do this is hydro electricity, so that even if a bauxite producing country wanted to produce its own aluminium it could not afford to do so: quite apart from the other considerations that we have already looked at. As a result of this, most bauxite producing countries have to export their ore to industrial nations which have large supplies of electricity. These include Canada (the Kitimat Project in northern British Columbia), Norway, West Germany, France and Switzerland. One African country at least produces both bauxite and aluminium. This country is Ghana whose Volta Dam generates enough electricity to do this.

First let us look at those countries which produce bauxite.

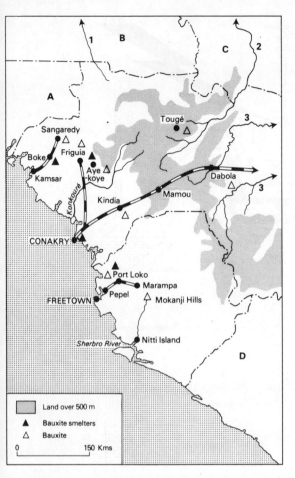

Fig. 128   The bauxite deposits of Guinea and Sierra Leone

Guinea

It seems as if most of western Guinea, from the Futa Djallon highlands to the coast, has wide and varied deposits of this red-brown clay. Certainly there are bauxite mines dotted all over the region, and it is no surprise to learn that, with an estimated 8 billion tonnes, Guinea has about two thirds of the world's known bauxite. Her production at present is about 12 million tonnes of ore a year.

One of Guinea's earliest bauxite mines is found at Friguia (formerly Fria) shown on Fig. 128 where one of the most modern processing plants in the world carries out primary smelting to produce alumina. In 1978 it produced 700 000 tonnes and it was hoped to double this within a year or two. Two further smelters at Boke and Conakry also process bauxite, much of which is sent to the aluminium smelter at Tema in Ghana.

Conakry exports much of Guinea's ore and will expand greatly to cope with exports from the new fields; one already in production at Kindia and partially owned by the Russians, and two more are to be developed at Dabola (Yugoslav finance) and Tougé (Swiss finance).

However, Kamsar is the main bauxite port, the largest bauxite exporting port in the world with an annual capacity of 9 million tonnes. It is linked by a 153 kilometre railway to Sangaredy, a huge open-cast mine in which Guinea has a 65% share. Unfortunately this ore does not undergo primary smelting as yet. A new field at Ayekoye, with a reserve of 500 million tonnes, is shortly to be started and will necessitate that the capacity of both Kamsar and the railway be greatly increased. It is hoped that this project will produce 2 million tonnes of alumina and, ultimately, 150 000 tonnes of finished aluminium. Before aluminium can be produced however, a new dam on the Konkouré River will have to be built, for which help is already being sought from the World Bank. In Guinea we have another example of a country in the throes of mono-production; but at least Guinea does have, at present, most of the world's supply: unlike Mauretania and Swaziland with their iron ore.

Sierra Leone

Another West African country which has considerable deposits of bauxite is Sierra Leone, where, at the Mokanji Hills mine, a Swiss owned company produces at least 700 000 tonnes a year. Huge mechanical shovels at this open-cast mine load a continuous stream of large lorries which take it by road to Nitti Island on the Sherbro River from where it is exported.

This is a complicated operation as from Nitti Island barges have to take the ore to a deep water loading anchorage 32 kilometres out in the Sherbro. An even bigger mine is to be opened at Port Loko. It is expected that reserves will be about 1 000 000 tonnes with a 47% aluminium content, which should yield about 1 million tonnes of alumina for thirty years or more. An alumina plant will also be built at Port Loko and this, together will easy mining conditions and low transport costs — the old iron ore port of Pepel and its railways are near at hand — should offset the lower than usual ore quality.

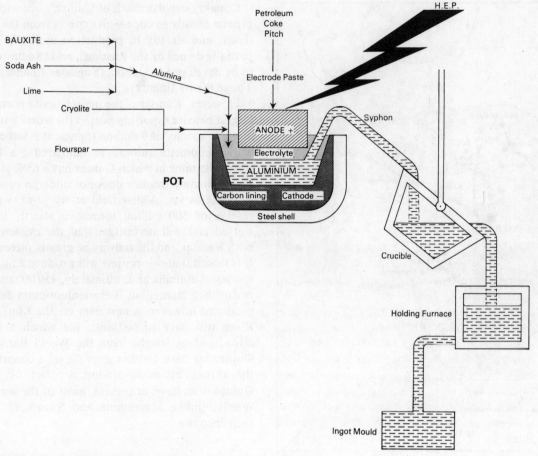

Fig. 129   How aluminium is made

The VALCO smelter at Tema, Ghana

Ghana

Ghana has large deposits of bauxite but only the Awaso deposits are being exploited so far. Although there is an aluminium factory at Tema, Ghana does not at present produce alumina to be used there: it comes from countries like Guinea, and even Cameroon, whose smelter at Edea produces alumina from local bauxite. However, the new power station at Kpong and a new railway to the Aya deposits could change this. The aluminium smelter located in Fig. 115 also introduced a fifth pot-line in 1978 thus increasing capacity. See also p. 107.

Question and answer session

1   How is aluminium made?
    It takes 4 tonnes of bauxite to yield 2 tonnes of alumina after the primary smelting. This two tonnes of alumina is added to about three

An open-cast bauxite mine in Ghana

tonnes of other material and, when finished, produces one tonne of aluminium. The alumina is reduced to aluminium metal in an electrolytic cell called a *pot*. These pots are installed in long lines called pot lines. The molten liquid of the electrolyte dissolves the alumina powder and conducts the electricity which is introduced by the anode. About 16 000 kilowatt hours of power (equal to about 13 tonnes of coal) is needed to make 1 tonne of aluminium. As the electric charge passes into the mixture the alumina is separated into aluminium and oxygen. The aluminium sinks to the bottom and is syphoned off (Fig. 129).

Before it is cast into ingots, alloying ingredients are added if needed.

Another way of looking at the power used is that the amount of electricity needed to make one tonne of aluminium would supply a normal African household's total electricity for something like 5 years. Only a power project the size of the Volta Dam could produce enough, cheaply enough, to do it.

2   What is rutile?

It is the source of titanium oxide, an extremely important additive in paint manufacture; and also the ore of the metal titanium which is so important in the aero-space industry because of its light weight, tremendous heat resistance and non corrosive qualities.

It is hoped Sierra Leone will be the world's largest producer at 150 000 tonnes a year; all of which will be exported through Freetown.

Tin

Without this remarkable metal our lives would not be so well ordered, particularly in Africa where refrigeration is not always possible. It has one extremely important use as a major ingredient used in making tin cans, millions and millions of which are used every day and then just thrown away.

Rolling aluminium at Port Harcourt

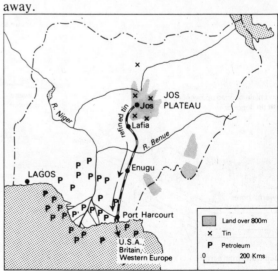

Fig. 130   Nigeria's tin and oil deposits

159

Tin mining, Jos, Nigeria Compare this with Fig. 131

Only a few African countries have discovered recoverable deposits of tin so far. Zimbabwe mines tin at Wankie, not far from the coal mines there. There are quite large deposits at Kyerwa near Bukoba in north-west Tanzania, while in Shaba province of Zaïre it is mined at Bukama close to the River Lualaba about 150 kilometres north of Tenke.

It is Nigeria who, at present, has the largest deposits of tin ore or *cassiterite* as it is called. It is found on the Jos (Bauchi) Plateau: a great granite topped range of hills and mountains, halfway between the River Benue and Kano as shown in Fig. 130. On the Plateau the cassiterite deposits are found in old, dry river valleys and old river-borne alluvial gravels probably deposited millions of years ago.

There are various ways of excavating the ore, most of which in Nigeria, involve open-cast methods of one sort or another. Small deposits are often mined by hand by large numbers of people. They use ground sluicing to recover the cassiterite. In this method they dig shallow channels across the deposits, fill them with water and throw shovel fulls of cassiterite into the moving water. The heavy cassiterite sinks and the waste is washed away, leaving the cassiterite to be recovered at intervals. This is too inefficient for large scale recovery so other methods have to be used. One is by 'gravel pumping' in which the ore is washed loose by blasts of water from powerful hoses shown in Fig. 131. The resulting mixture, a watery muddy mass, is pumped over a series of trays. The heavy cassiterite stays on the trays while the rest washes away.

For really large and deep deposits the ore is also excavated by massive mechanical grabs which take out huge loads with each grab. The ore is then dumped into *draglines* which are narrow, stepped, walled channels through which water is passed. Once again the waste is washed away and the cassiterite is left behind on the floor of the dragline.

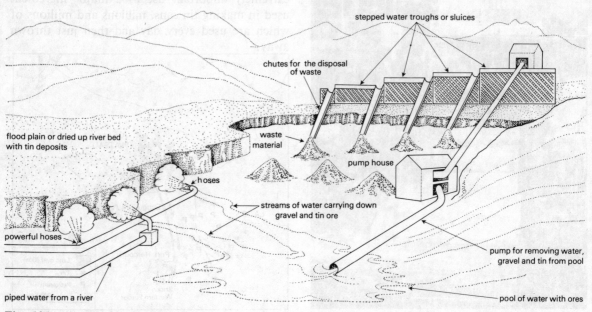

Fig. 131 A gravel pump tin mine

160

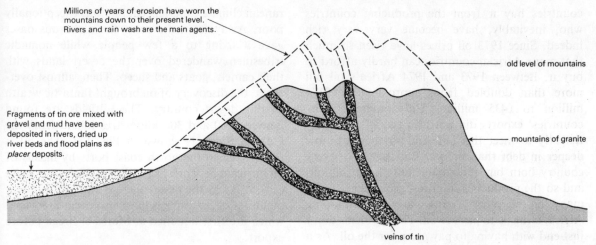

Millions of years of erosion have worn the mountains down to their present level. Rivers and rain wash are the main agents.

Fragments of tin ore mixed with gravel and mud have been deposited in rivers, dried up river beds and flood plains as *placer* deposits.

old level of mountains

mountains of granite

veins of tin

Fig. 132   How tin occurs

After the cassiterite is collected it goes to the separating or dressing mills where smelting and refining take place. Along with the tin ore, about 80% of which is tin itself, another very rare ore is also found. This is columbite which has to be separated from the cassiterite before smelting. It is the ore of the metal niobium and Nigeria is the world's largest producer of this valuable metal which is used in alloys for surgical instruments and aero-space engines. After smelting the tin is cooled into blocks of pure metal known as ingots and then railed to Port Harcourt for export to countries with large tin plate industries like USA, Britain and other West European countries.

Unfortunately, cassiterite is, like all other minerals, a wasting asset; and Nigeria's deposits are likely to be exhausted by the end of the century. However, this will not be the disaster to Nigeria that mine exhaustion is to some countries. She is extremely fortunate in having many other minerals, huge oil deposits, a developing heavy industry and an agricultural industry which is remarkable in its variety. Her Green Revolution is also well under way: something which is extremely difficult in a country like Mauretania. Monoproduction should not be a problem in Nigeria. See p. 162.

Question and answer session

1   Where did the cassiterite come from?
It is thought to have occurred in long veins in the granite rocks of Jos: placed there by subterranean volcanic activity and explained in Fig. 132. Then, as millions of years of erosion took place, it was washed away with other materials. Being heavy it tended to gather together in the deposits we know today.

2   How is tin plate made?
Iron is needed for this as tin on its own isn't strong enough. First of all the iron is rolled into very thin sheets which are then dipped into molten (melted or liquid) tin. A tin layer of tin is left on the iron sheet, which is then dipped in very hot palm oil to ensure an even spread of tin over the iron. When it cools tin plate is the result. It is very light, easily bent into any shape and keeps food perfectly for very long periods until it is wanted.

N.B. Another, more modern, method is to coat the iron sheet by electro-plating. This dispenses with the need for palm oil.

Petroleum: a mixed blessing for Africa

The economy of the modern world is almost completely dependant on petroleum, and without it the world would grind to a halt. Air, sea, road and rail transport depend almost entirely upon it; and so, until alternatives have been found, all countries which need it, must have it.

Natural gas is often found with oil deposits and is becoming an increasingly important cooking fuel in modern Africa; particularly where electricity supplies are short. The big petroleum companies bring both oil and gas to those African countries without their own deposits. These countries buy it from the producing countries who, inevitably, have become very very rich indeed. Since 1973 oil prices have risen so much that many African countries can hardly afford to buy it. Between 1973 and 1974 Africa's oil bill more than doubled from approximately £174 million to £435 million. Unfortunately many countries' exports did not also rise in price sufficiently to meet this bill, and so they are now deeper in debt than before. But they, like every country both big and small, must have this oil; and so the producing countries grow richer while many of the others, particularly in developing Africa, struggle to pay for oil. The problems don't just end with having to pay more for the oil. As a result of oil prices goods cost more to produce and transport, so inevitably the ordinary family has to pay more for the goods it buys.

Africa produces quite a lot of oil. More is found every year, particularly south of the Sahara. Africa now produces well over 10% of the world's supply but consumes only about 3%. First let us look at some of the North African producers.

Libya

Libya was just a desert country with only a narrow fringe of coastline which permitted settled agriculture, because only there was a form of Mediter-

ranean climate experienced. She was exceptionally poor. Away from the coast the numerous oases gave a living to a few people while nomadic tribesmen wandered over the desert lands with their camels, goats and sheep. Then, almost overnight, the discovery of oil brought fantastic wealth to this desert country. The oilfields are found between 200 and 300 kilometres inland from the Gulf of Sidra as shown in Fig. 133. The oil is transferred to the north coast ports by means of an intricate network of pipelines which were quite easy to lay as the desert there is fairly flat. Great quantites of natural gas have also been discovered which are first liquefied at Marsa el Brega before export.

Libyan oil is very popular indeed with the purchasing countries as it is sulphur free, and this is a great asset in industrial countries with a polution problem. A further factor which gave added impetus to oil exploration in Libya was the closure of the Suez Canal in 1967. Transport costs between Libya and North West Europe were immeasurably cheaper than those of the Middle East fields around the Persian Gulf. Along with the oil, vast quantities of artesian water were also discovered as mentioned earlier.

To a country which only has 1% of its land surface fit for agriculture because of the desert conditions, this was a wonderful bonus; and

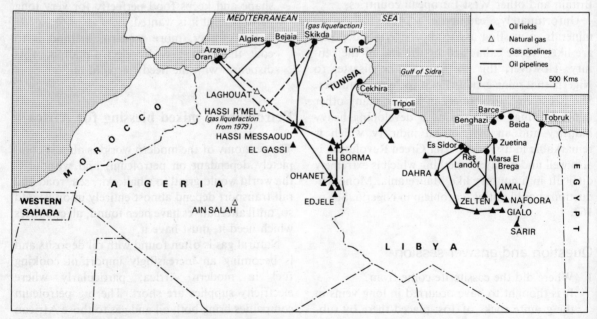

Fig. 133 Oil production in Libya and Algeria

Crude Oil Production in Libya

	Million metric tonnes
1968	125.0
1970	159.3
1972	105.0
1974	73.4
1976	93.4
1978	98.7
1979	99.2

already the desert is becoming productive around the oilfields. For agriculture in general however, the oil industry has brought a major problem: that of a diminished labour supply. The high wages now offered on the oilfields and in allied industries in the towns, have attracted many people away from the land. Although this is hardly surprising it is a great pity, as the oil cannot last forever: less than thirty years in fact, unless more is discovered. Libya's output has dropped a little between 1972 and 1978 because of this consideration, as she wishes to make it last as long as possible as shown in the figures above.

Algeria

Algeria is Libya's western neighbour and has been almost as fortunate as Libya with oil discoveries.

Since 1955, when oil and natural gas were first discovered, progress has been very rapid indeed. Like Libya, Algeria can only use a fraction of the oil she produces and so she sells it: mostly to France. However, she has made sure that many industries are developed to benefit her people. For instance, most of her oil is refined in Algeria before it is exported. There are pipeline-supplied refineries at Oran, Arzew, Algiers and Skikda as well as the terminal at Bejaja, from where crude oil is exported. There is a gas liquefaction plant at Skikda where gas is cooled into liquid form before export. In 1979 the new liquefaction plant at Hassi

An oil well at Hassi Messaoud in Algeria

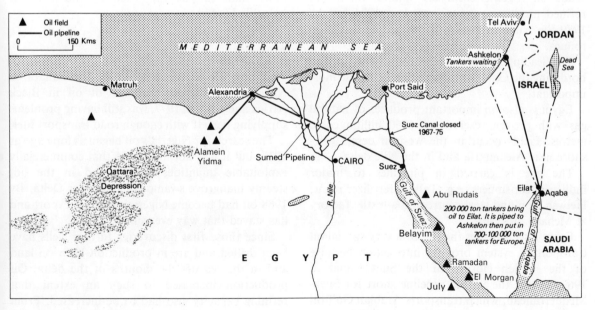

Fig. 134   Oil in Egypt

R'Mel came on stream. In association with Japan this plant, 550 kilometres south of Algiers, will produce over 2 million tonnes of liquid gas, and 8 million tonnes of condensate every year. Her gas is also taking an ever increasing share in supplying the power for Algeria's rapidly developing industries of which fertilisers, petrochemicals, cement, steel, mechanical and motor engineering, plastics, textiles and those based on forest products are just a few.

Algeria is rather more fortunate than many of her desert oil producing neighbours in that she is able to have a much wider economic base. Twelve per cent of her land is, or could be, productive; she has iron ore as well. So with wise use of the oil revenues there will be other economic activities to take the oil's place when it is finished.

Egypt

Egypt is Libya's eastern neighbour and also has oil deposits. The earliest discoveries of oil were made in the delta region and later wells were drilled in the western desert, however today over 80% of the oil produced comes from fields around or under the Gulf of Suez. An indication of the progress of oil exploration and exploitation can be seen in the production figures for 1974 when crude petroleum output was 7.5 million tonnes compared with 32.5 million tonnes in 1981. Only 2.3 million tonnes of crude oil together with 0.9 million tonnes of refined products were exported in 1974 but by 1980 the crude exports had reached 15.7 million tonnes.

The leading producers are four fields in and bordering the Gulf, with Ramadan being the most important.

Egypt is also an important producer of natural gas with proven' reserves of 1060 billion cubic metres. Fields occur in the western desert, offshore near Alexandria and in the Nile delta.

The gas is carried in pipelines to major industrial consumers, e.g. Talkha fertilizer plant, Helwan iron and steel centre and a textile factory at Mehalla el Kubra.

Egypt also provides the site of a very special oil transporting system brought into action because of the sudden closure of the Suez Canal in 1967. This is the Sumed pipeline short for Suez-Mediterranean, which transports Arabian Gulf oil brought by huge tankers from countries like Iran,

Drilling for oil in the Niger delta
What natural vegetation might those remnants in the foreground come from?

Arabia, Bahrain and Kuwait. The oil is pumped to Alexandria where it is reloaded onto tankers for ports in the Mediterranean countries (Fig. 134).

Egypt has the biggest population of all North Africa's countries at approximately 41 million. It is increasing by about 3% a year so she has welcomed the oil discoveries. Her population will be about 70 million at the end of the century: far more than can be supported by the available irrigable lands.

Nigeria

And now let us move south of the Sahara to Nigeria; the biggest producer of oil in Black Africa and who, in 1977, was still having problems supplying herself with enough road transport fuel.

The search for Nigeria's oil began as long ago as 1937, but it was not until 1956 that commercially exploitable quantities were found in the hot steamy mangrove swamps of the Niger Delta. By 1968 oil had become Nigeria's leading export and has stayed that way ever since.

Since those first discoveries further wells have been drilled and are in production both on land and in the sea off the mouths of the delta. Oil production increased to such an extent that refining capacity also had to be increased. From 650 000 barrels a day in 1972 when she became a member of OPEC, her production peaked at over 2 million barrels per day in the late seventies. With Japanese help at least 5 more wells were discovered by 1980.

By 1978 Nigeria was the eighth largest oil producer in the world and, with her huge oil income, began many new industrial projects. Nearly a million people entered Nigeria from Ghana, many illegally, to take jobs in the booming Nigerian economy.

Then world recession struck, countries bought less oil and Nigeria's production dropped to 700 000 barrels per day. Refineries at Port Harcourt, Warri and Kaduna worked short time. So also did the gas liquifaction plant at Warri. Nigeria's oil income was cut severely.

By 1982 production was back to 1.3 million barrels per day, but the price of oil was so low that Nigeria's income remained unable to cope with all the projects that had been started or planned.

Because of the race for oil, agriculture was neglected as the people left the land for well paid jobs in oil based industry and projects. The population grew to over 80 million and from being a palm oil exporter Nigeria became an importer in 1982. The same happened with soya beans and groundnuts. Rice imports rose to 15 million Naira, meat imports to 4 million, frozen and canned fish cost 145 million, cereal flour 165 million and dairy products 136 million. All these have to be paid for in precious foreign exchange, yet Nigeria was once self sufficient. A heavy price indeed for neglecting the most valuable resource of all: land. And so the Green Revolution started in 1980.

Nigeria is not the only oil producer in Black Africa. Gabon's offshore wells produced 130 000 barrels per day in 1982. The income helps finance her new railway. She looks able to maintain this output for at least another 10 years. And after it is finished . . .?

Angola's production in 1982 was 122 000 barrels per day, most of it from offshore Cabinda. New wells have been discovered south of the Zaïre estuary and look certain to double her production. They are in shallow water and cheap to operate, being near Zaïre's small field in the same area. Angola probably has the greatest potential of all of Atlantic Africa's new producers; particularly, when peace comes to Namibia and Angola's southern coasts can be safely explored and developed.

Ivory Coast's new wells produced 9000 barrels

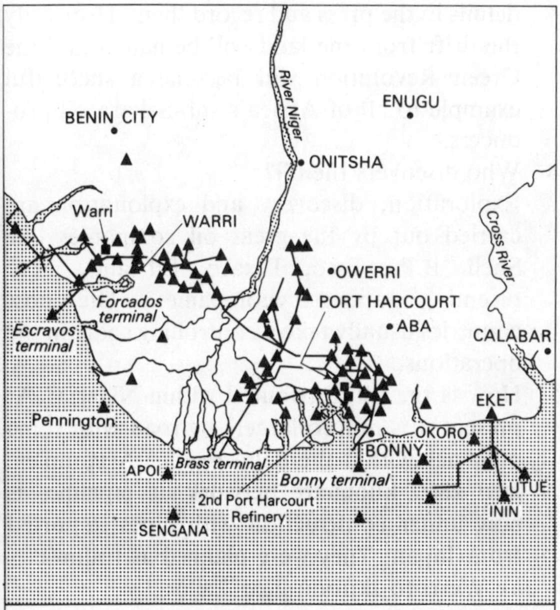

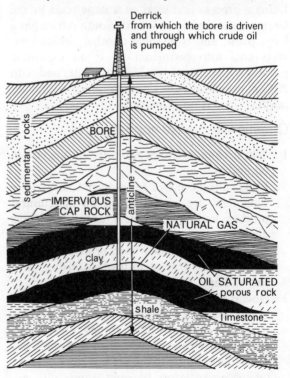

Fig. 135 Nigerian oil fields

Fig. 136 Section through a typical oil field

165

per day in 1982 but new offshore wells south-west of Abidjan will greatly increase this.

Finally, the most exciting recent discoveries were made in Sudan in 1980 in the White Nile Valley. See Fig. 83. Official resources are put at 200 – 300 million barrels but far more is confidently predicted in areas along the Chad Border (is there a connection with severe unrest along Sudan's borders with Libya and Chad?), the Sudd region around Wan and Rombek (see Fig. 83) and offshore in the Red Sea. At present a twin pipeline is proposed from the main field at Unity to Swakin, where a new port is being built. Completion is hoped for in 1985 – 86. The Unity oil is very thick and viscous and needs to be more fluid before it will flow easily. One pipeline will carry a liquid dilutant to the oil field to mix with the oil. It will then be piped back to the coast for export. This will bring in much needed foreign exchange to Africa's biggest country, whose vast mineral and agricultural potential suffers from lack of money.

Finally South Africa, the richest country in the whole of Africa has, so far, no oil reserves of her own. She is totally dependent on outside supplies for nearly 80% of her needs. The other 25%? Using a process first used on a large scale by the Germans during World War II, South Africa has a large plant, and is building another, which converts coal into petroleum. It is an expensive process but she considers it worthwhile; and with 20% of the world's known coal reserves within her borders there is no shortage of raw material.

Question and answer session

1   Which countries were worst hit by the rise in oil prices?
Principally those, like Tanzania or Chad, whose economies are largely based on agricultural products and exports. Prices for farm products did not rise enough to offset the oil price rise. Others, like Zambia whose principal export, copper, fell in price instead of rising, also suffered and are still suffering badly.

2   How is oil formed?
It takes millions of years to form and develops from the remains of living things. The sea has millions of creatures, both fish and shellfish, which die and sink to the sea bed to be covered by successive layers of sand, mud, silt, etc. Over the millions of years the fleshy parts of

the dead marine creatures mix with the fine rock materials and the layers become thicker and thicker. Slowly the organic remains become, under great pressure, a greasy, gassy, oily mass which is lighter than water and so slowly, very slowly, soaks upward through the rock layers until it is stopped by a dense, hard rock layer.

The Earth is never still as we have seen, and sometimes the layers of rock become folded. Eventually the oils and gasses rise further, to collect in the anticlinal parts of the fold as shown in Fig. 136; and it is these anticlinal collections that the drillers have to find.

3   What is the Green Revolution?
It was started by President Shagari with the aim of making Nigeria self sufficient in food by 1985. Eleven River Basin Authorities have been formed. Dams and water works will be built. Irrigation canals will be extended over 275 000 hectares and farms will be increasingly mechanised. Subsidies, grants and credit will be extended to farmers. 600 kilometres of feeder roads and 140 earth dams will be built, 85 wells and 215 bore holes sunk.

An emergency has occurred and Nigeria is meeting it with her own money plus a huge loan from the World Bank. Watch for further details in the press and record them. Hopefully the drift from the land will be halted and the Green Revolution will become a successful example to all of Africa's sub-Sahara oil producers.

4   Who discovers the oil?
Exploration, discovery and exploitation are carried out by the great oil companies like Shell, B.P., Esso, Texaco, Elf and, more recently, Japanese companies. The host countries usually take a controlling share in the operations.

5   How is the oil distributed within Nigeria? At present it is moved largely by road with some pipelines within the delta region. A complete new 2800 kilometre network of pipelines is now under construction with pipes imported from Japan. They were planned as follows:
a) Warri to Ikirodu near Lagos
b) Ikorodu to Lagos and district
c) Warri to the new refinery at Kaduna
d) Kaduna to various points in the north-east
e) Port Harcourt to the east.

12 Population and the location of settlement

In some parts of Africa there are vast numbers of people whilst in others there are very few. In certain places human beings are so congested, that housing facilities are inadequate and people have to sleep in houses made of cardboard boxes and covered with polythene sheeting. There are other regions of Africa where space is almost limitless yet no one lives there.

Overcrowding in Cairo In conditions like these disease can easily spread.

Part of the Namib Desert

The reasons for the rather disjointed distribution and density of Africa's population are many; but, in the main, they are found to be connected with the immediate environment. An abundance, or otherwise, of the earth's life-giving riches, makes the difference between whether or not a place or a region is settled. Some people refer to this as the natural environment, others refer to the natural conditions. We could just simply refer to our surroundings, which are made up of the earth on which we live and the various physical influences which affect it. There are high mountain peaks and ranges surrounded by broad and rolling plains, with rivers, both big and small, and the deserts. There are the low lying swamps, and the highest mountain valleys in which can sometimes be seen glaciers. Our surroundings include our climate: the amount of rain which falls, how reliable it is or if there is any rain at all: how hot or cold it is, how many hot months, how many cool months or if it is hot or cold all the time.

The natural vegetation helps make up our surroundings: the trees, the grass, the bushes or, perhaps, the lack of them. The soil also is a very important factor in the make up of our surroundings: how fertile or infertile it is and how hard or easy it is to cultivate.

All of these factors contribute to the natural environment, the natural conditions or, quite simply, our surroundings; and the degree to which a place, an area, a region or country is populated is almost entirely dependent on the way nature has arranged them.

Sometimes the natural conditions make life easy for humans, in which case people move to such areas. Sometimes natural conditions make life difficult, thus ensuring that few if any people are encouraged to build a life in them. However, it is possible to alter the existing natural conditions in certain circumstances; although the difficulties and expense involved restrict great changes.

Examples of man's attempts at fighting against and changing these conditions are numerous in Africa. All the big dams have achieved this, the great irrigation schemes are doing it as well. Arguably nowhere in Africa is there more of a fight to alter the environment than in the Sudan. Nevertheless, all these attempts are insignificant by comparison to the great whole of Africa. Their very expense, frequently colossal, is a limiting factor; and we are inevitably driven back to the basic fact that certain areas are more heavily populated than others.

The reasons why people live where they do all point towards one simple fact; which is that people congregate and settle where nature's gifts are in the greatest profusion. The basic requirements of man are food and water. If these are available then man can manage his other needs like shelter and clothing and the development of a social order. The more of nature's gifts that are available the greater will be the concentration of people. This is as true of Africa as it is anywhere else in the world. You only have to look at the photographs in this book for evidence of that. Where then do people live in Africa? And why?

Read again the section on Aswan and the River Nile. Look at Fig. 92 which shows population densities of Egypt. You will see that almost all of Egypt's population is concentrated in a narrow strip either side of the Nile and in the delta lands. The reason for this is not hard to find when one studies the climate graphs for places like Cairo, Aswan or Wadi Halfa in Sudan. See the example in Fig. 137. Along this strip of the Nile no more than 25 mm of rain falls in any one year. Desert conditions

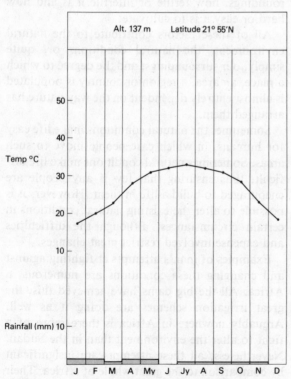

Fig. 137 Climate graph for Wadi Halfa

prevail everywhere away from the life giving Nile and so it is not surprising that the vast majority of Egypt's, and Sudan's population are concentrated along this narrow strip of fertile, well watered valley land which used to be annually rejuvenated by the Nile's floods: donations as it were, from East Africa and Ethiopia. For the last 1700 kilometres of its northward journey the Nile flows through the desert: a great elongated green snake of a valley in a desert sea of yellows, browns and greys. It is hardly surprising that the Nile Valley has been densely settled by man for many thousands of years, long before the time of Christ. Apart from scattered oases there was nowhere else in the region which afforded water to drink and the means of growing food.

Let us stay with the Nile, moving southwards to the Sudd, where the Bahr el Jebel (Nile) from the south meets with the hundreds of rivers, both big and small, which flow from all directions between west and the south-east, to form the White Nile at Malakal. During the flood season this area becomes a huge 20 000 square kilometres swamp interspersed with a few islands of drier, higher land. There are great expanses of floating papyrus and thick forest lines the rivers. Because of this seasonal flooding which brings swamp conditions, few people can live there. There is too much water and the soils are water-logged, making cultivation impossible.

Let us look now at Ethiopia — a land of extremes. There are many mountains, some of them flat topped, with great narrow valleys carved deeply through them. Large areas of the Ethiopian Highlands, as they are called, are over 3000 metres high, as shown in Fig. 139. There are smaller areas of 4000 metres high where temperatures are always cold, and the nights in particular are below freezing. Little or nothing will grow at that altitude because temperatures are too low and the heavy rainfall of the lower slopes is not available. Roads are difficult to build and railways almost impossible.

The natural conditions of the highlands of Ethiopia are thus not conducive to great concentrations of people. Similarly in the Danakil Desert, which is below sea level and often extremely hot, the conditions again make it impossible for many people to live here.

Somalia is another example, almost completely made up of semi-desert. Cultivation is impossible

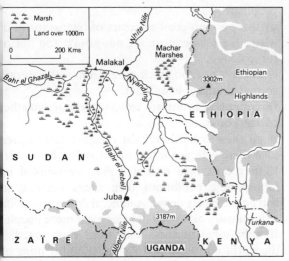

Fig. 138   The Sudd region

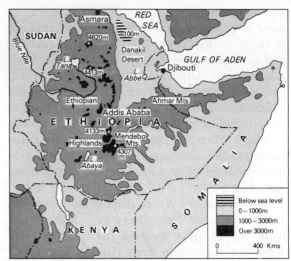

Fig. 139   Relief features of Ethiopia

and only a difficult semi-nomadic pastoralism exists as a way of life. The land just cannot support more than a few people. It was in Somalia that the natural conditions became so hostile in the early 1970's, that thousands of drought stricken nomads and their cattle died. Somalia became the scene of one of the greatest mass rescues of all time, planned by the Somalis them-

Part of the Ethiopian Highlands   Notice the different levels.

selves and executed with Russian aircraft. As a result 110 000 nomads have been resettled in the fertile lower valleys of the Juba and Shebelle rivers and along the coasts. They are now being taught to cultivate and to fish: skills which will take several years to perfect. These new areas can only support so many people however; and it is inevitable that most of the great wide empty plains of Somalia will remain that way, hostile and unwelcoming to man.

Look at Fig. 139 again, at those areas between 1000 – 3000 metres. In some of these areas there are quite a lot of people as there is plenty of rain and many rivers whose valleys are fertile and warm for much of the year. The people there can grow food and graze their cattle; but because the land is hilly and very steep, movement is not easy. However some of the higher valleys can be very cold and windy at times, and so great concentrations of people have not developed.

Wide expanses of Africa have fertile, cultivable soils. The southern lands of Mali, Upper Volta, Niger and Chad are examples. These lands which, as yet, have been unable to support large numbers of people, are the lands of the sahel, that halfway region between the desert and the savanna where the rains have recently been failing with resulting starvation of people and cattle. Areas like these cannot support many people even though the soils are fertile, because the rains are unreliable and there are too few rivers as a result. Once again the environment is winning its battle against people. The battle isn't quite so intense in the long grass savanna areas, even though the dry seasons can be quite long. The rains are a little more reliable and in rather greater amounts. Life is easier for men and animals because they know that at least some rain will fall. Although there isn't much, it *will* come. Nevertheless life can still be hard in the savanna lands where the tsetse fly is often a danger. Soil erosion is a problem and the rains can be short. When this happens people can become hungry and so, once again, we cannot expect great concentrations of people except along the rivers and streams.

In some parts of Africa there is too much rain and temperatures are always very high. When these two elements combine the result is thick dense rain forest with many rivers and steaming swamps. In conditions like these mosquitoes and other harmful insects abound. The anopheles mosquito thrives in hot damp swampy conditions where pools of water lie undisturbed for days on end. The **malaria** that they bring to humans **kills and hospitalises more people in Africa than any other known disease or illness**. The mosquito can be fought but not with complete success; and so we find that swampy rain forest conditions deter dense settlement. There are thousands of square kilometres of this sort of forest in northern Zaïre where the tiny pygmy leads a life devoted to hunting for, and collecting, his food.

In a few limited areas of Africa the natural conditions are almost perfect for human settlement. There are rich, fertile soils in a climate where temperatures range between 16°C – 27°C and rainfall is plentiful and reliable at between 1000 mm and 2000 mm. The land is fairly flat which makes cultivation reasonably simple, there are many rivers and streams for water and fishing and movement over the whole area is relatively easy. There are not many places like this in Africa, so wherever they occur there is always a heavy concentration of settlement as shown in Fig. 140.

Let us now summarise the points made so far and then they can be easily remembered. They are important and should always be considered when population matters are discussed. Most people tend to concentrate where

a) there is a sufficiency of water, whether it comes from rivers or rain or both.

b) soils are rich, fertile and easily cultivated.

c) the land is not too mountainous so that movement becomes difficult and cultivation presents problems.

d) there are no great extremes of temperatures o where the temperature are not always too hot o too cold.

e) there is not too much water from rivers or rain so that drainage is difficult.

f) communications are reasonably easy, whethe by land or water.

If all these conditions exist together in one are then there will be a large concentration of people If they exist in a restricted area surrounded by inhospitable conditions then the concentration will be extremely dense. A mineral discovery which aids industry as well, will bring even more people. If only some of these conditions exist together there will not be so many people; and if none of these conditions exist then few, if any, people will be able to settle there.

Some people have to live in a harsh and unkind environment, largely because they have had in the past little or no choice in the matter. The Pygmies of the rain forest were probably driven there by larger more warlike people. The same thing happened to the Bushmen who now cling precariously to their lives in the depths of the Kalahari. Both groups moved to these places because there was nowhere else to go which wasn't wanted by other bigger, stronger and more numerous people.

Town and city development

Hundreds of thousands of people, millions in some cases, live in towns and cities throughout the African continent. They do not grow food because there is no land on which to grow it. All the available land has been taken up by housing, office blocks, industrial sites, shops, roads and railway stations. They do not collect water from a well. Instead they turn on a tap. Only a very small percentage of Africa's people live in towns and cities: about 10% in fact. This is not really very surprising as Africa is not a continent of great urban development, by virtue of the fact that her greatest natural resource is her land. She is an agricultural continent, a continent of farms both big and small, a continent of rangelands and plantations, of deserts, lakes and mountains.

There are however several great cities and a greater number of large towns and ports; all of which are gradually becoming larger in popula-

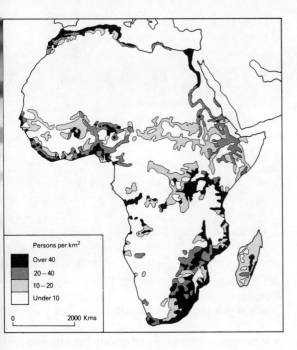

Fig. 140 Population distribution in Africa

tion, more widespread in area and more comprehensive in function. There are many reasons why towns and cities develop in certain places and the ones which grow to be the biggest are the ones which have the most reasons for being there.

Many towns in Africa, as elsewhere, have grown near rivers. This is only natural because rivers provide drinking water. In the beginning crops can grow on the nearby fertile valley soils and there is ample water for irrigation. Perhaps a town grows at an easy place for crossing the river: a ford where the water is shallow. At such a place merchants would wait to sell goods to travellers. Shops would be a natural development, followed by houses. Small service industries develop such as vehicle repair, weapon repair and manufacture and simple foods are made ready for sale.

People also use rivers as routeways. Their valleys form an easy route through steep hilly land, and across mountains. It is inevitable that travellers along river valleys meet with those crossing the rivers and that they should discuss matters of mutual interest, trade with each other and generally spend a little time before moving on. Inevitably a town at such a place grows larger, if only because it becomes a collecting and distributive centre for the surrounding farm lands. The bigger the river, the fewer the crossing places on it

and the richer the surrounding farm land, the bigger and more important will be the towns at the meeting places. Examples include Bamako on the River Niger in Mali, Kisangani on the River Lualaba and, to a smaller extent, Livingstone on the River Zambezi. Roads often develop along river valleys and these make the river towns even more important as there are then two means of transport. Bamako is a case in point.

While towns which grow up at crossing places on a river often do not become exceptionally large and important, those which grow at the meeting place or confluence of two big rivers almost always do. Khartoum is one such town, a town so big that it qualifies as being referred to as a city.

Khartoum as shown in Fig. 141 has grown up at the meeting place of three great river routes: the Nile from the north, the White Nile from the south and the Blue Nile from the south-east. It became the great crossing place for east-west travel, the pilgrimage route of devout Muslims on their way to and from Mecca, and so there was an east-west land route crossing the point at which three river routes met. Khartoum had to become important and the development of more road and rail routes through it only added to its importance. Another consideration in the old days was defence. Natural defensive barriers made it that much easier to hold off attackers. In times of war people tend to rush to a safe place, one that is easily defended. What more suitable place than Khartoum, defended on two sides of a triangle by wide and deep rivers.

Look again at the Nile. We have seen already that its valley and its delta were the only places in this arid land where people could live. Naturally they travelled up and down the whole valley so what more suitable place for a town and meeting place than Cairo at the head of that great delta; the point where so many distributaries shown in Fig. 92 branched out on their way to the sea. It was natural that Cairo should become the meeting place of the Nile Valley routeway and movements from east and west.

Other towns develop and grow at the end or beginning of a long overland route like those which cross the Sahara. Having crossed this burning wasteland, travellers wanted food, shelter and rest; after which they wanted to trade. In this way towns like Kano, Niamey and Ndjamena grew.

Many long routeways end at a coast, at an inlet,

171

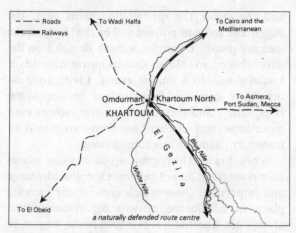

Fig. 141   Sketch map to show the situation of Khartoum

Khartoum
Which way is the camera facing?

a river mouth or sheltered bay. Ships called to trade, buying goods from inland and selling goods from other lands. Gradually a port develops: a meeting place of land and sea routes. Alexandria is one such port where Mediterranean sea traffic met the traffic of the Nile Valley. Built on a bar which encloses a large deltaic lagoon, Alexandria provides easy access to Cairo and the Nile and has done so for several thousands of years.

The Portuguese explored Africa's coasts in the 15th century; finally reaching East Africa where they chose several fine harbours to act as shelter for their ships and trading centres. The finest of all these harbours was Mombasa, the island commanding the entrance to two fine deep water havens, sheltered from strong winds and storms, and being an island, easy to defend. When the Arabs superceded the Portuguese, Mombasa grew in importance as their slave traders and merchants roamed far into East Africa's interior. Later a railway was built; and as a result, Mombasa has gone from strength to strength, becoming the export outlet for a huge area.

For a port to become really great and important however, something more than just a good harbour is necessary. All ports trade to a certain extent; they all have an import and export traffic, but it is the size and the scope of the traffic which counts. For a port to become great there must be a rich and large area behind it with fertile farmlands and a great many people. There should be minerals, preferably those which support a large industry in the big towns of the interior. As a result of this large and prosperous interior, ships

will bring a wide variety of goods for sale and will buy and take away other goods.

It is this *hinterland* of a port which decides its potential for development, that area over which the port holds influence, that area which the port helps by its activities. It handles that area's imports and exports. Thus, as we have seen in an earlier chapter, Mombasa's hinterland extends to Zambia's copper, Rwanda's tea and coffee exports and her petroleum imports, all of Uganda's surface trade and, before very long, some of Sudan's. Mombasa is an important port.

The greatest ports are those which not only have an extensive hinterland but which also control sea routes as well. Cape Town comes into this category having been settled by the Dutch as a transit port, a place where ships could take on stores and water for a continued journey to the Far Eastern colonies. It was the last great port of call before crossing the Indian Ocean. A country which can control Cape Town in these modern days can also control the sea ways in both directions. Therefore, apart from commerce, Cape Town has an important strategic position as well as being a base for exploration and research in the Antarctic.

There is another aspect to ports in that if, because of a large hinterland, they become very large, they will also develop industries based on their activities as ports. Oil refining is one such industry; flour milling is another. Industries such

Kilindini harbour Mombasa Notice the numerous railway lines and warehouses which line the dockside. What evidence is there that cargo handling is highly mechanised?
In which general direction was the camera facing?

as these are known as *port industries* and develop because it is convenient or most economical that certain commodities should be processed as soon as they arrive rather than be transported inland in their original state.

Wherever there is industry people will be attracted to it: particularly in Africa now that industrialisation is becoming very important. So much of Africa is inhospitable, so many of her people are poor. Industries provide good wages for the people who work in them; and with these wages food can be bought. So people drift to the towns, many of which are capital cities, hoping to obtain one of these well paid jobs. Unfortunately there are always too many people for too few jobs; and so while populations of cities grow, an increasing number of people are housed in substandard conditions: reluctant to return to what they consider is an even harsher, possibly landless, life in the rural areas.

Some towns start to develop for no other reason than that minerals are found. Probably the most famous of all towns of this type is Johannesburg. As we have seen coal, gold and iron ore were found in quick succession as a result of which her industries developed. All routes soon led to Johannesburg: road, rail and air links from all directions of the compass and from all the major

countries of the world. It has even become the nucleus of a satellite system of towns which have now combined to form one great *conurbation*. All this because of local coal, gold and iron ore.

Other towns grow because they are multi-route centres, places where all modes of transport converge. Some of the finest examples of this are Port Harcourt, or Brazzaville and Kinshasa. All the rivers of Zaïre and most of those in Congo and Central African Republic lead to Kinshasa and Brazzaville. River transport is tremendously important in these countries and Kinshasa and Brazzaville have become collecting and distributive centres as a result: particularly Kinshasa where road, rail, river and air traffic meet. Even sea traffic is near at hand at Matadi, Boma and Banana. These three ports supply Kinshasa, while Kinshasa supplies the hinterland and vice versa. They complement and grow with each other.

Finally, a few towns start for no other reason than the need for a new town. Such a town is Abuja, the new capital of Nigeria which will take 20 years to complete. The 8000 square kilometres Federal Capital Territory in which it stands lies to the north of the confluence of the Niger and Benue. See your atlas. The climate is good, the scenery is beautiful, it is central, easily accessible and with plenty of development land. The population density is very low and, and very important, it is ethnically neutral. Planning will ensure a city of wide roads and plenty of space: quite unlike the congested conurbation of Lagos: the old capital.

Group tasks

1 Make a list, with examples, of the various ways by which man tries to improve his environment here in Africa.
2 Select three densely populated regions in Africa: for example the Niger Valley between Gao and Niamey. Try to explain why this density is so by referring to the points made on page 167.
3 Study Fig. 141. Draw similar sketch maps for Cairo, Livingstone, Alexandria, Bamako and Kisangani.
4 Discuss with your teacher those industries which are best situated at a port.
5 Make a careful study of the historical geography of your country's capital city. Make a list of points which were important in assisting its growth.

13 Transport and trade

Transport and trade are inextricably connected. Without transport there can be no trade even between villages and towns, let alone between countries. Without transport there can be little or no agricultural or industrial growth. Without transport minerals stay in the ground, potentially rich farmland remains undeveloped and, a good point many would say, great forest lands remain undisturbed.

In order to develop economically, countries must be able to export their produce. This produce must be transported to the point of export or the market so roads and railways are vitally important. If the goods are being exported the port must have good loading and unloading facilities and plenty of space for railways to reach the quaysides and for storage facilities. If the produce is very valuable it can come and go by air, so roads and railways are needed to reach the airport. An airport itself is needed, large enough to take heavy cargo planes. In addition an efficient riverine and lake transport system, if available, is very welcome.

It is plain that for any country, let alone developing countries, an efficient transport infrastructure is absolutely essential. A brief look at a few examples will serve to illustrate these points.

The Gambia

The Gambia had no natural borders, as can be seen on your atlas map. Her borders were fixed by Britain and France in 1889. About 480 kilometres long and varying in width, but on average 50 kilometres wide: a thin, narrow twisting country whose borders follow the shape of the main meanders of the Gambia River. The country was surrounded completely by Senegal except for her coastline, opening onto the Atlantic Ocean. It was thus logical that by one means or another Francophone Senegal and Anglophone Gambia would unite. This occurred, peacefully, on February 1st 1982 when the Confederation of Senegambia came into being. Part of the ria coast of West Africa, the Gambia River and its estuary form a major trunk route from one end of the country to the other; from the border in the east to the huge sheltered estuary in the west, commanded by the capital Banjul.

Not only was Gambia the smallest nation in Africa, she was also the poorest in terms of natural resources. All she had was her soil, a climate ideal for producing tropical continental crops like groundnuts and cotton, and the finest natural waterway in Africa: the wide and deep Gambia River which is used by ocean going cargo ships as far upstream as Kaur, 240 kilometres from the coast.

The Gambia was a classic example of a country whose total economy, and total trade, depends on one product only: groundnuts. They formed 95% of her exports, and for a few months each year the

A groundnut sailing cutter on the Gambia River
Name the months between which this photograph might have been taken.

river was alive with canoes, barges and cargo ships; and then there was nothing until the next season's harvest.

The river transport system is run by an unwieldy combination consisting of the Gambia River Transport Company which is made up of 4 French and 2 British groundnut trading companies, the Gambia Oilseed Marketing Board and the Gambia Co-operative Union. It operates at a loss even though the freight rate from Basse to Banjul is almost the same as that from Kaur to Liverpool in England. At each up-country buying station there can be as many as 5 licensed buying agents, each with his own store. Each agent's nuts must be kept separate until they are officially delivered to the G.O.M.B. stations at Kaur or Banjul. Thus the G.R.T. must send separate boats for each agent's load. Some agents' trading posts are found on tiny, narrow twisting creeks which are difficult to navigate. Thus it is difficult to put together modern barge trains even though a few are available.

Handling facilities at many river ports are slow and inefficient and barges have to be dropped off at each little station; to be loaded and picked up again by the pulling tug as it returns from upriver. At Kaur and Banjul there are long queues for unloading after a journey which takes at least ten days, but should only take seven.

Apart from barge trains, big sailing canoes, built to a 400 year old design, operate almost as efficiently; each carrying a 200 tonne load. They can carry, in fact, the same load as some of the modern Gambia river barges which cost £40 – 50 000. The worst and most inescapable inefficiency is that the G.R.T. fleet can only operate for about 5 months of the year: in the dry season, when the nuts are harvested, moved and exported. For the remaining 6 – 7 months the fleet lies idle, but still swallows up thousands of pounds a month in costs such as wages and maintenance, which have to be paid. If a wet season crop could be introduced the fleet could then be used throughout the year. At least there is a cash crop and the river transport system does see that it gets exported eventually.

The Tanzam (Tazara) Railway

This is the great new railway shown in Fig. 142 which runs from Kapiri Mposhi in Zambia to Dar es Salaam. It was opened in October 1975. Built by the Chinese it has 147 stations, 310 bridges and 21 tunnels. It highlights two of the problems which have to be solved in modern Africa: that of the landlocked countries and that of remote areas.

The two main reasons for the Tazara were to open up the Southern Highlands of Tanzania and, equally important, to help with Zambia's export

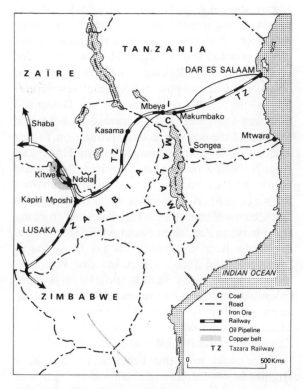

Fig. 142   The Tazara Railway

A station on the Tazara Railway

175

trade of copper and imports of manufactured goods. On and off, throughout the last 15 years, Zambia's trade routes to the sea have been blocked. Tazara was meant to partially solve this problem. Indeed by 1977 Dar es Salaam was handling over 40% of Zambia's trade. There have been problems. Dar es Salaam's handling facilities were not up to the swift throughput of Zambia's trade as well as trade from Rwanda, Burundi and Zaïre. Kapiri Mposhi railhead sometimes took a month to turn round wagons and send them back. Short of foreign exchange, Zambia sometimes cannot pay Tazara and Dar es Salaam Harbour Board for services rendered. Rolling stock keeps breaking down, the Chinese powered locomotives weren't up to the challenge presented by Tanzania's Southern Highlands and frequently broke down. Because of the delays and uncertainties on Tazara and on other routes through Mozambique and Angola, both Zambia and Zaire have had to use South African routes. Apart from Zimbabwe Railways and S.A.R. another route used is called the 'Zeerust Connection'. This is a road trucking route between Zeerust in South Africa (just across the border from Gaborone) through Botswana to Kazungula and then to Lusaka. See Fig. 148. Gradually, however, Tazara and Dar es Salaam delays are becoming shorter and efficiency is being improved. This is vital because of civil unrest in Mozambique, Malawi and Angola in which Zambia's alternative rail routes are situated.

There could be further benefits. The Southern Highlands of Tanzania are almost as rich and

fertile as those of Kenya. Rainfall is good and reliable, the volcanic soils very fertile and capable of growing large quantities of coffee, tea, maize, bananas, pyrethrum, and wheat as well as supporting a large dairy farming industry but previously transport was bad. The main roads were poor and feeder roads were worse. There were no railways and the whole region was inaccessible to a major port. Now however, the position is very different as there is a new tarmac main road and the Tazara as well. Agriculture could now expand because trade will be possible. That is not all. There are large coal and iron ore deposits either side of Mbeya, to the north (iron ore) and south (coal). With the aid of the Chinese, rail links to these deposits will bring the coal and iron together near Mbeya for the establishment of a basic iron and steel industry: the only one in Black Africa for over 1000 kilometres in any direction. What is more there are titanium deposits near Mbeya. This is a metal used in the production of high class steels.

The Tazara also goes through the Kilomebero Valley in Tanzania. Already plans are in action to increase its already great sugar and rice areas, reclaiming more land from the mosquito-infected swamps. 3500 hectares of new farmlands, many new villages and new feeder roads to the railway will be developed in phase two of the project.

Not only will Tanzania approach self sufficiency in sugar and rice, but there will be more jobs and prosperity. The Tazara could even bring more work to Mtwara on the south coast and prosperity to the Songea and Njombe regions of southern Tanzania when the modernised road link is opened between Sorgea and the Tazara at Makumbako.

The Tazara is now helping another all but landlocked country: Zaïre, who, despite her size, has a coastline of less than 50 kilometres. The Tazara now carries Zaïre's small soda ash and salt exports and, once Dar es Salaam can handle it, will take her copper as well.

Zaïre is a potential economic giant. But apart from Shaba province and the alluvial diamonds of Tshikapa and Mbuji Mayi her mineral resources are virtually untapped. One major reason is the absence of an efficient transport system. Products from the interior have to undergo at least five changes, in a disjointed pattern of rail and river transport if the goal is Kinshasa, Matadi and

Copper bars being loaded at Dar es Salaam

Banana. No wonder Zaïre is concentrating on the completion of the Banana – Alatadi – Kinshasa – Ilebo railway: The Trans Zaïre, Fig. 85. So far all Zaïre railways are, and have been, aimed at the exploitation of wasting assets: her minerals for export to Japan and the West. Hopefully a by-product of mineral exploitation will be feeder roads to help agriculture and food production. As the century draws to a close any country which has food enough to export to other countries could become very wealthy indeed. In the meantime the Tazara is helping out with Zaïre's mineral export problems.

The Trans-Cameroon Railway

This is another railway which has been of great help to more than one country. Designed to link the north of Cameroon with the port, it reached Ngaoundéré in the early 1970's and already has led to much agricultural development. Cattle of the Adamawa highlands are transported to the coast markets and escape the tsetse ridden trek through the southern lands. Cocoa and coffee production has expanded, so also has cotton and groundnut production in the tropical continental northlands. The railway has also assisted in the exploitation of

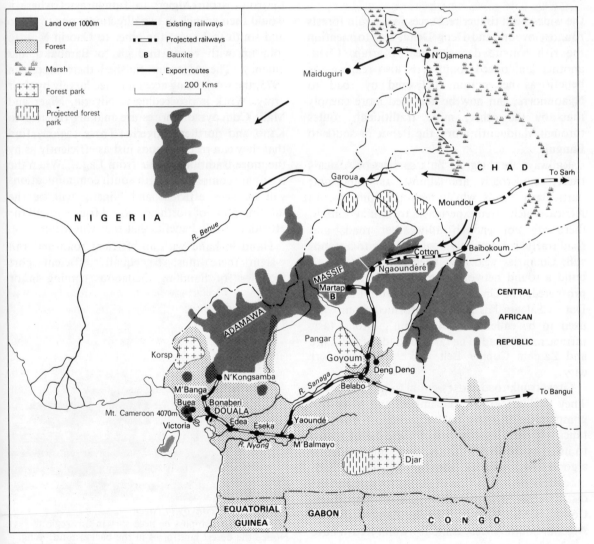

Fig. 143   The Trans-Cameroon Railway

177

The old main road from Tanzania to Zambia
What is the problem here?

the widespread timber resources in the rain forests round Goyoum and Deng Deng, not to mention the rich bauxite deposits near Martap. Chad, another landlocked country, is also reaping the benefit as her cotton, delivered by road to Ngaoundéré, can now be exported more cheaply than by the other, more traditional, routes through Maiduguri, along the Benue or south to Bangui.

Railways are the great bulk carriers of Africa's trade, but roads are almost as important; particularly roads which feed the railways. In Africa, which often experiences torrential rainfall, there are not enough all-weather roads and road traffic is frequently bogged down to a standstill. Countries who have been able to afford to build a sound network of roads have inevitably prospered. The Great North Road from Lusaka to Dar es Salaam has been transformed from what used to be called the 'Hell Run', into a fast, tarmac motor road. The tarmac roads of the Zaïre and Zambia Copper Belt make road transport easy.

Great trunk roads are essential to every country. They facilitate export and import and make fast communication easy; but to increase the importance and carrying capacity of these major roads, to use them really efficiently, there must again be a good feeder network from the agricultural lands on either side. Collection of goods for sale and the distribution of imports is just as important. Countries like Nigeria, Ghana, Zambia, Egypt, Algeria, South Africa, Zimbabwe and Kenya have worked hard on this aspect.

Nigeria is also the terminus (or the beginning) of two great road projects; they are the Trans-Sahara Highway and the east-west Trans-Africa Highway from Nairobi. Hundreds of kilometres of these roads will pass through Nigeria; but expense is the great problem. Much of the Trans-Africa will pass through sparsely populated regions of Zaïre, the Central African Republic and Cameroon, none of whom can afford their share of the expenses at present. But it will be completed and international trade between African countries will benefit as well as the export trade of the landlocked countries.

The other great route, the Trans-Sahara, is being built from both north and south. It was finally decided in 1970, with U.N. advice, to take the route from Algiers to Tamanrasset where it would then branch in two directions: one to Kano and south to Lagos, the other to Gao in Mali to join up with roads through to Bambako and Niamey. The Algerians finished their stretch in 1975, the work being accomplished largely by their army. Work is proceeding in Nigeria, Niger and Mali. Convoys of lorries are making the trip to Kano and northern Nigeria. These regions find that they can receive goods just as efficiently as by the more traditional route from Lagos. When the roads are completed, north-south communications will be very efficient and Nigeria will be the meeting place of north and east Africa with all the attendant trade benefits that that will mean.

Hand in hand with an efficient road and rail system there must be equally efficient port facilities for handling the goods coming in or

A desert lorry convoy in Niger
Why would a compass be necessary in this region?
Notice the desert landforms in the background. What are they called?

178

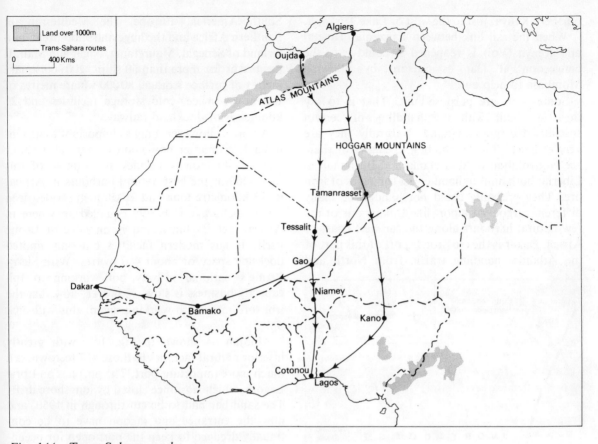

Fig. 144   Trans-Sahara roads

going out. Africa's 37 000 kilometre coastline does not have very many good natural harbours, but despite this she now has a large number of man-made ones which work with varying degrees of efficiency. The greatest problems tend to occur when ports of fairly long standing have to cope with a sudden and heavy increase in traffic. For instance, had Dar es Salaam been able to grow at leisure with a gradually increasing freight from the Tazara all would have been well. This was not possible. All Zambia's outlets were suddenly closed and only the Tazara was left. The problems were too great and there were many protracted delays. It was not until 1983 that Dar es Salaam was able to get on top of the problem. Mombasa, on the other hand, has had no such sudden demands, although she did handle some Zambian cargo in the seventies. Nevertheless Mombasa is one of the busiest and best organised ports along the whole eastern African coast. It handles all Uganda's trade as well as that of Kenya, Rwanda and Burundi. Huge cranes,

recently installed, and many kilometres of railways line the dockside and deal with incoming and outgoing cargo. Before long her hinterland will extend into southern Sudan with the completion of the new road to Juba through

A tanker anchored off the Bonny oil terminal

179

northern Kenya, just to the west of Lake Turkana.

When the rail link between Tanzania (Taveta) and Kenya (Voi) is reopened it could ease the congestion at Dar es Salaam by allowing Mombasa to help out.

Some ports are purpose-built. That is to say they are built with the handling of certain specialised cargoes in mind. Naturally they are very efficient. Two of the best examples of these are Nouadhibou in Mauretania and Buchanan in Liberia: both built to handle vast tonnages of iron ore. They probably could not handle the many different cargoes of a port like Dakar; one of the few natural harbours along the far west coast of Africa. Dakar is the crossroads port of this part of the Atlantic, handling traffic from North and South America, Europe, the Mediterranean, Southern Africa and the huge and widespread hinterland of Senegal, Mauretania, Niger and Mali. It has berths for more than 60 ships, 200 000 square metres of surface storage, 80 000 square metres of warehouse space, cold storage facilities and 21 kilometres of dockland railway.

A port, is however, only as important as its hinterland, no matter how good its natural harbour may be. Freetown provides an example of this fact. One of the best natural harbours in Africa, its 13 kilometre long and $2\frac{1}{2}$ kilometre wide, deep water anchorage is hardly equalled anywhere in Africa. Yet its hinterland is only Sierra Leone itself. It has modern facilities but only limited dockside space of about 400 metres. With Sierra Leone's national railway not working to full capacity business is slow. However, now that the iron ore mines are working again, this will pick up.

Abidjan as shown in Fig. 145, with greatly inferior natural facilities to those of Freetown, is a much more important port. The port lies on Ebrie Lagoon which was once closed by longshore drift. The sand bar had to be cut through in 1950, and now the entrance and lagoon have to be continually dredged to keep the port open for ocean-going vessels. The reason for Abidjan's importance is that, not only is Ivory Coast's economy rapidly expanding, it is the only outlet for the large cattle and cotton trade of the Upper Volta savanna lands. Abidjan's hinterland is thus Upper Volta as well as Ivory Coast; and a railway extends along almost the whole route, through Bouake, Bobo Dioulasso to Ouagadougou. Roads converge on Ouagadougou from all directions and provide the railway with a great deal of business. Apart from the normal facilities there are special ones for bananas, oil tankers and fishing, as well as for timber.

Apapa, the port for Lagos, is another port built on a lagoon whose opening has to be dredged regularly to maintain depth. The same problem occurs with all the Niger delta ports, which is not surprising when one considers the nature of deltaic expansion. Apapa was another port which was thrown out of gear by sudden increased traffic. Her traffic trebled between 1974 and 1975. Oil exports rose and so imports rose dramatically with them, much of them extremely heavy duty machinery and construction equipment for which

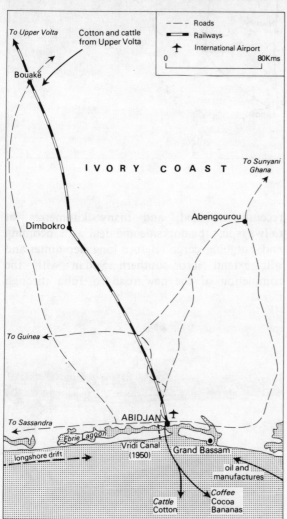

Fig. 145   Sketch map to show the situation of Abidjan

A container being loaded for Apapa in Nigeria

there were no suitable cranes for unloading. As many as 400 vessels queued to unload there. These delays were the reason for increased trans-Saharan traffic to northern Nigeria. Goods were delivered more quickly that way and only now are conditions improving. By 1980 Apapa had six new berths; Port Harcourt, Warri and Calabar had four each. However Nigeria's economy is expanding at such a rate that even these improvements may well not be sufficient. But at least the administrative move to Abuja, the new capital, will ease the city's congestion.

We have mentioned just a few of Africa's ports. There are many more. For almost all of them, facilities for the growing container trade are being installed as quickly as possible. In this method cargo is enclosed in great rectangular crates which
a) use space on the ship much more efficiently,
b) make unloading and loading much easier and quicker,
c) cut down on loss from theft.
Lorries and railway wagons line up at the dockside and receive their load straight from the crane. It is bolted to the vehicle floor and moves off straight away to its destination. The opposite occurs with container cargo being delivered to the docks.

These then are the problems which occur with ports which serve rapidly developing countries. Traffic has so far seemed to outpace handling facilities. Problems such as these do not happen at old established ports like Cape Town, Durban and Dakar. As the years have passed their facilities

Durban harbour
What problem has to be overcome in this harbour?
How is it achieved?
What important feature can be seen in the foreground?

have been able to expand at a planned rate.

Cape Town is exposed to winter gales from the north-west but a system of breakwaters and separate docks now protects ships from these.

Durban is the largest port south of the Equator. Built on a lagoon with a shallow sand-filled entrance, it has to be dredged regularly to be kept open. The reason for Durban's greatness is its rich hinterland which includes the great industrial region of the Rand to which it is connected by efficient road and rail links. Its specialist facilities are very comprehensive. It can load coal on to ships at 2000 tonnes per hour and pipelines facilitate the movement of oil. South Africa's manganese is loaded by conveyor belt on to waiting ships while the huge grain elevator can store 42 000 tonnes. There are cooling facilities for the export of citrus and deciduous fruits and the sugar loading terminal is one of the biggest in the world. Her ship repair and maintenance facilities are the equal of anything in the southern hemisphere.

So it is plain that, together with a comprehensive road and rail system, it is essential that the ports they serve are able to cope with the traffic and cargo that is brought to them. For the developing ports there is a very fortunate aspect to current problems. All modernisation really will be modern, with the latest and most up-to-date facilities for both specialist and general cargo.

So far we have looked at road, railways, rivers and ports, but trade and transport does not finish with them. The modern world also uses air transport, and in this field Africa is as important as anywhere else. Many cities in Africa receive regular visits from airlines all over the world as shown in Fig. 146; particularly air route centres like Nairobi and Johannesburg. From them a network of smaller aircraft fly to smaller towns. N'Djamena, for instance, is one of the most important air cargo centres north of the Equator. From there cargo is relayed to many countries and airports all over north central Africa.

Most aircraft carry passengers, however a lot of freight (cargo) is also carried, and some planes just carry that and nothing else. Charges for air freight are very high so anything flown as freight must be very special. Diamonds are always sent by air because they are very valuable and make large profits. Gold, although heavy, is often sent by air because of its great value.

Sometimes farm produce is exported by air because it means that out of season fruit and vegetables can be sent to Europe. In Europe the winters are long and cold and little or nothing can grow for about five months. In inter-tropical Africa however, fruit, vegetables and flowers grow throughout the year, provided they are given water. People in Europe will pay high prices for them and so, as they deteriorate quickly, these products go by air.

There is a very simple rule about air cargo; if the customer is prepared to pay, most things can be flown. For this reason Kenya Airways flies butter to Zambia. There are many daily flights from Dakar, Abidjan and Nairobi to European cities, carrying carnations, pineapples, avocado pears, Indian vegetables, French beans, passion fruit and mangoes. In 1975 Kenya exported 2.5 thousand tonnes of cut flowers, mostly carnations, to West Germany. She exported 2.7 thousand tonnes of Indian vegetables to London in 1975. All told Kenya earned in 1975 over £5 million from this trade.

As you can see air transport is important; so important that it kept Zambia's wheels turning in the early days after UDI in Zimbabwe, when all her oil had to be air-freighted into the country.

Another important point about air transport is that it is often the only way in which certain places can be reached efficiently and quickly. This is certainly so in a country like Zaïre where surface transport leaves much to be desired. It is in Zaïre that a most comprehensive network of airfields is being established over an area of millions of square kilometres. Existing airfields are being modernised and new ones built. When the project is complete Mbandaka, Kisangani, Mbuji Mayi, Kindu, Kananga and Gemina will all have international class airports as well as that at Kinshasa. From these centres a radiating service to smaller airfields will be established. Ironically the project is proceeding slowly because of surface transport problems with imported materials!

Economic unions

On their own, countries with small populations and limited natural resources often have a struggle to maintain the standard of living of their people. On a much more smaller scale little farmers have similar problems with their few hectares of land. The solution to their problems is often to form a co-operative in which, although still retaining

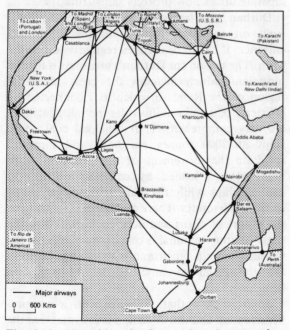

Fig. 146 Nairobi and other major airports of Africa

their individualism, they receive the benefits of buying, selling and marketing on a large scale. It is thought that much the same benefits can be achieved by an economic union between countries; in which the buying, selling, industrial, agricultural, mineral exploitation and taxation policies are rationalised in order to eliminate too much senseless competition. Carried to its logical conclusion separate identities are supposed to be merged into one, with a common political system as well. This has proved impossible in all instances so far. It is the ultimate aim of the first large post war economic union: that of the European Economic Community. The E.E.C. is not progressing smoothly because it is extremely difficult for individual nations to forget their identity and the interests of their people in favour of a supposed overall benefit to the whole organisation. However, the benefits are there for all to see, which is why the countries of the E.E.C. fight to make a success of their union.

In Africa the success rate has not, to date, been good. The Union of Northern Rhodesia, Southern Rhodesia and Nyasaland did not last long because Southern Rhodesia felt that she was subsidising the other two. They split to become Malawi (Nyasaland), Zambia (Northern Rhodesia) and Rhodesia (now Zimbabwe). This was a pity because together they could have become rich and powerful. The East Africa community had serious difficulties, both political and financial, and finally collapsed. It was hard for military dictatorship,

communism and capitalism to live together amicably. So far, 1983, the borders are still closed between Kenya and Tanzania. In fact, Zambia's and Zimbabwe's trade with Kenya now has to use a road and lake route over 3000 kilometres and 21 days long by way of Burundi and Rwanda because of this closure. So, all the early attempts at economic unions failed. Perhaps Senegambia and the Mano River Union will have a happier fate.

The Mano River Union

The Mano River Union came into being in April 1977 when Sierra Leone and Liberia agreed to unite their economies for, hopefully, their common good. They have a common customs tariff for most goods and commodities. There is complete mobility of trade, goods, capital and labour within their borders. The Mano River bridge was built to create a physical union as well. This year, 1983, the construction of the Freetown — Monrovia Highway begins. The E.E.C. has advised on an Industrial Development Unit: some industries for Mano River Union consumption and some for export. These will be free of competition within the Union. Rural development and agriculture based industries will be encouraged as well as free exchange of advice on farm practices, pest control, marketing. The Union has joint membership of international commodity agreements. In 1980 Guinea joined the Union and will take a full part as from 1984. It is to be hoped that language problems and political ideologies will not stand in the way of future progress.

Trade balances

These sound rather complicated but, in effect, they are tragically simple for many developing countries. They can be likened to a man who earns his living by repairing bicycles. If he does not spend all he earns, he saves money. With the money he saves he can buy other things: new tools, a bigger shop or one or more assistants. If he spends all he earns he will live and eat adequately but he will not grow wealthier. If he spends more than he earns he will end up badly in debt and have to ask other people to lend him money. He will get deeper and deeper into debt

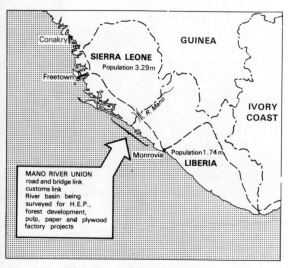

Fig. 147   The Mano River Union

until no one will lend him any more. Our first man has a *favourable* trade balance, our second man has a *balanced* trade and our third man has an *unfavourable* trade balance.

So it is with countries to a certain extent. If they wish to expand their economy in order to become wealthier they must earn through exports more than they spend through imports. This is not always easy, because before they can export they sometimes need to spend money they do not have. To exploit a mineral deposit is terribly expensive

and so they have to borrow or take a foreign company into partnership. The company exploits the deposit at its expense and the country takes a share of the profits.

Botswana is just such a country. Independent but completely landlocked at shown in Fig. 148, within south central Africa, she was, in 1971, on the U.N.'s list of the twenty-five least developed countries. She is 570 000 square kilometres in area, most of which is taken up by the Kalahari and its arid margins. Drought is frequent and only in the

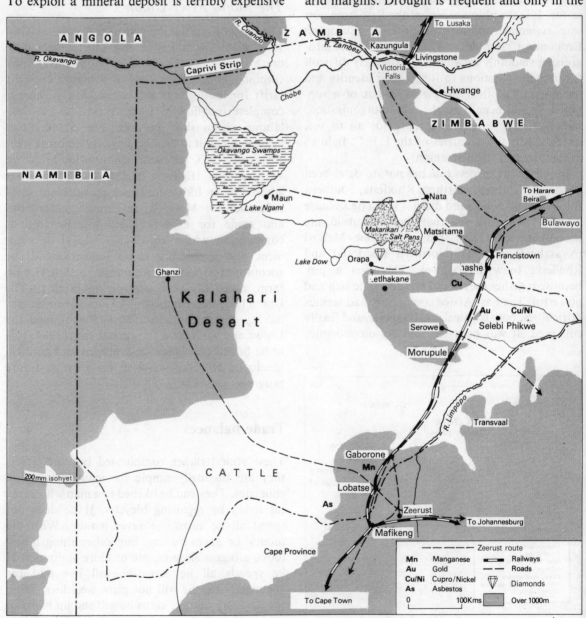

Fig. 148 Botswana

184

The diamond recovery plant at Orapa, Botswana
Is Orapa a 'pipe' or an alluvial mine?

Chobe Valley area is large-scale tree life possible. Over 500 000 of her 750 000 population live near the border with South Africa. The rest of the country is almost empty of people. The San are finding that opportunities for hunting are becoming more and more restricted because of increased ranching and game reserves. The better watered north also has a low population because of the tsetse problem. Over 60 000 of her more able bodied men work in the South African mines. Before 1967 her exports were mostly meat, meat products, hides and skins; all of which had to go through South Africa. There was, and still is, no other way. Her exports did not pay for her imports and she depended on South African and British financial help to stay solvent. Then in 1967 diamonds were discovered at Orapa. The pipe there is the second largest in Africa and contains a 20% quantity of gem stones. Botswana could not develop it alone and the South African owned De Beers Company undertook it. Botswana's share in the venture had to be paid for out of profits and so to begin with she received little money; but imports rose dramatically and her unfavourable trade balance widened. Nobody minded too much because it was hoped that soon profits would begin to overtake expenses.

Then the huge copper and nickel deposits were discovered at Selebi Phikwe. These are being exploited, and production nearly trebled between 1974 and 1975; but with copper prices so low Botswana's 15% share was not much help as the company made a loss in 1975. Botswana's share in that loss was 15%. Her trade balance remained very unfavourable! The latest discovery has meant that Botswana's worries might soon grow less. Much more money had to be spent. The government felt this was justified because, combined with other minerals this development could provide a sound future. Another diamond deposit was found 40 kilometres south of Orapa at a village called Letlhakane. Production started in 1977 with at least 40% of the diamonds being gemstones. Botswana also negotiated a 50% share in the company working the mine. All this was at the expense of other aspects of Botswana's economy; and while her income from minerals gradually increased, that from agriculture declined sadly.

In the years since 1980 however, things have been improving. Export earnings reached P447 million in 1982 and the overall balance of payments deficit was wiped out leaving a credit balance. Thus for 1983 more money became available for further development in farming, water supplies, communications and education. The recent rise in world copper prices in 1983 will be a great help. Soon perhaps, the vast artesian waters beneath the Kalahari will be exploited for more ranching. Huge areas on the perimeters of the Okavango swamps could be reclaimed. No doubt further mineral exploitation will also take place.

Throughout Black Africa the story is a similar one: spending heavily as an investment for the future and using borrowed money to do it. Unfortunately some countries will take longer to reap the benefits of this investment than others.

Question and answer session

1   Why can Zaïre's produce not be transported all the way by river transport?
Zaïre's rivers flow for hundreds of kilometres along smooth deep water channels. Unfortunately their courses are punctuated by many violent and swiftly flowing waterfalls and rapids through which no boat or barge could survive.

2   Why are metal ores not exported by air?
It would be far too expensive and completely unnecessary. Ores do not deteriorate and therefore speed is not so important.

3   What other forms of transport are used to move produce?
Don't forget the way Swaziland moves her asbestos. Another interesting method is found in the phosphate mines of Bu Craa in what is at present known as Western Sahara. The phosphates are transported by a 96 kilometre long conveyor belt from the mines to El Aaiun from where it is exported. As there is no deep water harbour a jetty, several kilometres long, has been built out to sea in order that ships may load in safety. Find El Aaiun on your atlas. Bu Craa is south-east of it.

Group tasks

1   Make a list of the railway development projects mentioned in this book and the purpose of each one. Add to this list by studying your newspaper.

2   Write a brief paragraph to explain the extent of the following ports' hinterlands:
Alexandria, Lobito, Maputo, Mogadishu.
Which do you think has the least trade and why?

3   Discuss with your friends the problems of landlocked countries. Ask your teacher to chair a class discussion and to collate your findings for the benefit of all.

4   How do people get to work in the big cities of your country? What would happen to city life and work if these methods of transport broke down?

5   If you live in a village make a traffic study in its centre of all the means of transport used to enter it. Record the numbers of *each* type of transport entering from *each* direction during the course of a two hour period of your choice. Include bicycles and animal transport as well as other types of wheeled vehicles. Record your results in the form of a bar graph.

6   Study Fig. 149. Try to give an explanation for the export performance of each country shown. Ask your teacher to help.

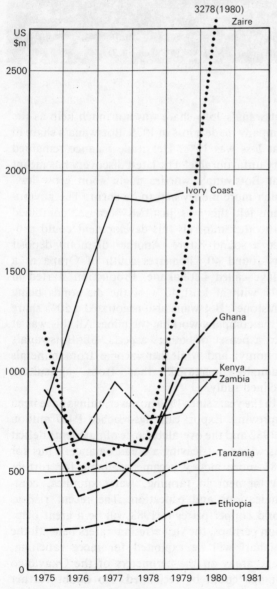

Fig. 149   Africa's exports

186

14 Fishing

Fish are one of the world's most important and palatable sources of protein. They abound in most of Africa's lakes and rivers, while off most of her coasts an almost inexhaustible harvest of fish is available. They could provide millions more people with a more balanced diet than the largely carbohydrate based diet of maize or millet, which is the fare of so many of Africa's people. This is not to say that there is no fishing carried out in Africa. Quite the reverse, particularly in her lakes and rivers. Generally speaking however, Africa is not catching enough of her own fish. Other countries are doing this, rich ones who can afford big ships and expensive equipment. Gradually things are changing. African countries are beginning to claim a greater share of the sea's riches as we shall see.

In the meantime let us just look at fishing in Africa's lakes and rivers; the sort of fish available and the methods used to catch them. There are many methods used to catch them. Some are simple while others are complicated and laborious.

The biggest fish to be found in Africa's lakes and rivers is the Nile Perch: a fish which can grow to monstrous proportions for a fresh water fish. Some have been caught which have weighed almost 150 kilograms. They are caught in the Victoria Nile between Lake Victoria and Lake Albert (Lake Mobuto Sese Seko) and Lake Turkana in Kenya. For some years now they have also been caught in Lake Victoria.

Many people catch the Nile Perch for fun. These are the tourists who pay a lot of money just for a few hours fishing. They use a rod and line and fish from a powerful motor boat. The fishing lodges keep the catch, refrigerate it and send it by air to big cities like Nairobi, where it is a very expensive but popular food.

It is not such fun for the El Molo tribe who live on the south-eastern shores of Lake Turkana and whose health has been adversely affected by the high fluoride content of the lake's waters. There are less than 300 of them and they depend for food on the fish they catch from the lake. A few years ago they used spears to catch the fish. Not only was this difficult it was also dangerous, as Lake Turkana is infested with crocodiles. It is only in recent years that methods have been changing so that now the El Molo have been provided with small boats, nets and, for the biggest fish, stout lines and hooks. This is not the end of the story. A survey is being conducted by the Kenya Government aimed at a planned commercial exploitation of Lake Turkana's teeming fish life: a survey which will determine the

Nile Perch from Lake Turkana
Compare their size with the men.

A fine catch of Dagaa

optimum number of fish that the lake can provide without the fish population decreasing.

Lake Tanganyika is another lake, this time an exceptionally deep one, which has an abundant fish life: possibly the richest in the whole of East and Central Africa. There are many fishing villages along the shores on the Tanzanian side and the annual catch approximates very closely to 50 000 tonnes. The best known of Lake Tanganyika's rich fish life is the Dagaa, or Kapenta as it is called in Zambia. At present the fishermen catch them at night using a method known as lamp attraction. They lower the open net into the water and then shine a lantern above the water which attracts swarms of these small fish. The nets are then quickly scooped up into the boat.

Lake Tanganyika could, in fact, yield many more fish than this; some experts consider it capable of sustaining an annual yield of 200 000 tonnes. To this end the United Nations is sponsoring a concerted effort towards the modernisation of Lake Tanganyika's fishing industry. Already a team of international experts is currently assisting with research, experimental fishing methods, administration, training of staff and fishermen; and marketing procedures such as preservation, storage and transport.

Already Zambia imports over 25 000 tonnes of Dagaa from Tanzania. After they are caught the fish are dried in the sun on the lakeside beaches. They are then sold in dried form, brined (salted) and packed in polythene bags. Soon however, a modern freezing plant will enable more of these fish to be processed and sold from the fish receiving station near Kigoma. Modern equipment will also soon permit the capture of the bigger fish in the deepest waters, far out way from the shores in the underfished part of the lake.

One of the most important fresh water fish in Africa is the Tilapia, a fish found nowhere else in the world. It is very tasty and therefore a popular food. Lake Rukwa, the Malagarasi swamp lands and Lake Chad contain millions of them. Lake Chad alone yields 20 000 tonnes a year. They are dried in the sun before being put on sale. In Zaïre, Malawi and Kenya artifical ponds are in wide use, containing specially grown Tilapia. This is known as *fish farming*, a practice which has only arrived in Africa on any scale within the last fifteen years. The fish in these ponds are fed with animal droppings until they are big enough to be consumed. They are frozen and sold in packets in many of East Africa's shops.

Lake George, in Uganda, supplies Tilapia for this industry. There is a large Tilapia population in the lake because of the hippo's droppings which fertilise and encourage a rich submarine plant life on which the fish feed.

Methods of catching fish

We have already mentioned spearing and lamp attraction. Another simple though rather inefficient method is used in shallow lakes and ponds where baskets are placed on their sides in the water and lots of people wade and stamp their way through the water to frighten fish into the baskets.

A much more efficient method is the gill net in which the holes are just big enough to allow the fishes' head through but not big enough for its body. The fish swims into the net and is caught by its gills, being unable to move either backwards or forwards. Gill nets may be used in several different ways: between boats, between people who wade round in a circle or spread right across a river so that the fish have to swim into the nets. The new modern nylon nets are very efficient and very hard wearing: an important attribute in Africa where replacements are often very expensive to obtain.

A wide variety of woven baskets is used all over Africa. One variety has a small hole in it, big enough for a fish to enter. It is placed on the river or lake bottom with bait inside it. The fish find their way in for the food, but invariably cannot get out. Another basket method involves a cone shaped basket which is held in swiftly-moving river waters so that unsuspecting fish are caught in the open end and the basket lifted out before they can escape. The simple hook and line is effective but can generally only catch one at a time, but this is as good a method as any for catching the large cat-fish which lie at the bottom, half buried in the mud, of most of Africa's rivers.

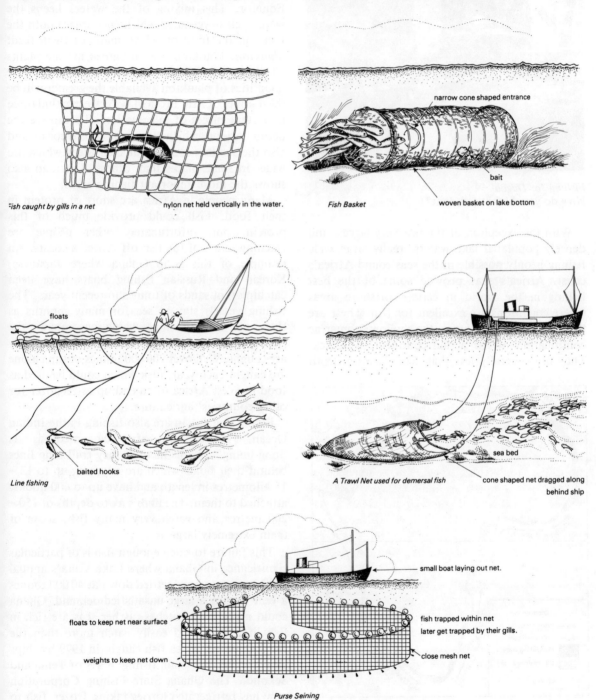

Fish caught by gills in a net — nylon net held vertically in the water.

Fish Basket — narrow cone shaped entrance, bait, woven basket on lake bottom

Line fishing — floats, baited hooks

A Trawl Net used for demersal fish — sea bed, cone shaped net dragged along behind ship

Purse Seining — floats to keep net near surface, weights to keep net down, small boat laying out net, fish trapped within net later get trapped by their gills, close mesh net

Fig. 150 The main methods of fishing in Africa

189

Fishing for Dagaa
How do you think it was done?

With the exception of the few very largest and densely populated lake waters, really large scale fishing is only possible in the seas round Africa's coast. Africa's seas provide some of the best fishing in the world in certain offshore areas where conditions are excellent for fish. These are the continental shelf areas, the shallow submarine continuation of the actual continent of Africa. They are generally less than 62 metres in depth

which means that sunlight can filter through the water and thus encourage the growth of sea plants on which some fish feed. In the best continental shelf areas there is an intermingling of cold and warm water: for instance the Benguela Current (cold) which flows northwards towards the Equator. This mixing of the waters keeps the water well oxygenated which encourages both the fish and the food on which many of them feed: *plankton*. Plankton are tiny green marine plants which grow and float in the water. The greater the quantities of plankton available the greater will be the number of fish. From Fig. 151 we can find three important pieces of information. We can see the ocean currents which flow around the coasts and also the shallow continental shelf areas which are wider in some places than others. The map also shows the most important fishing areas.

Many people in Africa are short of protein in their food. Fish could provide much of this protein, but unfortunately other people are catching much of the fish off Africa's coasts. An example of this is in Ghana where Japanese, Korean and Russian fishing boats have been catching thousands of tonnes in recent years. The fishing vessels stay at sea for many months as there are factory ships which accompany the fishing boats and process the fish as soon as they are caught. Well over 300 000 tonnes of tuna alone are caught each year. Fish which could be used as food in West Africa often end up as fertilizer for other countries' agriculture.

Russia and Japan are also fishing in the Indian Ocean, where one of their methods is 'long-lining'. In this method they trail long lines behind their boats which are anything up to 12 – 15 kilometres in length and have up to 400 hooks, attached to them. The lines sink to depths of 150 – 200 metres and catch very many fish, some of them extremely large.

This failure to catch enough fish is of particular significance in Ghana where Lake Volta's annual yields seems to have settled down at 40 000 tonnes a year leaving a large unsatisfied demand. Ghana could make large catches, as her seas are rich in fish life. She could easily catch more than the 188 000 tonnes of sea fish caught in 1979 by ships based on her two main fishing ports of Tema and Sekondi. The Ghana State Fishing Corporation now has refrigerated lorries taking frozen fish to many towns in Ghana. This has encouraged

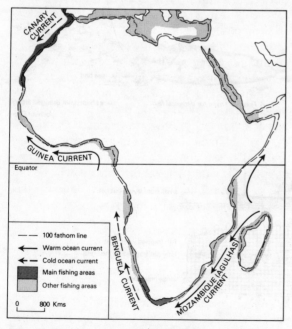

Fig. 151 The continental shelf areas of Africa

fishermen to catch more, knowing their sales are guaranteed.

The great problem is effective control of foreign fishing. For instance, Mauretania, Senegal and the Guineas have declared an extended territorial water limit of 200 nautical miles with particular reference to fishing. Countries like Russia, Poland, France, Spain and Portugal now need licences to fish within these limits.

But what can these countries do without an effective Navy? The foreign countries can fish as they wish. If they take out a licence for a certain quantity of fish they can ignore it and take what they want. So, there is a problem which, seemingly, can only be solved by either honourable behaviour by the foreign ships or by a powerful fleet of armed boats, maybe jointly owned and financed, which can enforce control. One example will suffice. Fish could earn Mauretania more money than her iron ore. Unfortunately Mauretania cannot enforce her regulations, so in 1981 foreign fishing fleets declared 120 000 tonnes of fish caught. This earned Mauretania $35 million. But Mauretania's fishing authorities knew that the figure had to be at least 10 times that amount. She thus lost over 200 million dollars as a result. Her main port is Nowadhibow, see Fig. 117. Here, fish from the cold Canary Current areas of the Atlantic are brought for processing. Cut, washed and dried in the sun they provide valuable food as well as fertilizers from the waste products.

Fish are a renewable asset, unlike say, minerals or oil. It is wicked to over-exploit these assets whether the commodity be fish, trees or, vitally important, the soil, so that they become exhausted.

There is one further example of over exploitation. Some foreign trawlers off West Africa's

Small fishing boats at anchor in Senegal These boats are not designed for deep sea fishing.

coasts fish TOTALLY catching even tiny fish which are tomorrow's big fish. They even jettison (throw overboard) a total catch if they find a shoal of more valuable fish before returning to port or to the factory ship.

Some hope lies in the fact that the west coast fishing fleets are being enlarged. By 1990 Senegal will have 26 tuna boats and 47 ocean trawlers. In 1981 Senegal's 8000 local fishermen caught 115 000 tonnes of fish. Exports to Mauretania and Mali earned $140 million. This was a drop on the 370 000 tonnes of 1976. By 1990 Senegal could be catching all her estimated 420 000 tonnes of renewable fish. Efficient, powerful and unified control of the west coast territorial waters is the answer. Africa is too short of food to allow edible fish to become fertilizer in Eastern or Western Europe.

There are many fish off South Africa's south coast where the continental shelf is quite wide, over 200 kilometres in places, and the warm waters of the Mozambique Current meet and mingle with those of the cold Benguela Current. These shallow, plankton rich waters provide the largest catches of all Africa's coasts. Walvis Bay and the Angola fishing ports have a multi-thousand tonne pilchard fishing industry. The cold Benguela Current provides ideal conditions for fish life. Factories can the fish and also produce fish oil and fertilizer.

Not all fish are *pelagic* living near the surface of the oceans. Many of them prefer the deeper waters of the continental shelf seas and are generally known as *demersal* fish. Naturally a different method is needed to catch them. One has already been mentioned: long lining, but an equally common method is trawling. The net is called a trawl and it is towed along behind a fishing boat called a trawler. As the trawl passes through a shoal of fish many are swept into the trawl and are trapped in the cod end. After a predetermined length of time has passed the trawl is winched in and is emptied on the ship's deck. Usually this occurs every 2 – 3 hours. See Fig. 150.

Question and answer session

1 What are pelagic fish?
  These are fish which swim and live in the waters close to the surface of the sea.
2 What are demersal fish?
  These are the fish which live in the deeper waters, nearer to, or on, the sea bed.

Index

Aberdare mountains, 10
Abidjan, 5, 180
Abuja, 173
Addis Ababa, 88
afforestation, 127, 128
air transport, 182
Akosombo, 106, 109
Alep pine, 132
alcohol, 73–4
Algeria, 2; forestry, 131–3; iron
　ore, 164; oil, 163–4
aluminium, 143–4, 156–9
Angola, 2; coffee, 57; oil, 165
Apapa, 180–1
Arabica, 57
arch, 7
arch dam, 180–1
asbestos, 142, 151
Aswan dam, 95, 110–3, 145
Atlas mountains, 27
Awash Valley Authority, 88–90

bagasse, 73
banket, 137
barchans, 21
bars, 3
bauxite, 143, 144, 156–9, 178
Benguela current, 27, 31, 190
bilharzia, 97, 108
Blackarm, 97
block mountains, 9
blow holes, 7
Bogoria (lake), 11
boll weevil, 68
boll worm, 97
Bomi hills, 150
Bomvu ridge, 147–8
Botswana, 184–5; cattle, 122;
　diamonds, 141
Buchanan, 150, 180

Burundi, 60
Bwana Mkubwa mine, 152

caldera, 11, 12
Caledon river, 114
Calueque dam, 104
Cameroon: coffee, 57; railways,
　177–8; tea, 60; timber, 131
Canary current, 32
cane, 73, 74
cassava, 53
cassiterite, 160, 161
cattle, 85: high lands, 123–4;
　savanna, 118–22
caving, 153–4
cedar, 133
Chad, 65, 67
chrome, 142
cirques, 19
cities, 170–3
climate: desert, 32–4; equatorial
　36–9; Mediterranean, 26–7;
　monsoon, 41; mountain, 39, 41;
　savanna, 34–6; trade wind
　coast, 39
coal, 138; Swaziland, 151;
　Tanzania, 176
coastal lands, 3–7
cocoa, 47–51
coffee, 56–9
coke, 146
columbite, 161
Conakry, 157
Confederation of Senegambia, 174
Congo, 130
continental shelf, 1, 3, 190
contour ploughing, 72
convection, 37
co-operatives, 113, 182–3
copper, 152–6, 176, 185
coral, 5, 6–7
cork, 133
cotton, 63–8, 97, 98, 145
crater, 10, 10–11

Dagaa, 188
dairy farming, 123–4
Dakar, 180
dams, 88–90, 91–5, 102–14
　passim, 145, 154, 180–1
De Beers company, 140, 185
delta, 16–17, 92, 93
delta scheme, 92
depression, 9, 27–31
desert, 168; continental, 32, 34;

formation, 120–1, 126; marine,
　32
diamonds, 140–2, 146, 185
dipping, 121
disease; bilharzia, 97, 108; cattle,
　117; cocoa, 51; coffee, 59;
　cotton, 67; malaria, 170; oil
　palm, 56; sugar cane, 75
distributaries, 17
doldrums, 24, 25, 36
Doué (river), 91
drainage, 17, see also rivers
Drakensberg mountains, 128,
　129
dredging, 5
drought, 117, 169
dunes, 21
Durban, 181

economic unions, 182–3
Egypt, 2; industrialisation, 145–6;
　oil, 164; settlement pattern, 168
El molo, 187
electricity, 108; see also dams,
　hydro electric power
environment, and population
　settlement, 167–70
Equator (thermal), 25, 26
erosion, 14, 19, 20–1, 131
Ethiopia, 2, 57, 85–90
Ethiopian highlands, 10, 168–9
Eucalyptus, 130, 131
exfoliation, 23

faults, 7, 8, 10
F'Derik, 148
fishing, 99, 108, 187–91
flood control, 107–8
flush, the, 61
fold mountains, 12–13
forest, 44, 128–31, 178
Free Zones, 146
Friguia, 157
front, 27–8
Fulani, 119–21

Gabon, 130, 165
Gambia, 174–5
gas, 161, 163–4, 165
geosyncline, 13, 14
Germiston, 140
geysers, 11
Gezira scheme, 95–9
Ghana, 2, 93; bauxite, 156, 158;
　cocoa, 47, 48, 51; forests,

129–30; industrialisation, 143–4;
  oil palms, 53
gill net, 188, 189
glaciers, 18–20
goats, 125–6
gold, 136–7
gorge, 16
grapes, 79–82
grasslands, 42–4
gravel pumping, 160
Great Fish river, 115
Great Usutu forest, 128
Green Oak, 133
green revolution, 165, 166
groundnuts, 174–5
Guiers, lake, 91, 92
Guinea, 152, 157

haematite, 148, 149
Hammar, 85
Harbel, 78
harbours, see ports
hardwoods, 129–31
Hendrik Verwoerd dam, 114
Heva tree, 76
hinterland, of ports, 180
Hoggar mountains, 10
horn, 19
horst mountains, 9
hydro electric power, 89–90, 102,
  103, 154

ice, 17–20
industrialisation, 88, 108, 134, 142
Inga dam, 102
inselbergs, 21, 22
inter tropical convergence zone,
  38, 39
iron 138–9, 147–52, 164, 176, 180
irrigation: Awash, 88–90; cane
  fields, 74; Niger, 92–3; Nile,
  94–100, 111–12; Senegal, 90–2
isobars, 29
Ivory Coast, 47; coffee, 57;
  forests, 131; oil palms, 53; oil
  (petroleum), 165–6; rubber, 77

Johannesberg, 134–5, 139–40
Jonglei canal, 99–100

Kafue river, 154
Kainji dam, 109–10
Kalahari, 2, 32, 34
Kamsar, 157
Karakul, 125

Kariba dam, 104, 154
Karoos, 124
Kenana sugar scheme, 98–9
Kenya, 2; coffee, 57, 58; cotton,
  64–5; sisal, 82–3; tea, 60, 61
Kericho, 60
Khartoum, 94, 171
Kimberley, 140
Knysna forest, 129
Koka dam, 88, 89–90
Kpong project, 109
Kunene (river), 103

LAMCO, 150
lagoons, 5
Lagos, 5
lakes, 17
landlocked countries, 175, 184–5
Langerberg mountains, 27
latex, 78
lava; 10–11, 12
Le Marinel, 102
leaf hopper, 97
leafcurl, 97
Lesotho Highlands Water Project,
  115
levee, 16, 17
Liberia, 2, 75, 77–8, 149–50
Libya, 162–3
Limpopo river, 14
loans, government, 121–2
long-lining, 190
longshore drift, 3

Magadi, lake, 11
magnetite, 149
malaria, 170
Malawi, 60
manganese, 142
Mano River Union, 183
Marampa mines, 149
Maasai, 2, 119
Mauretania, 90, 148–9, 191
Mauritius, 60
meanders, 16
Merino, 124, 125
mesa, 22–3
minerals, 173
Mokanji hills, 157
molasses, 73
Mombassa, 3, 172, 179
monsoon, 26, 41
moraine, 19–20
mosquito, 170
mountain climate, 39, 41

Mozambique, 2, 60, 66, 104, 105
Murchison (Kabalega) falls, 16
Mursi mountains, 85
Mursi, 85–8

Nagana, 117
Nairobi, 8
Naivasha, lake, 11
Namib desert, 32
Namibia, 2, 138
Nasser, lake, 110
Natal, 124, 129; sugar, 71–3
New Valley Project, 113
Nhlangano forest, 128
nickel, 142
Niger, 92–3, 109–10
Nigeria, 2; cotton, 65; forests,
  129–30; iron ore, 150–1; oil
  palms, 52; oil (petroleum), 165
  ores, 161; rubber, 76; sugar, 69;
  tin, 160–1
Nigerian Institue for Oil Palm
  Research (NIFOR), 53, 54
Nile, 5, 17, 94–100, 168, 171
Nile perch, 187
nomads, 85, 119–21, 169

oasis, 45
oil, 144, 161–6
Okoume, 130
Omo, 85, 86
Orange river, 14, 113–5
orchards, 133
Oualo, 91
overgrazing, 119, 120
Owendo, 130
oxbow, 16, 17

palm oil, 51–6
para statal body, 60, 62
pastoralism, 85–8, 169
petroleum from coal, 166
Plain of Death, the, 85–8
plankton, 190
plantation farming, 54, 55
plateau, 7, 10, 45–6, 47, 118
platinum, 142
population settlement, 170
ports, 5, 172–3, 179–82
Port Said Zone, 146
Portuguese, 172
pressure (atmospheric), 24–6, 29,
  35
Pretoria, 140

Qattara Depression Project, 146

Rahad river, 99
railways, 130, 147, 148, 175-8
rain shadow, 90
ranching, 121-2
Rand (Witwatersrand), 134-42
rattoon, 73
reef, 5
reef (gold bearing rock), 135, 136
refineries, 163
relief rain, 27, 41
rice, 92
Richard Toll scheme, 91-2
rift valley, 3
rivers, 3, 14-17, 171, 173
roads, 176
road transport, 178
Robusta, 57
rock fill dam, 122
Roseires dam, 104
rotation system, 98
rubber, 75-9
Ruacana dam, 104
Rustenberg mine, 142
rutile, 159
Rwanda, 60
Sahara, 32, 34
Sahel, 90-1, 92, 108, 120, 169
saltation, 22
saw mills, 129
scree, 21
sea fishing, 190-1
sedimantary rocks, 7, 13, 153
Seid, 97
semi arid region, 85-8
semi desert, see desert
Senegal, 90, 91; river, 90-2
Sennar dam, 95
Serir, 85
shaft mining, 141
sheep, 124-5
Sierra Leone, 149, 157
sisal, 82-4
sleeping sickness, 117
snow, see ice
softwoods, 129
Somalia, 169
South Africa, 2, 104, 106; iron
  ore, 150; Orange River scheme,

113-5; sheep farming, 124-5;
  tea, 60; viticulture, 80-2; see
  also Rand
spits, 3
Springs, 140
springs, hot, 11
steel 139, 151; see also iron
step faults, 8
Stope, 135, 137
subsistence economy, 47, 52-3
Sudan, 2; cotton, 63-4; exports,
  100; Gezira scheme, 95-9; oil,
  166; ranch, 122
Suez canal, 162
sugar, 69-75, 72-4, 98, 99, 110,
  176
Sumed pipeline, 164
Swaziland, 128-9, 147-8

Tahrir Province Scheme, 113
Tanganyika, lake, 188
Tanzania, 2; cotton, 65, 66-7;
  crops, 68; dairy farming, 123;
  iron, 151; railways, 176; sisal,
  82-3; tea, 60; tin, 160
Taoue river, 91, 92
tapping, 78
tarn, 19
Tazara railway, 175-7
tea, 59-63
Tema, 143-4
Tendaho, 89
textiles, 145-6
Thabazami, 139
Tibesti mountains, 10
Tilapia, 188
timber, see forests
Timbuktu, 92
tin, 159-61
towns, 170-3
trade, 171, 172
trade balances, 183-6
Trade Winds, 32, 34, 38, 39
Trans-Africa highway, 178
Trans-Cameroon highway, 177-8
Trans-Sahara highway, 178
transhumance, 121, 126
transport, 90, 130, 155; see also
  specific type
Transvaal, 115, 123

trash, 73
trawling, 191
trees, uses of, 127
tsetse fly, 56, 85, 117, 118, 120,
  125
Turkana, 2, 187

Uganda, 2; coffee, 57; cotton,
  65-6; sugar, 69; tea, 60
uranium, 137-8

VALCO, 108-9
valleys, 7-9, 18-19
Vanderbiljl Park, 140
vegetation, 42-6
Vereeniging, 140
Victoria falls, 16, 104
Victoria, lake, 8-9
viticulture, 79-82
volcanoes, 10-11
Volta: lake, 107-8; river, 106-9;
  dam, 143, 156

wattle, 129
weathering, 22; see also erosion
westerlies, 25, 27
wind, 20-1, 24-6
wine, 80, 81-2
Wologisi mountains, 150

Yatta plateau, 10
Yekepa, 150

Zaïre, 2; coffee, 57, 58; copper,
  152-3, 156; cotton, 66; dairy
  farming, 123; oil palms, 51, 53;
  railway, 176-7; rubber, 76;
  sugar, 69; tea, 60
Zaïre, river, 14, 102-3
Zambezi, 14, 104-5
Zambezi river authority, 122
Zambia, 2; air freight, 182;
  copper, 152, 153-6; dairy
  farming, 123; pastoralism, 122;
  railway, 175-6; sugar, 69; tea,
  60
Zeerust Connection, 176
Zimbabwe, 60, 160